EYEWITNESS TO THE CIVIL WAR
Volume II

The Bloody Struggle

The Civil War in the East, 1862

Union sharpshooter

EYEWITNESS TO THE CIVIL WAR
Volume II

The Bloody Struggle
The Civil War in the East, 1862

Edited by
Albert A. Nofi

GALLERY BOOKS
An Imprint of W. H. Smith Publishers Inc.
112 Madison Avenue
New York City 10016

This one's for M.S.N.

ACKNOWLEDGMENTS

Several people rendered considerable assistance in the preparation of this volume: Helena Rubenstein, Daniel Scott Palter, and the Staff of West End Games generously gave me access to the company library, with its extensive Civil War collection. The staffs of the New York Public Library and the Brooklyn College Library were of enormous assistance. I am, in addition, indebted to Dr. David G. Martin and to Prof. John Boardman for their assistance and advice.

As always, special thanks are due to my wife, Mary S. Nofi, and my daughter, Marilyn J. Spencer, for their patience and understanding as they once more endured the disruption attendant upon the preparation of a volume.

Library of Congress Cataloging-in-Publication Data

The Bloody struggle.

  (Eyewitness history of the Civil War; v. 2)
  Bibliography: p. 173
  1. United States—History—Civil War, 1861-1865—Campaigns.   2. United States—History—Civil War, 1861-1865—Personal narratives.   I. Nofi, Albert A.
II. Series.
E470.2.B66 1988   973.7'32   88-5057
ISBN 0-8317-3082-X

Prepared by Combined Books
26 Summit Grove, Suite 207
Bryn Mawr, PA 19010

Project Director: Robert L. Pigeon
Project Coordinator: Antoinette Bauer
Editor of the Series: Albert A. Nofi
Photographic Research: John Cannan
Photographs: Tim Scott
Layout: Lizbeth Nauta

Produced by Wieser and Wieser, Inc.
118 East 25th Street, New York, NY 10010

Rebel line behind the stone wall at Fredericksburg

CONTENTS

Preface to the Series		6
Introduction		7
I.	Before the Battle	9
II.	The Peninsular Campaign	19
III.	Jackson's Valley Campaign	57
IV.	The Second Bull Run Campaign	77
V.	The Antietam Campaign	103
VI.	Fredericksburg	147
VII.	Winter, 1862–1863	167
	Sources	173

PREFACE TO THE SERIES

Well over a century after its conclusion, the Civil War remains the gravest crisis in the history of the Republic since the attainment of independence. It was a vast complex struggle which touched the lives of far more Americans than any other war in which the nation has fought. A conflict of momentous import, it still retains an immediate and continuing impact on the life of the nation. The story of the Civil War has been told on numerous occasions and in numerous ways. The literature is enormous, ranging from erudite scholarly tomes to dry official reports, from informative popular histories to vicious partisan tracts. All these have their value. Yet none can ever be entirely satisfactory. After all these years there exists no better way of looking at the Civil War than to see it through the eyes of those who lived through it, the thousands upon thousands for whom the war was a daily reality.

The Civil War was probably the first war in history in which most of the troops could read and write. As a result, there exists an enormous number of first-hand accounts. The range of materials is equally large, from private letters to multi-volume memoirs. These cover everything from the minutia of daily life to serious historical treatments, from amusing anecdotes to vituperative personal attacks. Nothing surpasses such original documents for developing an understanding of the events as they were perceived by the people who lived through them, for the flavor of the times, the emotions of the struggle, the force of the issues, the impact of the events. Such materials have been drawn upon several times already for the creation of a number of anthologies of first-hand accounts of the war, or of particular aspects of it. Yet the amount of material available is so vast, the stories to be told so numerous, that there still remains much material which has not received wide circulation. It was an awareness of this fact which led to the creation of the present series, *Eyewitness to the Civil War.*

Each volume in *Eyewitness to the Civil War* covers a distinct aspect of the war as seen by the people who lived through it, as ex-pressed in their personal letters, private diaries, historical accounts, and even in their songs. The typical volume contains around two dozen items selected from among many thousands. These items deal with events ranging from small, otherwise forgotten, incidents to great historic battles. In most cases, the events depicted were personally witnessed by the authors. In a few instances accounts by contemporary authors who did not personally witness the events have been included, especially when the writer was someone of particularly interesting identity or possessed an unusual perspective on the events.

In preparing *Eyewitness to the Civil War,* the editor has made no effort to attempt a balanced presentation. As a consequence, many events are treated from only a Northern point of view, while others have an equally Southern slant, and still others are seen from two or three different perspectives. The purpose of the work is neither to achieve historical accuracy nor political balance, but to see events as they were experienced and understood by some of the people who lived through them. There will thus be redundancies, contradictions, and errors, not to mention outright falsehoods.

All of the selections appear almost exactly as they did on their original publication, save for the occasional eliding of extraneous materials. Where necessary, the editor has created titles for selections which lacked such. For the most part, he has avoided the inclusion of explanatory notes, confining himself to the insertion of occasional comments in brackets. Where explanatory notes appear in the original, they have been included only when they seemed of particular importance. In addition, the editor has refrained from modernizing the many little differences in spelling, capitalization, grammar, usage, and syntax, which have developed since the Civil War. Needless to say, there has been no attempt to impose a uniformity of style. Thus, in *Eyewitness to the Civil War* the participants speak for themselves in their own voices.

Confederate dead at the stone wall after the battle of Fredericksburg

Introduction
REBELLION BECOMES WAR

The events of 1861 had been traumatic for the American people, both in the North and South. In little more than five months the Union, which had endured for over eighty years, had split in two. Rival armies of inept though enthusiastic volunteers soon took to the field, the Northerners seeking to reaffirm the Union while their Southern erstwhile countrymen sought to deny it. At first enthusiasm knew no bounds. On both sides it was widely held that the matter would be over in a few weeks and at little cost. The first major clash of the war, along Virginia's Bull Run Creek in July of 1861, came as a shock to both sides, as the Confederate forces drove the Union troops back in considerable disorder after a long, confused struggle. The butcher's bill seemed enormous, a combined total of 4878, including 847 dead. But the battle decided little. Nor did it lay to rest the illusion that the war would be ended quickly. However, Bull Run did turn enthusiasm into determination.

Both sides were intent upon renewing the struggle at the earliest opportunity, as soon as the resources of the nation were mobilized.

Although war was becoming generalized all along the frontier between the North and South, attentions remained focused primarily on the eastern theater. Washington and Richmond were too close—barely a hundred miles apart—for people raised on the memory of Napoleon to believe that the struggle could not be ended with one or two great victories in the field. It was an enticing illusion, one which continues to haunt the public and the military mind despite the advent of the industrial age which enables nations to tap seemingly endless resources and struggle on and on until a decision is reached as much by utter exhaustion as by political and military skill.

However, as 1861 turned into 1862, no one understood this. While the raw recruits of both North and South were molded

7

rapidly into trained soldiers in camps not a day's ride apart, their leaders planned for a new campaign in the spring, one which would yield a quick and favorable decision. But when the armies did march again, the brutal realities of war swiftly intruded themselves. The war in the eastern theater in 1862 was characterized by an almost continuous series of campaigns. The human suffering was enormous, the loss of life making it the costliest year of the war. And in the end, much had been decided, yet little had changed.

Confederate soldiers prepare for battle.

I

BEFORE THE BATTLE

IN THE EASTERN THEATER THE WINTER OF 1861–1862 WAS A RELATIVELY QUIET ONE, AS the armies made ready for a decisive struggle as soon as the weather permitted large scale operations. There was much to be done. Troops had to be recruited, equipped, and trained. Plans had to be made, supplies gathered. And the home front had to be sustained.

A dying Yankee color bearer demonstrates his devotion to his flag.

★★★

JULIA WARD HOWE

The Writing of "The Battle Hymn of the Republic"

Julia Ward Howe(1819–1910), the daughter of a wealthy New York banker and mother of six, was noted as an abolitionist, women's rights advocate, writer, poetess, and reformer. Editor, with husband Samuel G. Howe, of the abolitionist periodical Commonwealth *she had several books to her credit even before the Civil War. After the war she wrote several more books and became prominent in the international peace movement. Despite all of this noteworthy activity,, Mrs. Howe is today best remembered for "The Battle Hymn of the Republic." The song*

first appeared in print in the February 1862 issue of The Atlantic Monthly, *for which she was paid $4, at the time nearly a week's pay for a laborer. The song rapidly became one of the most popular, and certainly the most enduring, of all Civil War songs. In this selection from her* Reminiscences, 1819–1899 *(Boston, 1899), she tells how she came to write it, inspired by a visit to the camps of the Army of the Potomac in the company of Governor John A. Andrew of Massachusetts and several other friends.*

I distinctly remember that a feeling of discouragement came over me as I drew near the city of Washington. I thought of the women of my acquaintance whose sons or husbands were fighting our great battle, the women themselves serving in the hospitals, or busying themselves with the work of the Sanitary Commission. My husband was be-

yond the age of military service, my eldest son but a stripling; my youngest was a child of not more than two years. I could not leave my nursery to follow the march of our armies; neither had I the practical deftness which the preparing and packing of sanitary stores demanded. Something seemed to say to me, "You would be glad to serve, but you cannot help any one; you have nothing to give, and there is nothing for you to do." Yet, because of my sincere desire, a word was given me to say, which did strengthen the hearts of those who fought in the field and of those who languished in the prison.

We were invited one day to attend a review of troops at some distance from the town. While we were engaged in watching the maneuvers, a sudden movement of the enemy necessitated immediate action. The review was discontinued, and we saw a detachment of soldiers gallop to the assistance of a small body of our men who were in imminent danger of being surrounded and cut off from retreat. The regiments remaining on the field were ordered to march to their cantonments. We returned to the city very slowly, of necessity, for the troops nearly filled the road. My dear minister was in the carriage with me, as were several other friends. To beguile the rather tedious drive, we sang from time to time snatches of the army songs so popular at that time, concluding, I think, with: John Brown's body lies a-moldering in the ground; His soul is marching on.

The soldiers seemed to like this and answered back, "Good for you!" Mr. Clark said, "Mrs. Howe, why do you not write some good words for that stirring tune?" I replied that I had often wished to do this but had not as yet found in my mind any leading toward it.

I went to bed that night as usual and slept, according to my wont, quite soundly. I awoke in the gray of the morning twilight, and as I lay waiting for the dawn, the long lines of the desired poem began to twine themselves in my mind. Having thought out all the stanzas, I said to myself, "I must get up and write these verses down, lest I fall asleep again and forget them." So with a sudden effort I sprang out of bed and found in the dimness an old stump of a pen which I remembered to have used the day before. I scrawled the verses almost without looking at the paper. I had learned to do this when, on previous occasions, attacks of versification had visited me in the night and I feared to have recourse to a light lest I should wake the baby, who slept near me. I was always obliged to decipher my scrawl before another night should intervene, as it was only legible while the matter was fresh in my mind. At this time, having completed my writing, I returned to bed and fell asleep, saying to myself, "I like this better than most things that I have written."

The poem, which was soon after published in the *Atlantic Monthly*, was somewhat praised on its appearance, but the vicissitudes of the war so engrossed public attention that small heed was taken of literary matters. I knew and was content to know that the poem soon found its way to the camps, as I heard from time to time of its being sung in chorus by the soldiers.

THE BATTLE HYMN OF THE REPUBLIC

Mine eyes have seen the glory of the coming of the Lord:
He is trampling out the vintage where the grapes of wrath are stored;
He hath loosed the fateful lightning of his terrible swift sword:
His truth is marching on.

Chorus
Glory, glory hallelujah,
Glory, glory hallelujah,
Glory, glory hallelujah,
His truth is marching on.

I have seen Him in the watch fires of a hundred circling camps;
They have builded Him an altar in the evening dews and damps;
I can read His righteous sentence by the dim and flaring lamps.
His day is marching on.

I have read a fiery gospel writ in burnished rows of steel:
"As ye deal with my contemners, so with you my grace shall deal;
Let the Hero, born of woman, crush the serpent with his heel,
Since God is marching on."

He has sounded forth the trumpet that shall never call retreat;
He is sifting out the hearts of men before his judgment seat:
Oh! be swift, my soul, to answer Him! be jubilant, my feet!
Our God is marching on.

In the beauty of the lilies Christ was born across the sea,
With a glory in His bosom that transfigures you and me:
As He died to make men holy, let us die to make men free,
While God is marching on.

★★★

GEORGE B. McCLELLAN
McClellan Takes Command

One of the most distinguished junior officers of the Old Army, West Pointer George B. McClellan (1826–1885) left the service in 1857 to go into railroading, rising to the presidency of the Ohio & Mississippi. At the onset of the Civil War he returned to active duty, initially with the Ohio State Militia. He later commanded with some success in western Virginia—now West Virginia—and soon after Bull Run was given command of the Union forces about Washington. Not long afterwards he was made general-in-chief of all the Union armies. A first-rate organizer, administrator, and disciplinarian, McClellan soon shaped the dispirited, ill-equipped troops into the Army of the Potomac, which he led with some success, but little brilliance for over a year. McClellan's account of the creation of The Army of the Potomac, his experiences in the first winter of the war, and his plans for the coming campaign show the flaws in his character which made him something less than a great captain. It is drawn from that most valuable of Civil War anthologies, **Battles and Leaders of the Civil War,** *edited by Robert U. Johnson and Clarence C. Buell (New York, 1887), a multi-volume compilation of articles, letters, and such originally published in* **The Century Magazine.**

In July, 1861, after having secured solidly for the Union that part of western Virginia north of the Kanawha and west of the mountains, I was suddenly called to Washington on the day succeeding the first battle of Bull Run. Reaching the capital on the 26th, I found myself assigned to the command of that city and of the troops gathered around it.

All was chaos and despondency; the city was filled with intoxicated stragglers, and an attack was expected. The troops numbered less than fifty thousand, many of whom were so demoralized and undisciplined that they could not be relied upon even for defensive purposes. Moreover, the term of service of a large part had already expired, or was on the point of doing so. On the Maryland side of the Potomac no troops were posted on the roads leading into the city, nor were there any intrenchments. On the Virginia side the condition of affairs was better in these respects, but far from satisfactory. Sufficient and fit material of war did not exist. The situation was difficult and fraught with danger.

The first and most pressing demand was the immediate safety of the capital and the Government. This was secured by enforcing the most rigid discipline, by organizing permanent brigades under regular officers, and by placing the troops in good defensive positions, far enough to the front to afford room for manœuvring and to enable the brigades to support each other.

The contingency of the enemy's crossing the Potomac above the city was foreseen and promptly provided for. [As General Beauregard observed, had] he attempted this "about three months after the battle of Manassas," he would, upon reaching "the rear of Washington," have found it covered by respectable works, amply garrisoned, with a sufficient disposable force to move upon his rear and force him to "a decisive engagement." It would have been the greatest possible good fortune for us if he had made this movement at the time in question, or even some weeks earlier. It was only for a very few days after the battle of Bull Run that the movement was practicable, and every day added to its difficulty.

Two things were at once clear: first, that a large and thoroughly organized army was necessary to bring the war to a successful conclusion; second, that Washington must be so strongly fortified as to set at rest any reasonable apprehensions of its being carried by a sudden attack, in order that the active army might be free to move with the maximum strength and on any line of operations without regard to the safety of the capital.

These two herculean tasks were entered upon without delay or hesitation. They were carried to a successful conclusion, without regard to that impatient and unceasing clamor—inevitable among a people unaccustomed to war—which finally forced the hand of the general charged with their execution. He regarded their completion as essential to the salvation of his country, and determined to accomplish them, even if sacrificed in the endeavor. Nor has he, even at this distant day, and after much bitter experience, any regret that he persisted in his determination. Washington was surrounded by a line of strong detached works, armed with garrison artillery, and secure against assault. Intermediate points were occupied by smaller works, battery epaulements, infantry intrenchments, etc. The result was a line of defenses which could easily be held by a comparatively small garrison against any assault, and could be reduced only by the slow operations of a regular siege, requiring much time and material, and affording full opportunity to bring all the resources of the country to its relief. At no time during the war was the enemy able to undertake the siege of Washington, nor, if respectably garrisoned, could it ever have been in danger from an assault. The maximum garrison necessary to hold the place against a siege from any and every quarter was 34,000 troops, with 40 field-guns; this included the requisite reserves.

With regard to the formation of the Army of the Potomac, it must suffice to say that everything was to be created from the very foundation. Raw men and officers were to be disciplined and instructed. The regular army was too small to furnish more than a portion of the general officers, and a very small portion of the staff, so that the staff-departments and staff-officers were to be fashioned mainly out of the intelligent and enthusiastic, but perfectly raw, material furnished. Artillery, small-arms, and ammunition were to be fabricated, or purchased from abroad; wagons, ambulances, bridge trains, camp equipage, hospital stores, and all the vast impedimenta and material indispensable for an army in the field, were to be manufactured. So great was the

difficulty of procuring small-arms that the armament of the infantry was not satisfactorily completed until the winter, and a large part of the field-batteries were not ready for service until the spring of 1862. As soon as possible divisions were organized, the formation being essentially completed in November.

On the 1st of November, upon the retirement of General Winfield Scott, I succeeded to the command of all the armies, except the Department of Virginia, which comprised the country within sixty miles of Fort Monroe. Upon assuming the general command, I found that the West was far behind the East in its state of preparation, and much of my time and large quantities of material were consumed in pushing the organization of the Western armies. Meanwhile the various coast expeditions were employed in seizing important points of the enemy's sea-board, to facilitate the prevention of blockade-running, and to cut or threaten the lines of communication near the coast, with reference to subsequent operations.

The plan of campaign which I adopted for the spring of 1862 was to push forward the armies of Generals Halleck and Buell to occupy Memphis, Nashville, and Knoxville, and the line of the Memphis and Danville Railroad, so as to deprive the

General McClellan (standing, at left) **and his staff gave discipline to the dispirited Army of the Potomac.**

enemy of that important line, and force him to adopt the circuitous routes by Augusta, Branchville, and Charleston. It was also intended to seize Washington, North Carolina, at the earliest practicable moment, and to open the Mississippi by effecting a junction between Generals Halleck and Butler. This movement of the Western armies was to be followed by that of the Army of the Potomac from Urbana, on the lower Rappahannock, to West Point and Richmond, intending, if we failed to gain Richmond by a rapid march, to cross the James and attack the city in rear, with the James as a line of supply.

So long as Mr. Cameron was Secretary of War I received the cordial support of that department; but when he resigned, the whole state of affairs changed. I had never met Mr. Stanton before reaching Washington, in 1861. He at once sought me and professed the utmost personal affection, the expression of which was exceeded only by the bitterness of his denunciation of the Government and its policy. I was unaware of his appointment as Secretary of War until after it had been made, whereupon he called to ascertain whether I desired him to accept, saying that to do so would involve a total sacrifice of his personal interests, and that the only inducement would be the desire to assist me in my work. Having no reason to doubt his sincerity, I desired him to accept, whereupon he consented, and with great effusion exclaimed: "Now we two will save the country."

On the next day the President came to my house to explain why he had appointed Mr. Stanton without consulting me; his reason being that he supposed Stanton to be a great friend of mine, and that the appointment would naturally be satisfactory, and that he feared that if I had known it beforehand it would be said that I had dragooned him into it.

The more serious difficulties of my position began with Mr. Stanton's accession to the War Office. It at once became very difficult to approach him, even for the transaction of ordinary current business, and our personal relations at once ceased. The impatience of the Executive immediately became extreme, and I can attribute it only to the influence of the new Secretary, who did many things to break up the free and confidential intercourse that had heretofore existed between the President and myself. The Government soon manifested great impatience in regard to the opening of the Baltimore and Ohio Railroad and the destruction of the Confederate batteries on the Potomac. The first object could be permanently attained only by occupying the Shenandoah Valley with a force strong enough to resist any attack by the Confederate army then at Manassas; the second only by a general advance of the Army of the Potomac, driving the enemy back of the Rapidan. My own view was that the movement of the Army of the Potomac from Urbana would accomplish both of these objects, by forcing the enemy to abandon all his positions and fall back on Richmond. I was therefore unwilling to interfere with this plan by a premature advance, the effect of which must be ei-

ther to commit us to the overland route, or to minimize the advantages of the urbana movement. I wished to hold the enemy at Manassas to the last moment—if possible until the advance from Urbana had actually commenced, for neither the reopening of the railroad nor the destruction of the batteries was worth the danger involved.

The positive order of the President, probably issued under the pressure of the Secretary of War,

forced me to undertake the opening of the railway. For this purpose I went to Harper's Ferry in February, intending to throw over a force sufficient to occupy Winchester. To do this it was necessary to have a reliable bridge across the Potomac—to insure supplies and prompt reënforcements. The pontoon-bridge, thrown as a preliminary, could not be absolutely trusted on a river so liable to heavy freshets; therefore it was determined to construct a canal-boat bridge. It was discovered, however, when the attempt was made, that the lift-lock from the canal to the river was too narrow for the boats by some four or five inches, and I therefore decided to rebuild the railroad bridge, and content myself with occupying Charlestown until its completion, postponing to the same time the advance to Winchester. I had fully explained my intentions to the President and Secretary before leaving Washington, providing for pre-

A coward is removed from the ranks of the Army of the Potomac.

cisely such a contingency. While at Harper's Ferry I learned that the President was dissatisfied with my action, and on reaching Washington I laid a full explanation before the Secretary, with which he expressed himself entirely satisfied, and told me that the President was already so, and that it was unnecessary for me to communicate with him on the subject. I then proceeded with the preparations necessary to force the evacuation of the Potomac batteries. On the very day appointed for the division commanders to come to headquarters to receive their final orders, the President sent for me. I then learned that he had received no explanation of the Harper's Ferry affair, and that the Secretary was not authorized to make the statement already referred to; but after my repetition of it the President became fully satisfied with my course. He then, however, said that there was another "very ugly matter" which he desired to talk about, and that was the movement by the lower Chesapeake. He said that it had been suggested that I proposed this movement with the "traitorous" purpose of leaving Washington uncovered and exposed to attack. I very promptly objected to the coupling of any such adjective with my purposes, whereon he disclaimed any intention of conveying the idea that he expressed his own opinion, as he merely repeated the suggestions of others. I then explained the purpose and effect of fortifying Washington, and, as I thought, removed his apprehensions, but informed him that the division commanders were to be at headquarters that morning, and suggested that my plans should be laid before them that they might give their opinion as to whether the capital would be endangered; I also said that in order to leave them perfectly untrammeled I would not attend the meeting. Accordingly they met on the 8th of March and approved my plans.

On the same day was issued, without my knowledge, the order forming army corps and assigning the senior general officers to their command. My own views were that, as the command of army corps involved great responsibility and demanded ability of a high order, it was safer to postpone their formation until trial in the field had shown which general officers could best perform those vital functions. An incompetent division commander could not often jeopardize the safety of an army; while an unfit corps commander could easily lose a battle and frustrate the best-conceived plan of campaign. Of the four corps commanders, one only had commanded so much as a regiment in the field prior to the Bull Run campaign. On the next day intelligence arrived that the enemy was abandoning his positions. I crossed to the Virginia side to receive information more promptly and decide upon what should be done. During the night I determined to advance the whole army, to take advantage of any opportunity to strike the enemy, to break up the permanent camps, give the troops a little experience on the march and in bivouac, get rid of extra baggage, and test the working of the staff-departments. If this were done at all, it must be done promptly, and by moving the troops by divisions, without waiting to form the army corps. Accordingly, I telegraphed to the Secretary, explaining the state of the case and asking authority to postpone the army corps formation until the completion of the movement. The reply was an abrupt and unreasonable refusal. I again telegraphed, explaining the situation and throwing the responsibility upon the Secretary, whereupon he gave way.

Meanwhile, as far back as the 27th of February, orders had been given for collecting the transportation necessary to carry out the Urbana movement. This conclusion had been reached after full discussion. On the 27th of January had been issued the President's General War Order No. 1, directing a general movement of the land and naval forces against the enemy on the 22d of February. On the 31st of January was issued the President's Special War Order No. 1, directing the Army of the Potomac to advance to the attack of Manassas on the 22d of February. The President, however, permitted me to state my objections to this order, which I did, at length, in a letter of February 3d, to the Secretary of War. As the President's order was not insisted upon, although never formally revoked, it is to be assumed that my letter produced, for a time at least, the desired effect. When Manassas had been abandoned by the enemy and he had withdrawn behind the Rapidan, the Urbana movement lost much of its promise, as the enemy was now in position to reach Richmond before we could do so. The alternative remained of making Fort Monroe and its vicinity the base of operations.

★★★

JOHN B. GORDON
The First Winter of the War

Georgian John B. Gordon (1832–1904) was a lawyer and businessman in Virginia when the Civil War broke out. He raised a company of volunteers and was accepted into Confederate service as a captain. Accompanied by his wife, he served in all the campaigns of the Army of Northern Virginia. By the autumn of 1862 he had risen to brigadier general. At the end of the war he commanded the II Corps of the Army of Northern Virginia, and was one of Robert E. Lee's most capable subordinates. After the war

he served Georgia in the state legislature, as governor, and in the U.S. Senate. His account of life in the Army of Northern Virginia during the first winter of the war is drawn from his excellent memoir, Reminiscences of the Civil War *(New York, 1904).*

The North soon rallied after the defeat at Bull Run. Her armies were placed under the immediate command of that brilliant young chieftain, George B. McClellan, whose genius as organizer, ability as disciplinarian, and magnetism in contact with his men, rapidly advanced his heavily reënforced army to a high plane of efficiency. The pride felt in him was manifested by the title "Young Napoleon," bestowed upon him by his admiring countrymen. No advance, however, was made by his army until the following spring. The Confederate army, under General Joseph E. Johnston, was occupied during the remaining months of summer and fall, mainly in drilling, recruiting its ranks, doing picket duty, and, as winter approached, in gathering supplies and preparing, as far as possible, for protection against Virginia freezes and snows.

My men were winter-quartered in the dense pine thickets on the rough hills that border the Occoquan. Christmas came, and was to be made as joyous as our surroundings would permit, by a genuine Southern eggnog with our friends. The country was scoured far and near for eggs, which were exceedingly scarce. Of sugar we still had at that time a reasonable supply, but our small store of eggs and the other ingredients could not be increased in all the country round about. Mrs. Gordon superintended the preparation of this favorite Christmas beverage, and at last the delicious potion was ready. All stood anxiously waiting with camp cups in hand. The servant started toward the company with full and foaming bowl, holding it out before him with almost painful care. He had taken but a few steps when he struck his toe against the uneven floor of the rude quarters and stumbled. The scattered fragments of crockery and the aroma of the wasted nectar marked the melancholy wreck of our Christmas cheer.

The winter was a severe one and the men suffered greatly—not only for want of sufficient preparation, but because those from farther South were unaccustomed to so cold a climate. There was much sickness in camp. It was amazing to see the large number of country boys who had never had the measles. Indeed, it seemed to me that they ran through the whole catalogue of complaints to which boyhood and even babyhood are subjected. They had everything almost except teething, nettle-rash, and whooping-cough. I rather think some of them were afflicted with this latter disease. Those who are disposed to wonder that Southern troops should suffer so much from a Virginia winter will better appreci-

ate the occasional severity of that climate when told of the incident which I now relate. General R. A. Alger, of the Union army, ex-Governor of Michigan and ex-Secretary of War, states that he was himself on picket duty in winter and at night in this same section of Virginia. It was his duty as officer in charge to visit during the night the different picket posts and see that the men were on the alert, so as to avoid surprises. It was an intensely cold night, and on one of his rounds, a few hours before daylight, he approached a post where a solitary picket stood on guard. As he neared the post he was greatly surprised to find that the soldier did not halt him and force him to give the countersign. He could plainly see the soldier standing on his post, leaning against a tree, and was indignant because he supposed he had found one of his men asleep on duty, when to remain awake and watchful was essential to the army's safety. Walking up to his man, he took him by the arm to arouse him from sleep and place him under immediate arrest. He was horrified to find that the sentinel was dead. Frozen, literally frozen, was this faithful picket, but still standing at the post of duty where his commander had placed him, his form erect and rigid—dead on his post!

Even at that early period the Southern men were scantily clad, though we had not then reached the straits to which we came as the war progressed, and of which a simple-hearted countrywoman gave an approximate conception when she naïvely explained that her son's only pair of socks did not wear out, because "when the feet of the socks got full of holes I just knitted new feet to the tops, and when the tops wore out I just knitted new tops to the feet."

This remarkable deficiency in heavy clothing among the Southern troops even at the beginning of the war is easily explained. We were an agricultural people. Farming or planting was fairly remunerative and brought comfort, with not only financial but personal independence, which induced a large majority of our population to cling to rural life and its delightful occupations. Little attention, comparatively, was paid to mining or manufacturing. The railroads were constructed through cotton belts rather than through coal-and iron-fields. There were some factories for the manufacture of cloth, but these were mainly engaged upon cotton fabrics, and those which produced woollens or heavy goods were few and of limited capacity. It will be seen that in this situation, with small milling facilities, with great armies on our hands, and our ports closed against foreign importations, we were reduced to the dangerous extremity of blockade-running, and to the still more hazardous contingency of capturing now and then overcoats and trousers from the Union forces. . . .

At last after the winter months, each one of which seemed to us almost a year, the snows on the Occoquan melted. The buds began to swell, the dogwood to blossom, and the wild onions, which the men gathered by the bushel and ate, began to shed their pungent odor on the soft warm air. With the spring came also the marching and the fighting. General McClellan landed his splendid army at Yorktown, and threatened Richmond from the Virginia peninsula. The rush then came to relieve from capture the small force of General Magruder and to confront General McClellan's army at his new base of operations. Striking camp and moving to the nearest depot, we were soon on the way to Yorktown. The long trains packed with their living Confederate freight were hurried along with the utmost possible speed. As the crowded train upon which I sat rushed under full head of steam down grade on this single track, it was met by another train of empty cars flying with great speed in the opposite direction. The crash of the fearful collision and its harrowing results are indescribable. Nearly every car on the densely packed train was telescoped and torn in pieces; and men, knapsacks, arms, and shivered seats were hurled to the front and piled in horrid mass against the crushed timbers and ironwork. Many were killed, many maimed for life, and the marvel is that any escaped unhurt. Mrs. Gordon, who was with me on this ill-fated train, was saved, by a merciful Providence, without the slightest injury. Her hands were busied with the wounded, while I superintended the cutting away of débris to rescue the maimed and remove the dead.

Robert E. Lee, who would decisively defeat the befuddled McClellan during the Peninsular Campaign and assume the leadership of the Army of Virginia

II

THE PENINSULAR CAMPAIGN

AS 1862 OPENED, UNION PLANS FOR AN OFFENSIVE MATURED. DESPITE SOME MISGIV-ings on the part of President Abraham Lincoln, the Union commander, Maj. Gen. George B. McClellan, proposed to move against Richmond by sea. He would use the Union's superior maritime resources to place the Army of the Potomac on the peninsula between the York and the James Rivers in eastern Virginia, some 70 miles southeast of the Confederate capital, thereby flanking the enemy army concentrated before Washington. Brilliantly conceived, the campaign proved a failure, through a combination of poor execution, bad luck, and the emergence of Robert E. Lee at the head of the Confederate forces before Richmond.

★★★

GEORGE B. McCLELLAN
The Movement to the Peninsula

McClellan's peninsular operation got off to a slow start. Even before the troops were scheduled to embark, Confederate Gen. Joseph E. Johnston pulled his army back from its camps in north central Virginia to the line of the Rappahannock. Though McClellan hailed this move as a victory achieved by pure military skill, others were not so impressed. Lincoln believed that the peninsular adventure was no longer necessary, and possibly dangerous, since

Johnston's army was now considerably closer to Richmond than had been the case. Despite the President's misgivings, McClellan insisted that the undertaking go forward. Further complicating matters was a relative shortage of shipping, which made it necessary to move the troops by individual divisions rather than whole corps. Nevertheless, by mid-March the Army of the Potomac began to move.

Civilians watch as Federal transports embark troops at Alexandria.

On the 17th of March the leading division embarked at Alexandria. The campaign was undertaken with the intention of taking some 145,000 troops, to be increased by a division of 10,000 drawn from the troops in the vicinity of Fort Monroe, giving a total of 155,000. Strenuous efforts were made to induce the President to take away Blenker's German division of 10,000 men. Of his own volition he at first declined, but the day before I left Washington he yielded to the non-military pressure and reluctantly gave the order, thus reducing the expected force to 145,000.

While at Fairfax Court House, on the 12th of March, I learned that there had appeared in the daily papers the order relieving me from the general command of all the armies and confining my authority to the Department of the Potomac. I had received no previous intimation of the intention of the Government in this respect. Thus, when I embarked for Fort Monroe on the 1st of April, my command extended from Philadelphia to Richmond, from the Alleghanies, including the Shenandoah, to the Atlantic;

for an order had been issued a few days previous placing Fort Monroe and the Department of Virginia under my command, and authorizing me to withdraw from the troops therein ten thousand, to form a division to be added to the First Corps.

The fortifications of Washington were at this time completed and armed. I had already given instructions for the refortification of Manassas, the reopening of the Manassas Gap Railroad, the protection of its bridges by blockhouses, the intrenchment of a position for a brigade at or near the railroad crossing of the Shenandoah, and an intrenched post at Chester Gap. I left about 42,000 trooops for the immediate defense of Washington, and more than 35,000 for the Shenandoah Valley—an abundance to insure the safety of Washington and to check any attempt to recover the lower Shenandoah and threaten Maryland. Beyond this force, the reserves of the Northern States were all available.

On my arrival at Fort Monroe on the 2d of April, I found five divisions of infantry, Sykes's brigade of regulars, two regiments of cavalry, and a portion of the reserve artillery disembarked. Another cavalry regiment and a part of a fourth had arrived, but were still on shipboard; comparatively few wagons had come. On the same day came a telegram stating that the Department of Virginia was withdrawn from my control, and forbidding me to form the division of ten thousand men without General Wool's sanction. I was thus deprived of the command of the base of operations, and the ultimate strength of the army was reduced to 135,000—another serious departure from the plan of campaign. Of the troops disembarked, only four divisions, the regulars, the majority of the reserve artillery, and a part of the cavalry, could be moved, in consequence of the lack of transportation. Casey's division was unable to leave Newport News until the 16th, from the impossibility of supplying it with wagons.

The best information obtainable represented the Confederate troops around Yorktown as numbering at least fifteen thousand, with about an equal force at Norfolk; and it was clear that the army lately at Manassas, now mostly near Gordonsville, was in position to be thrown promptly to the Peninsula. It was represented that Yorktown was surrounded by strong earth-works, and that the Warwick River, instead of stretching across the Peninsula to Yorktown,—as proved to be the case,—came down to Lee's Mills from the North, running parallel with and not crossing the road from Newport News to Williamsburg. It was also known that there were intrenched positions of more or less strength at Young's Mills, on the Newport News road, and at Big Bethel, Howard's Bridge, and Ship's Point, on or near the Hampton and Yorktown road, and at Williamsburg.

On my arrival at Fort Monroe, I learned, in an interview with Flag-Officer Goldsborough, that he could not protect the James as a line of supply, and that he could furnish no vessels to take an active part in the reduction of the batteries at York and Gloucester or to run by and gain their rear. He could only aid in the final attack after our land batteries had essentially silenced their fire.

I thus found myself with 53,000 men in condition to move, faced by the conditions of the problem just stated. Information was received that Yorktown was already being reënforced from Norfolk, and it was apprehended that the main Confederate army would promptly follow the same course. I therefore determined to move at once with the force in hand, and endeavor to seize a point—near the Halfway House—between Yorktown and Williamsburg. . . . The advance commenced on the morning of the 4th of April. . . .

★★★

WARREN LEE GOSS
Yorktown and Williamsburg

Warren Lee Goss was a young volunteer with the 2nd Massachusetts Artillery. He served in all the campaigns in the eastern theater. After the war he wrote about his adventures in a series of articles which first appeared in The Century Magazine *and later were published in* Battles and Leaders of the Civil War. *Eventually a somewhat modified version of his memoirs was collected together as* Recollections of a Private: A Story of the Army of the Potomac (New York, 1890). *This selection, from* Battles and Leaders, *gives a vivid picture of the army as it marched to the front during the opening days of the Peninsular Campaign and of the fighting around Yorktown and Williamsburg, where McClellan was successfully held for several precious weeks by a relatively insignificant Confederate force, with almost fatal consequences for the subsequent course of the campaign.*

It was with open-eyed wonder that, as part of McClellan's army, we arrived at Old Point Comfort and gazed upon Fort Monroe, huge and frowning. Negroes were everywhere, and went about their work with an air of importance born of their new-found freedom. These were the "contrabands" for whom General [Benjamin] Butler had recently invented that sobriquet. We pitched our tents amid the charred and blackened ruins of what had been the beautiful and aristocratic village of Hampton. The first thing I noticed about the ruins, unaccustomed as I was to Southern architecture, was the absence of cellars. The only building left standing of all the village was the massive old Episcopal church. Here

Washington had worshiped, and its broad aisles had echoed to the footsteps of armed men during the Revolution. In the church-yard the tombs had been broken open. Many tombstones were broken and overthrown, and at the corner of the church a big hole showed that some one with a greater desire for possessing curiosities than reverence for ancient landmarks had been digging for the corner-stone and its buried mementos.

Along the shore which looks toward Fort Monroe were landed artillery, baggage-wagons, pontoon trains and boats, and the level land back of this was crowded with the tents of the soldiers. Here and there were groups frying hard-tack and bacon. Near at hand was the irrepressible army mule, hitched to and eating out of pontoon boats; those who had eaten their ration of grain and hay were trying their teeth, with promise of success, in eating the boats. An army mule was hungrier than a soldier, and would eat anything, especially a pontoon boat or rubber blanket. The scene was a busy one. The red cap, white leggins, and baggy trousers of the Zouaves mingled with the blue uniforms and dark trimmings of the regular infantry-men, the short jackets and yellow trimmings of the cavalry, the red stripes of the artillery, and the dark blue with orange trimmings of the engineers; together with the ragged, many-colored costumes of the black laborers and teamsters, all busy at something.

One morning we broke camp and went marching up the Peninsula. The roads were very poor and muddy with recent rains, and were crowded with the indescribable material of the vast army which was slowly creeping through the mud over the flat, wooded country. It was a bright day in April—a perfect Virginia day; the grass was green beneath our feet, the buds of the trees were just unrolling into leaves under the warming sun of spring, and in the woods the birds were singing. The march was at first orderly, but under the unaccustomed burden of heavy equipments and knapsacks, and the warmth of the weather, the men straggled along the roads, mingling with the baggage-wagons, ambulances, and pontoon trains, in seeming confusion.

During our second day's march it rained, and the muddy roads, cut up and kneaded, as it were, by the teams preceding us, left them in a state of semi-liquid filth hardly possible to describe or imagine. When we arrived at Big Bethel the rain was coming down in sheets. A dozen houses of very ordinary character, scattered over an area of a third of a mile, constituted what was called the village. Just outside and west of the town was an insignificant building from which the place takes its name. It did not seem large enough or of sufficient consequence to give name to a hamlet as small as Big Bethel. Before our arrival it had evidently been occupied as officers' barracks for the enemy, and looked very little like a church.

I visited one of the dwelling-houses just outside the fortifications (if the insignificant rifle-pits could be called such) for the purpose of obtaining some-thing more palatable than hard-tack, salt beef, or pork, which, with coffee, comprised the marching rations. The woman of the house was communicative, and expressed her surprise at the great number of Yanks who had "come down to invade our soil." She said she had a son in the Confederate army, or, as she expressed it, "in our army," and then tearfully said she should tremble for her boy every time she heard of a battle. I expressed the opinion that we should go into Richmond without much fighting. "No!" said she, with the emphasis of conviction, "you all will drink hot blood before you all get thar!"

While wandering about, I came to the house of a Mrs. T——, whose husband was said to be a captain in the Confederate service and a "fire-eating" secessionist. Here some of our men were put on guard for a short time, until relieved by guards from other parts of the army as they came up, whereupon we went on. A large, good-looking woman, about forty years old, who, I learned, was Mrs. T——, was crying profusely, and I could not induce her to tell me why. One of the soldiers said her grief was caused by the fact that some of our men had helped themselves to the contents of cupboard and cellar. She was superintending the loading of an old farm-wagon, into which she was putting a large family of colored people, with numerous bundles. The only white person on the load as it started away was the mistress, who sat amid her dark chattels in desolation and tears. Returning to the house, after this exodus, I found letters, papers, and odds and ends of various kinds littering the floor; whether overturned in the haste of the mistress or by the visiting soldiers, I could only guess. No other building at Big Bethel was so devastated, and I did not see another building so treated on our whole route. The men detailed to guard it declined to protect the property of one who was in arms fighting against us.

After leaving Big Bethel we began to feel the weight of our knapsacks. Castaway overcoats, blankets, parade-coats, and shoes were scattered along the route in reckless profusion, being dropped by the overloaded soldiers, as if after plowing the roads with heavy teams they were sowing them for a harvest. I lightened my knapsack without much regret, for I could not see the wisdom of carrying a blanket or overcoat when I could pick one up almost anywhere along the march. Very likely the same philosophy actuated those who preceded me or came after. The colored people along our route occupied themselves in picking up this scattered property. They had on their faces a distrustful look, as if uncertain of the tenure of their harvest. The march up the peninsula seemed very slow, yet it was impossible to increase our speed, owing to the bad condition of the roads. I learned in time that marching on paper and the actual march made two very different impressions. I can easily understand and excuse our fireside heroes, who fought their or our battles at home over comfortable breakfast-tables, without impediments of any kind to circumscribe their fancied operations; it is so much easier to man-œuvre and fight large armies around the corner gro-cery, than to fight, march, and manœuvre in mud and rain, in the face of a brave and vigilant enemy.

The baggage-trains were a notable spectacle. To each baggage-wagon were attached four or six mules, driven usually by a colored man, with only one rein, or line, and that line attached to the bit of the near leading mule, while the driver rode in a saddle upon the near wheel mule. Each train was accompanied by a guard, and while the guard urged the drivers the drivers urged the mules. The drivers were usually expert, and understood well the wayward, sportive natures of the creatures over whose destinies they presided. On our way to Yorktown our pontoon and baggage trains were sometimes blocked for miles, and the heaviest trains were often unloaded by the guard to facilitate their removal from the mud. It did seem at times as if there were needless delays with the trains, partly due, no doubt, to fear of danger ahead. While I was guarding our pontoon train, after leaving Big Bethel, the teams stopped all along the line. Hurrying to the front, I found one of the lead-ing teams badly mired, but not enough to justify the stopping of the whole train. The lazy colored driver was comfortably asleep in the saddle. "Get that team out of the mud!" I yelled, bringing him to his senses. He flourished his long whip, shouted his mule lingo at the team, and the mules pulled frantically, but not together. "Can't you make your mules pull to-

Battery guns bombard ships during the first day's firing at Yorktown.

gether?" I inquired. "Dem mules pull right smart!" said the driver. Cocking and capping my unloaded musket, I brought it to the shoulder and again commanded the driver, "Get that team out of the mud!" The negro rolled his eyes wildly and woke up all over. He first patted his saddle mule, spoke to each one, and then, flourishing his long whip with a crack like a pistol, shouted, "Go 'long dar!! what I feed yo' fo'!" and the mule team left the slough in a very expeditious manner.

When procuring luxuries of eggs or milk, we paid the people at first in silver, and they gave us local scrip in change; but we found on attempting to pay it out again that they were rather reluctant to receive it, even at that early state in Confederate finance,

and much preferred Yankee silver or notes.

On the afternoon of April 5th, 1862, the advance of our column was brought to a standstill, with the right in front of Yorktown, and the left by the enemy's works at Lee's mills. We pitched our camp on Wormley Creek, near the Moore house, on the York River, in sight of the enemy's water-battery and their defensive works at Gloucester Point. One of the impediments to an immediate attack on Yorktown was the difficulty of using light artillery in the muddy fields in our front, and at that time the topography of the country ahead was but little understood, and had to be learned by reconnoissance in force. We had settled down to the siege of Yorktown; began bridging the streams between us and the enemy, constructing and improving the roads for the rapid transit of supplies, and for the advance. The first parallel was opened about a mile from the enemy's fortifications, extending along the entire front of their works, which reached from the York River on the left to Warwick Creek on the right, along a line about four miles in length. Fourteen batteries and three redoubts were planted, heavily armed with ordnance.

We were near Battery No. 1, not far from the York River. On it were mounted several 200-pounder guns, which commanded the enemy's water-batteries. One day I was in a redoubt on the left, and saw General McClellan with the Prince de Joinville, examining the enemy's works through their fieldglasses. They very soon drew the fire of the observant enemy, who opened with one of their heavy guns on the group, sending the first shot howling and hissing over and very close to their heads; another, quickly following it, struck in the parapet of the redoubt. The French prince, seemingly quite startled, jumped and glanced nervously around, while McClellan quietly knocked the ashes from his cigar.

Several of our war-vessels made their appearance in the York River, and occasionally threw a shot at the enemy's works; but most of them were kept busy at Hampton Roads, watching for the iron-clad *Merrimac*, which was still afloat. The firing from the enemy's lines was of little consequence, not amounting to over ten or twelve shots each day, a number of these being directed at the huge balloon which went up daily on a tour of inspection, from near General Fitz John Porter's headquarters. One day the balloon broke from its mooring of ropes and sailed majestically over the enemy's works; but fortunately for its occupants it soon met a countercurrent of air which returned it safe to our lines. The month of April was a dreary one, much of the time rainy and uncomfortable. It was a common expectation among us that we were about to end the rebellion. One of my comrades wrote home to his father that we should probably finish up the war in season for him to be at home to teach the village school the following winter; in fact, I believe he partly engaged to teach it. Another wrote to his mother: "We have got them hemmed in on every

side, and the only reason they don't run is because they can't." We had at last corduroyed every road and bridged every creek; our guns and mortars were in position; Battery No 1. had actually opened on the enemy's works, Saturday, May 3d, 1862, and it was expected that our whole line would open on them in the morning. About 2 o'clock of Saturday night, or rather of Sunday morning, while on guard duty, I observed a bright illumination, as if a fire had broken out within the enemy's lines. Several guns were fired from their works during the early morning hours, but soon after daylight of May 4th it was reported that they had abandoned their works in our front, and we very quickly found the report to be

Observation balloon *Intrepid* prepares to launch for a reconnoitering expedition.

true. As soon as I was relieved from guard duty, I went over on "French leave" to view our enemy's fortifications. They were prodigiously strong. A few tumble-down tents and houses and seventy pieces of heavy ordnance had been abandoned as the price of the enemy's safe retreat.

As soon as it was known that the Confederates had abandoned the works at Yorktown, the commanding general sent the cavalry and horse artillery under Stoneman in pursuit to harass the retreating column. The infantry divisions of Smith (Fourth Corps) and Hooker (Third Corps) were sent forward by two roads to support the light column. General Sumner (the officer second in rank in the Army of the Potomac) was directed to proceed to the front and assume command until McClellan's arrival. Stoneman overtook Johnston's rear-guard about noon, six miles from Williamsburg, and skirmished with the cavalry of Stuart, following sharply until 4 o'clock, when he was confronted by a line of redoubts before Williamsburg. The works consisted of a large fort (Magruder) at the junction of two roads running from Yorktown to Williamsburg, and small redoubts on each side of this, making an irregular chain of fortifications extending, with the creeks upon which they rested on either flank, across the peninsula.

Pickets converse before battle of Yorktown, a common circumstance.

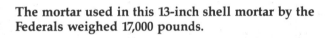

The mortar used in this 13-inch shell mortar by the Federals weighed 17,000 pounds.

G. MOXLEY SORREL
The Peninsula and Williamsburg

Confederate Capt. Gilbert Moxley Sorrel (1838–1901) was also in the Peninsula in April and May of 1862. Before the war Sorrel, a native Georgian, had been a railroad clerk and militiaman in the Georgia Hussars. He began the war in Charleston Harbor during the attack on Fort Sumter. Shortly before First Bull Run he was made a captain and volunteer aide-de-camp on the staff of Brig. Gen. James Longstreet. He spent the next three years in various staff positions with Longstreet, particularly distinguishing himself in the Wilderness in early 1864. *He was promoted brigadier and given a brigade and subsequently a division which he led ably. Severely wounded early in 1865, he was still incapacitated at the end of the war. After the war he became a merchant and shipper and found time to write* Recollections of a Confederate Staff Officer *(New York, 1905), one of the most perceptive and readable memoirs to come out of the struggle, from which the following selection, which elaborates on operations in the Peninsula, has been taken.*

. . . I must hasten to the Peninsula, where at Yorktown and along the lines of the little Warwick River, McClellan and Johnston are frowning at each other; the former, as usual, tripling the Confederate force and bawling for more men. Persons and things I have left behind will probably come into these jottings in the loose way they fall from the pen.

Longstreet with his staff and some of his regiments were among the first arrivals to face McClellan and gave great relief to [John B.] Magruder. This officer, a major-general, commanding some 10,000 to 12,000 men, had offered a most extraordinary and successful defense. It was a wonderful piece of bluff and could have won only against McClellan. Yorktown was strongly armed and well defended. Thence stretching across the Peninsula was a sluggish little stream known as the Warwick River. It was fordable in almost all places, in some nearly dry-shod.

Magruder's engineers had strengthened the defenses by some dams that gathered a good spread of water to be passed in an attack. The Warwick, of many miles extent, was necessarily thinly defended. Magruder put his whole force behind it, an attenuated line, up and down which he constantly rode in full sight of the enemy. He was known in the old Army as "Prince John," from the splendor of his appearance and his dress. Of commanding form and loving display, he had assembled a numerous staff, all, like himself, in the most showy uniforms. To these he added a fine troop of cavalry, and when the cavalcade at a full gallop inspected the thin lines of the Warwick, it was a sight for men and gods. I am persuaded he so impressed "Little Mac" that he sang out for more men and thus lost his opportunity. In very truth he was so strong and Magruder so weak that the Union ramrods should have sufficed to

break the defense and gobble up the magnificent "Prince John."

Longstreet's arrival was therefore a great relief, and soon Johnston had his army in full position, making McClellan almost frantic; he more than doubled Johnston's actual strength. A strong attack should have prevailed to drive us away; and if briskly followed, eventually into the York River. But Johnston knew his man, as did indeed every Confederate leader later on. Lee, Longstreet, Jackson, the Hills all knowing his points, while serving in the U.S. Army, could now rightly measure him. McClellan was a lovable man, an admirable organizer, but with little taste for battle unless largely outnumbering his opponent. Here in the trenches occurred remarkable scenes. Many of the Southern regiments had enlisted for only twelve months and the time expired in April. Re-enlistments and elections of the officers took place under fire of the enemy! Our men were splendid, and with rare exceptions they refused home and re-enlisted, this time for the war.

Inactivity continued for some time, Longstreet commanding the center with his own and other troops, until it was soon apparent to Johnston that Richmond was too much exposed to attacks on the north side of the James River. The capital must be covered; besides, both our flanks were endangered by the enemy's immense superiority on the water. Preparations therefore began for a move, and on the night of May 3 the army was successfully drawn from its trenches and started on its deliberate, well-ordered retreat. On May 5 our rearguard was overtaken and attacked in force at Williamsburg, Longstreet in command, with a considerable part of the army. It was a stubborn, all-day fight, with serious losses on both sides, but the enemy was beaten off and we resumed the march that night, the Federals having enough of it. We were not again molested. This was our first severe fight, and the steadiness and order of officers and men appeared to be very satisfactory. I was promoted to be major soon afterwards, the commission dating May 5, the day of the action. There was a gruesome but affecting sight

General McClellan's army proceeds through woods and water on way from Williamsburg.

during the battle. Colonel Mott, of high reputation, had brought from his State the Nineteenth Mississippi Infantry. It was hotly engaged in a long, fierce fight, and Mott fell. His black servant in the rear immediately took a horse and went to the firing line for his master's body. I met the two coming out of the fire and smoke. The devoted negro had straddled the stiffened limbs of his master on the saddle before him, covered his face with a handkerchief, and thus rescued his beloved master's body for interment with his fathers on the old Mississippi estate.

The celebrated L. Q. C. Lamar was lieutenant-colonel of the regiment, and succeeded to the command, until forced by physical disability, he retired to Richmond for other service. The army moving on soon neared the capital and took up the several positions assigned its divisions. McClellan's huge force following, threw itself across the Chickahominy, and the siege of Richmond may be said to have begun.

On the withdrawal of the army from the Peninsula, Norfolk and Gloucester Point became indefensible and the destruction of immense quantities of material both for field use and for construction had to be submitted to. The blow was not made lighter by the loss of the famous *Virginia*, formerly the *Merrimac*, that did such havoc at Newport News. She could not be permitted to fall into the enemy's hands and was of too deep draft for service on the James River. Her commander, Admiral Josiah Tatnall, was therefore reluctantly forced to her destruction. She was blown up and disappeared. Other vessels, cruisers and gun-boats, boilers, engines, and great quantities of material for construction had to be destroyed for similar reasons. The loss was bitter to us, as so much could have been done with it all for a little fighting navy.

It was during the action at Williamsburg that I was ready to shout for joy at seeing my old troop, the Georgia Hussars, in a gallant charge. Their regiment, the Jeff Davis Legion, had been prematurely thrown at the enemy in a position he was thought about leaving. The cavalry colonel was wrong. Our Georgians went forward in fine style, expecting to carry everything, but quickly found themselves in a very hot place. The enemy was not retiring, but on the contrary gave the Legion so warm a reception as to empty many saddles. They all came back pell-mell, "the devil take the hind-most," my Hussar comrades wondering what their colonel had got them "into that galley for!" It was a severe lesson but a salutary one, and the regiment was not again caught that way. Longstreet saw them close by as they dashed forward, and said, "They must soon come back; the colonel is ahead of the right moment."

General Johnston was present on the field all day, but seeing Longstreet, the rearguard commander, carrying things very handsomely, generously forbore any interference and left the battle to his handling. He sent the latter such additional troops as he had to call for from time to time. When night came it was horrible. There were many dead and wounded and the weather nasty; the roads ankle deep in mud and slush. But the march had to be again taken up.

On the retreat from Yorktown, Brigadier-General [Gabriel J.] Rains was commanding the rearguard. He was a brother of the other Rains who at Augusta, Georgia, achieved the apparently impossible task of supplying ammunition. Both brothers were given to experiments in explosives and fond of that study. When Gabriel began moving out on our march he amused himself planting shells and other explosives in the roadway after us to tickle the pursuers. Hearing this I reported the matter to Longstreet, who instantly stopped it. He caused me to write Rains a rather severe note, reminding him that such practises were not considered in the limits of legitimate warfare, and that if he would put them aside and pay some attention to his brigade his march would be better and his stragglers not so numerous. This officer did not remain long on duty in the field. His talents, like those of his more celebrated brother, lay elsewhere.

After getting into position before Richmond, less than a month intervened between the reorganization and strengthening of the army and change of its commander.

EVANDER McIVOR LAW
Lee Takes Command

As the Confederate forces retired from the Peninsula they were followed in somewhat leisurely fashion by McClellan's Army of the Potomac. By 24 May both armies were in position before *Richmond. Now commenced the most serious phase of the campaign, as Federal troops deployed along the east bank of the Chickahominy River, not five miles from the Confederate cap-*

The swampy area of the Chickahominy was enundated by heavy rain on May 30 which threatened Federal movement.

ital. The Battle of Seven Pines/Fair Oaks (31 May–1 June 1862) followed, as Confederate commander Gen. Joseph E. Johnston attempted to destroy the Union IV Corps under Maj. Gen. Erasmus D. Keyes, exposed on the south side of the Chickahominy. The effort was a failure, but had important consequences, as recounted by

Evander McIvor Law, then serving as colonel of the 4th Alabama. The outbreak of the war had found Law (1836–1920), a graduate of the South Carolina Military Academy (The Citadel), teaching at a military high school in Tuskegee, Alabama. He recruited a company from among his students and served as its captain in the 4th

Alabama. By the end of 1861 he was in command of the regiment, serving with it in Longstreet's division. Law was an able officer and rose rapidly to brigadier, but no further, for he failed to get along with Longstreet, and served at the head of a brigade through some of the toughest fighting in the eastern theater. Towards the end of the war he served in the

Carolinas. Afterwards he moved to Florida, where he was active as a journalist and founder of the state's public education system. The following account of Seven Pines and its consequences is drawn from an article which Law wrote for The Southern Bivouac, *one of several magazines which were devoted to studying the conflict in the post-war years.*

The Federal army, holding the line of the Chickahominy from Mechanicsville to Bottom's bridge, at once commenced the construction of military bridges between those points, and before the end of May McClellan's left wing was advanced by throwing two corps of Heintzelman and Keyes across the river. The latter took position and entrenched on a line running in front of "Seven Pines" on the Williamsburg road, with its right extending across the York River Railroad in front of Fair Oaks station. Heintzelman was placed in supporting distance in the rear, near Savage's station. McClellan's outposts were now within five miles of Richmond. Almost near enough to realize President Lincoln's suggestion, when he inquired by telegraph on May 26th, "Can you get near enough to throw shells into the city?" This amiable desire was not destined to be gratified, for during the afternoon and night of the 30th of May a heavy rain-storm occurred, flooding the low grounds of the Chickahominy and threatening the destruction of the military bridges constructed by the Federal army. The two wings were to a certain extent isolated, and General Johnston took advantage of this condition of affairs to attack Keyes' corps near Seven Pines on the 31st of May. This corps was assailed by D. H. Hill's division and thoroughly routed. Heintzelman came to its support, but by this time the divisions of Longstreet and G. W. Smith had united in the attack with D. H. Hill, and this corps fared little better than that of Keyes. By the most strenuous exertions Sumner's Federal corps was thrown across the almost ruined bridges, during the afternoon and night of the 31st, and this timely reinforcement, together with the intervention of night, saved the left wing of McClellan's army from destruction.

The tardy movements of some of the Confederate commanders on the extreme right delayed the attack several hours beyond the time when it should have been made, and this delay was fatal to the complete success of General Johnston's plans. While G. W. Smith's division, to which I was attached, was warmly engaged near the junction of the "Nine Mile" road and the York River Railroad, General Johnston rode up and gave me an order as to the movements of my command. Night was rapidly approaching, and he seemed anxious to urge forward the attack with all possible speed so as to clear the field of the enemy before night. He was moving with the troops and personally directing the advance, when he received a severe wound in the shoulder

and was compelled to relinquish the command. The Confederates had been checked on their left wing by the arrival of Sumner's corps, and the fighting ceased just after dark. It was renewed on our right wing on the morning of the 1st of June without advantage to either side, and by 2 o'clock P.M. the battle was over, without having accomplished the purpose for which it was fought.

General G. W. Smith, an officer of acknowledged ability, succeeded General Johnston in command of the Confederate army on the night of the 31st of May. But during the afternoon of the next day, June 1st, he in turn relinquished the command to General [Robert E.] Lee, under orders from President Davis. Our right wing was at once withdrawn from its advanced position, and Smith's division on the left followed the next day. As I was standing near the Nine Mile road a day or two after the battle, General Lee passed along the road accompanied by two staff officers. I had never seen him before, and he was pointed out by some one near me. I observed the new commander of the "Army of Northern Virginia" very closely and with a great deal of interest. General Johnston was universally beloved and possessed the unbounded confidence of the army, and the commander who succeeded him must be "every inch a man" and a soldier to fill his place in their confidence and affection. General Lee had up to this time accomplished nothing to warrant the belief in his future greatness as a commander. He had made an unsuccessful campaign in Western Virginia the year before, and since that time had been on duty first at Charleston and then in Richmond. There was naturally a great deal of speculation among the soldiers as to how he would "pan out." The general tone, however, was one of confidence, which was invariably strengthened by a sight of the man himself. Calm, dignified, and commanding in his bearing, a countenance strikingly benevolent and self-possessed, a clear, honest eye that could look friend or enemy in the face; clean-shaven, except a closely-trimmed mustache which gave a touch of firmness to the well-shaped mouth; simply and neatly dressed in the uniform of his rank, felt hat, and top boots reaching to the knee; sitting on horse as if his home was in the saddle; such was Robert E. Lee as he appeared when he assumed command of the army of "Northern Virginia" in the early days of June 1862, never to relinquish it for a day, until its colors were furled for ever at Appomattox.

General Robert E. Lee

JAMES LONGSTREET

"The Seven Days," Including Frayser's Farm

Joseph Johnston had been an able commander, but his replacement, Robert E. Lee, was a brilliant one. Lee's assumption of command in Virginia ushered in a new phase in the war. Within days he was striking back at McClellan and the Army of the Potomac, in a series of battles known collectively as The Seven Days. The following account of these actions is by James Longstreet, who commanded Lee's right wing. Longstreet (1821–1904) was one of the most capable Confederate commanders. A West Pointer (1842), he served in Florida, Mexico, on the frontier, and in garrison. On the outbreak of the war he went South and was appointed a brigadier general in the Confederate Army. Thereafter he served in virtually every battle in the eastern theater, rising from brigade commander to corps commander. During the Peninsular Campaign he was still learning his trade and committed a number of unfortunate errors, but nevertheless managed to retain Lee's confidence. His account of The Seven Days is taken from Battles and Leaders of the Civil War.

When General Joseph E. Johnston was wounded at the battle of Seven Pines, and General Lee assumed his new duties as commander of the Army of Northern Virgina, General Stonewall Jackson was in the Shenandoah Valley, and the rest of the Confederate troops were east and north of Richmond in front of General George B. McClellan's army, then encamped about the Chickahominy River, 100,000 strong, and preparing for a regular siege of the Confederate capital. The situation required prompt and successful action by General Lee. Very early in June he called about him, on the noted Nine-mile road near Richmond, all his commanders, and asked each in turn his opinion of the military situation. I had my own views, but did not express them, believing that if they were important it was equally important that they should be unfolded privately to the commanding general. The next day I called on General Lee, and suggested my plan for driving the Federal forces away from the Chickahominy. McClellan had a small force at Mechanicsville, and farther back, at Beaver Dam Creek, a considerable portion of his army in a stronghold that was simply unassailable from the front. The banks of Beaver Dam Creek were so steep as to be impassable except on bridges. I proposed an echelon movement, and suggested that Jackson be called down from the Valley, and passed to the rear of the Federal right, in order to turn the position behind Beaver Dam, while the rest of the Confederate forces who were to emerge in the attack could cross the Chickahominy at points suitable for the succession in the move, and be ready to attack the Federals as soon as they were thrown from their position. After hearing me, General Lee sent General J. E. B. Stuart on his famous ride around Mc-

Clellan. The dashing horseman, with a strong reconnoitering force of cavalry, made a forced reconnoissance, passing above and around the Federal forces, recrossing the Chickahominy below them, and returning safe to Confederate headquarters. He made a favorable report of the situation and the practicability of the proposed plan. On the 23d of June General Jackson was summoned to General Lee's headquarters, and was there met by General A. P. Hill, General D. H. Hill, and myself. A conference resulted in the selection of the 26th as the day on which we should move against the Federal position at Beaver Dam. General Jackson was ordered down from the Valley. General A. P. Hill was to pass the Chickahominy with part of his division, and hold the rest in readiness to cross at Meadow Bridge, following Jackson's swoop along the dividing ridge between the Pamunkey and the Chickahominy. D. H. Hill and I were ordered to be in position on the Mechanicsville pike early on the 26th, ready to cross the river at Mechanicsville Bridge as soon as it was cleared by the advance of Jackson and A. P. Hill.

Thus matters stood when the morning of the 26th arrived. The weather was clear, and the roads were in fine condition. Everything seemed favorable to the move. But the morning passed and we received no tidings from Jackson. As noon approached, General Hill, who was to move behind Jackson, grew impatient at the delay and begged permission to hurry him up by a fusillade. General Lee consented, and General Hill opened his batteries on Mechanicsville, driving the Federals off. When D. H. Hill and I crossed at the Mechanicsville Bridge we found A. P. Hill severely engaged, trying to drive the Federals

Union men defend position at Ellerson's Mill.

from their strong position behind Beaver Dam Creek. Without Jackson to turn the Federal right, the battle could not be ours. Although the contest lasted until some time after night, the Confederates made no progress. The next day the fight was renewed, and the position was hotly contested by the Federals until 7 o'clock in the morning, when the advance of Jackson speedily caused the Federals to abandon their position, thus ending the battle.[1] It is easy to see that the battle of the previous day would have been a quick and bloodless Confederate victory if Jackson could have reached his position at the time appointed. In my judgment the evacuation of Beaver Dam Creek was very unwise on the part of the Federal commanders. We had attacked at Beaver Dam, and had failed to make an impression at that point, losing several thousand men and officers. This demonstrated that the position was safe. If the Federal commanders knew of Jackson's appraoch on the 26th, they had ample time to reënforce Porter's right before Friday morning (27th) with men and field defenses, to such extent as to make the remainder of the line to the right secure against assault. So that the Federals in withdrawing not only abandoned a strong position, but gave up the morale of their success, and transferred it to our somewhat disheartened forces; for, next to Malvern Hill, the sacrifice at Beaver Dam was unequaled in demoralization during the entire summer.

J.E.B. Stuart

1. According to General Fitz John Porter, it was not Jackson's approach, but information of that event, that caused the withdrawal of the Union troops, who, with the exception of "some batteries and infantry skirmishers," were withdrawn before sunrise on the 27th.

General A.P. Hill

From Beaver Dam we followed the Federals closely, encountering them again under Porter beyond Powhite Creek, where the battle of Gaines's Mill occurred. General A. P. Hill, being in advance, deployed his men and opened the attack without consulting me. A very severe battle followed. I came up with my reserve forces and was preparing to support Hill, who was suffering very severely, when I received an order from General Lee to make a demonstration against the Federal left, as the battle was not progressing to suit him. I threw in three brigades opposite the Federal left and engaged them in a severe skirmish with infantry and artillery. The battle then raged with great fierceness. General Jackson was again missing, and General Lee grew fearful of the result. Soon I received another message from General Lee, saying that unless I could do something the day seemed to be lost. I then determined to make the heaviest attack I could. The position in front of me was very strong. An open field led down to a difficult ravine a short distance beyond the Powhite Creek. From there the ground made a steep ascent, and was covered with trees and slashed timber and hastily made rifle-trenches. General Whiting came to me with two brigades of Jackson's men and asked me to put him in. I told him I was just organizing an

Federal left suffers several casualties at Gaines's Mill.

attack and would give him position. My column of attack then was R. H. Anderson's and Pickett's brigades, with Law's and Hood's of Whiting's division. We attacked and defeated the Federals on their left, capturing many thousand stand of arms, fifty-two pieces of artillery, a large quantity of supplies, and many prisoners,—among them General Reynolds, who afterward fell at Gettysburg. The Federals made some effort to reënforce and recover their lost ground, but failed, and during the afternoon and night withdrew their entire forces from that side of the Chickahominy, going in the direction of James River. On the 29th General Lee ascertained that McClellan was marching toward the James. He determined to make a vigorous move and strike the enemy a severe blow. He decided to intercept them in the neighborhood of Charles City cross-roads, and with that end in view planned a pursuit as follows: I was to march to a point below Frayser's farm with General A. P. Hill. General Holmes was to take up position below me on the New Market or River road, to be in readiness to coöperate with me and to attack such Federals as would come within his reach. Jackson was to pursue closely the Federal rear, crossing at the Grapevine Bridge, and coming in on the north of the cross-roads. Huger was to attend to the Federal right flank, and take position on the Charles City road west of the cross-roads. Thus we were to envelop the Federal rear and make the destruction of that part of McClellan's army sure. To reach my position south of the cross-roads, I had about sixteen miles to march. I marched 14 miles on the 29th, crossing over into the Darbytown road and moving down to its intersection, with the New Market road, where I camped for the night, about 3 miles southwest of Frayser's farm. On the morning of the 30th I moved two miles nearer up and made preparation to intercept the Federals as they retreated toward James River. General McCall, with a division of ten thousand Federals, was at the crossroads and about Frayser's farm. My division, being in advance, was deployed in front of the enemy. I placed such of my batteries as I could find position for, and kept Hill's troops in my rear. As I had twice as far to march as the other commanders, I considered it certain that Jackson and Huger would be in position when I was ready. After getting my troops in position I called upon General A. P. Hill to throw one of his brigades to cover my right and to hold the rest of his troops in readiness to give pursuit when the enemy had been dislodged. My line extended from near the Quaker road across the New Market road to the Federal

Wounded are examined at Savage's Station field hospital after the battle at Gaines's Mill.

right. The ground upon which I approached was much lower than that occupied by General McCall, and was greatly cut up by ravines and covered with heavy timber and tangled undergrowth. On account of these obstructions we were not disturbed while getting into position, except by the firing of a few shots that did no damage. Holmes got into position below me on the New Market road, and was afterward joined by Magruder, who had previously made an unsuccessful attack on the Federal rear-guard at Savage's Station.

By 11 o'clock our troops were in position, and we waited for the signal from Jackson and Huger. Everything was quiet on my part of the line, except occasional firing between my pickets and McCall's. I was in momentary expectation of the signal. About half-past 2 o'clock artillery firing was heard on my left, evidently at the point near White Oak Swamp where Huger was to attack. I very naturally supposed this firing to be the expected signal, and ordered some of my batteries to reply, as a signal that I was ready to coöperate. While the order to open was going around to the batteries, President Davis and General Lee, with their staff and followers, were with me in a little open field near the rear of my right. We were in pleasant conversation, anticipating fruitful results from the fight, when our batteries opened. Instantly the Federal batteries responded most spitefully. It was impossible for the enemy to see us as we sat on our horses in the little field, surrounded by tall, heavy timber and thick undergrowth; yet a battery by chance had our range and exact distance, and poured upon us a terrific fire. The second or third shell burst in the midst of us, killing two or three horses and wounding one or two men. Our little party speedily retired to safe quarters. The Federals doubtless had no idea that the Confederate President, commanding general, and division commanders were receiving point-blank shot from their batteries. Colonel Micah Jenkins was in front of us, and I sent him an order to silence the Federal battery, supposing that he could do so with his long-range rifles. He became engaged, and finally determined to charge the battery. That brought on a general fight between my division and the troops in front of us. Kemper on my right advanced his brigade over difficult ground and captured a battery. Jenkins moved his brigade forward and made a bold fight. He was followed by the other four brigades successively.

The enemy's line was broken, and he was partly dislodged from his position. The batteries were taken, but our line was very much broken up by the rough ground we had to move over, and we were not in sufficiently solid form to maintain a proper battle. The battle was continued, however, until we encountered succor from the corps of Generals Sumner and Heintzelman, when we were obliged to halt and hold the position the enemy had left. This line was held throughout the day, though at times, when vigorous combinations were made against me, McCall regained points along his line. Our counter-movements, however, finally pushed him back again, and more formidable efforts from our adversary were required. Other advances were made and reënforcements came to the support of the Federals, who contested the line with varying fortune, sometimes recovering batteries we had taken, and again losing them. Finally McCall's division was driven off, and fresh troops seemed to come in to their relief. Ten thousand men of A. P. Hill's division had been held in reserve, in the hope that Jackson and Huger would come up on our left, enabling us to dislodge the Federals, after which Hill's troops could be put in fresh to give pursuit, and follow them down to Harrison's Landing. Jackson found Grapevine Bridge destroyed and could not reach his position; while for some unaccountable reason Huger failed to take part, though near enough to do so. As neither Jackson nor Huger came up, and as night drew on, I put Hill in to relieve my troops. When he came into the fight the Federal line had been broken at every point except one. He formed his line and followed up in the position occupied by my troops. By night we succeeded in getting the entire field, though all of it was not actually occupied until we advanced in pursuit next day. As the enemy moved off they continued the fire of their artillery upon us from various points, and it was after 9 o'clock when the shells ceased to fall. Just before dark General McCall, while looking up a fragment of his division, found us where he supposed his troops were, and was taken prisoner. At the time he was brought in General Lee happened to be with us. As I had known General McCall pleasantly in our service together in the 4th Infantry, I moved to offer my hand as he dismounted. At the first motion, however, I saw he did not regard the occasion as one for renewing the old friendship, and I merely offered him some of my staff as an escort to Richmond. But for the succoring forces, which should have been engaged by Jackson, Huger, Holmes, and Magruder, McCall would have been entirely dislodged by the first attack. All of our other forces were within a radius of 3 miles, and in easy hearing of the battle, yet of the 50,000 none came in to coöperate. (Jackson should have done more for me than he did. When he wanted me at the Second Manassas, I marched two columns by night to clear the way at Thoroughfare Gap, and joined him in due season.) Hooker claimed at Glendale to have rolled me up and hurriedly thrown me over on Kearny,—tennis-like, I suppose; but McCall showed in his supplementary report that Hooker could as well claim, with a little tension of the hyperbole, that he had thrown me over the moon. On leaving Frayser's farm the Federals withdrew to Malvern Hill, and Lee concentrated his forces and followed them.

On the morning of July 1st, the day after the battle at Frayser's farm, we encountered the enemy at Malvern Hill, and General Lee asked me to make a reconnoissance and see if I could find a good position for the artillery. I found position offering good play for batteries across the Federal left over to the right, and suggested that sixty pieces should be put in

while Jackson engaged the Federal front. I suggested that a heavy play of this cross-fire on the Federals would so discomfit them as to warrant an assault by infantry. General Lee issued his orders accordingly, and designated the advance of Armistead's brigade as the signal for the grand assault. Later it was found that the ground over which our batteries were to pass into position on our right was so rough and obstructed that of the artillery ordered for us there only one or two batteries could go in at a time. As our guns in front did not engage, the result was the enemy concentrated the fire of fifty or sixty guns upon our isolated batteries, and tore them into fragments in a few minutes after they opened, piling horses upon each other and guns upon horses. Before

night, the fire from our batteries failing of execution, General Lee seemed to abandon the idea of an attack. He proposed to me to move around to the left with my own and A. P. Hill's division, turning the Federal right. I issued my order accordingly for the two divisions to go around and turn the Federal right, when in some way unknown to me the battle was drawn on. We were repulsed at all points with fearful slaughter, losing six thousand men and accomplishing nothing.

The Federals withdrew after the battle, and the next day I moved on around by the route which it was proposed we should take the day before. I followed the enemy to Harrison's Landing, and Jackson went down by another route in advance of Lee. As soon as we reached the front of the Federal position we put out our skirmish-lines, and I ordered an advance, intending to make another attack, but revoked it on Jackson urging me to wait until the arrival of General Lee. Very soon General Lee came, and, after carefully considering the position of the enemy and of their gun-boats on the James, decided that it would be better to forego any further operations. Our skirmish-lines were withdrawn, we ordered our troops back to their old lines around Richmond, and a month later McClellan's army was withdrawn to the North.

The Seven Days' Fighting, although a decided Confederate victory, was a succession of mishaps. If Jackson had arrived on the 26th,—the day of his own

Federal troops retreat during the Peninsular Campaign.

The Sixth Corps falls back before daylight
in retreat from the Chickahominy.

selection,—the Federals would have been driven back from Mechanicsville without a battle. His delay there, caused by obstructions placed in his road by the enemy, was the first mishap. He was too late in entering the fight at Gaines's Mill, and the destruction of Grapevine Bridge kept him from reaching Frayser's farm until the day after that battle. If he had been there, we might have destroyed or captured McClellan's army. Huger was in position for the battle of Frayser's farm, and after his batteries had misled me into opening the fight he subsided. Holmes and Magruder, who were on the New Market road to attack the Federals as they passed that way, failed to do so.

General McClellan's retreat was successfully managed; therefore we must give it credit for being well managed. He had 100,000 men, and insisted to the authorities at Washington that Lee had 200,000. In fact, Lee had only 90,000. General McClellan's plan to take Richmond by a siege was wise enough, and it would have been a success if the Confederates had consented to such a programme. In spite of McClellan's excellent plans, General Lee, with a force inferior in number, completely routed him, and while suffering less than McClellan, captured over six thousand of his men. General Lee's plans in the Seven Days' Fight were excellent, but were poorly executed. General McClellan was a very accomplished soldier and a very able engineer, but hardly equal to the position of field-marshal as a military chieftain. He organized the Army of the

Potomac cleverly, but did not handle it skillfully when in actual battle. Still I doubt if his retreat could have been better handled, though the rear of his army should have been more positively either in his own hands or in the hands of Sumner. Heintzelman crossed the White Oak Swamp prematurely and left the rear of McClellan's army exposed, which would have been fatal had Jackson come up and taken part in Magruder's affair of the 29th near Savage's Station.

I cannot close this sketch without referring to the Confederate commander when he came upon the scene for the first time. General Lee was an unusually handsome man, even in his advanced life. He seemed fresh from West Point, so trim was his figure and so elastic his step. Out of battle he was as gentle as a woman, but when the clash of arms came he loved fight, and urged his battle with wonderful determination. As a usual thing he was remarkably well-balanced—always so, except on one or two occasions of severe trial when he failed to maintain his exact equipoise. Lee's orders were always well considered and well chosen. He depended almost too much on his officers for their execution. Jackson was a very skillful man against such men as Shields, Banks, and Frémont, but when pitted against the best of the Federal commanders he did not appear so well. Without doubt the greatest man of rebellion times, the one matchless among forty millions for the peculiar difficulties of the period, was Abraham Lincoln.

* * *

FITZ JOHN PORTER
The Battle of Malvern Hill

The bloodiest action of The Seven Days was at Malvern Hill, on 1 July 1862, when, as already recounted by Longstreet, the Confederates attempted an assault of the well-entrenched Army of the Potomac. One of the finest accounts of this action is that of Fitz John Porter. Porter (1822–1901), a West Point graduate (1845), had a distinguished career in the Old Army, serving in Mexico and on the frontier. At the onset of the Civil War he rose rapidly and was named a brigadier general. So ably did he lead his divi-

sion in the early stages of the Peninsular Campaign that McClellan gave him V Corps. He commanded his corps through to the end of the year, but was cashiered early in 1862 for "willful failure to obey his orders" during the Second Bull Run Campaign, charges which he disputed for over 20 years, until partially vindicated in 1886. Porter's account of Malvern Hill is taken from Battles and Leaders of the Civil War.

Malvern Hill map shows approximate positions of brigades and batteries.

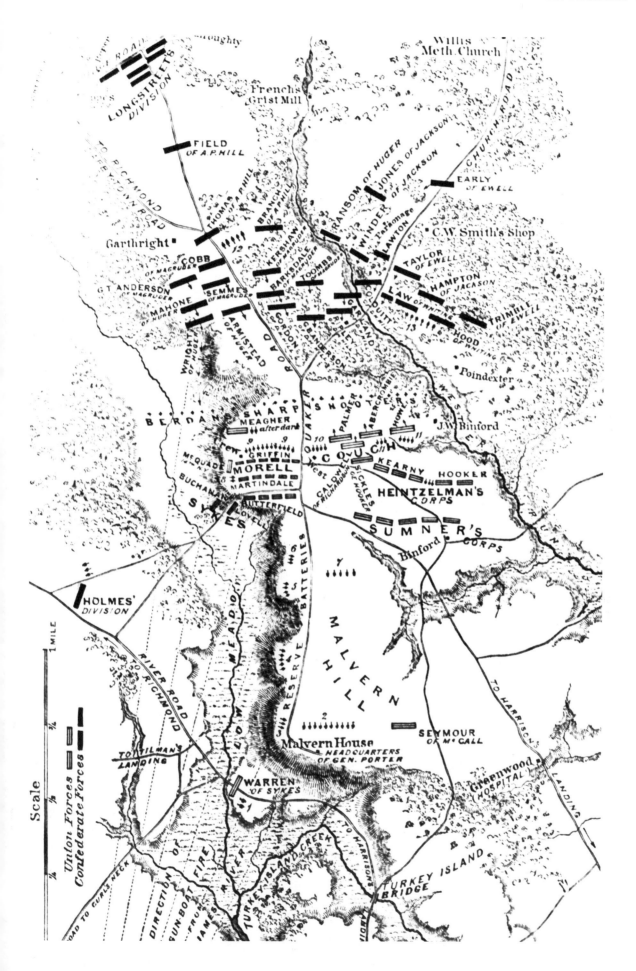

The final repulse of the Confederates at Malvern Hill was near Turkey Bend.

Our new field of battle embraced Malvern Hill, just north of Turkey Creek, and Crew's Hill, about one mile farther north. Both hills have given name to the interesting and eventful battle which took place on July 1st, and which I shall now attempt to describe.

The forces which on this occasion came under my control, and were engaged in or held ready to enter the contest, were my own corps, consisting of Morell's, Sykes's and McCall's divisions, Colonel H. J. Hunt's Artillery Reserve of one hundred pieces, including Colonel R. O. Tyler's Connecticut siege artillery, Couch's division of Keyes's corps, the brigades of John C. Caldwell and Thomas F. Meagher of Sumner's corps, and the brigade of D. E. Sickles of Heintzelman's corps. Though Couch was placed under my command, he was left uncontrolled by me, as will be seen hereafter. The other brigades were sent to me by their respective division commanders, in anticipation of my needs or at my request.

This new position, with its elements of great strength, was better adapted for a defensive battle than any with which we had been favored. It was elevated, and was more or less protected on each flank by small steams or by swamps, while the woods in front through which the enemy had to pass to attack us were in places marshy, and the timber so thick that artillery could not be brought up, and even troops were moved in it with difficulty. Slightly in rear of our line of battle on Crew's Hill the reserve artillery and infantry were held for immediate service. The hill concealed them from the view of the enemy and sheltered them to some extent from his fire. These hills, both to the east and west, were connected with the adjacent valleys by gradually sloping plains except at the Crew house, where for a little distance the slope was quite abrupt, and was easily protected by a small force. With the exception of the River road, all the roads from Richmond, along which the enemy would be obliged to approach, meet in front of Crew's Hill. This hill was flanked with ravines, enfiladed by our fire. The ground in front was sloping, and over it our artillery and infantry, themselves protected by the crest and ridges, had clear sweep for their fire. In all directions, for several hundred yards, the land over which an attacking force must advance was almost entirely cleared of forest and was generally cultivated.

I reached Malvern Hill some two hours before my command on Monday, June 30th; each division, as it came upon the field, was assigned to a position covering the approaches from Richmond along the River road and the debouches from the New Market, Charles City, and Williamsburg roads. Warren, with his brigade of about six hundred men, took position on the lowlands to the left, to guard against the approach of the enemy along the River road, or over the low, extensive, and cultivated plateau beyond and extending north along Crew's Hill. Warren's men were greatly in need of rest. The brigade had suffered greatly at Gaines's Mill, and was not expected to perform much more than picket duty, and it was large enough for the purpose designed, as it was not probable that any large force would be so reckless as to advance on that road. Warren was supported by the 11th U. S. Infantry, under Major Floyd-Jones, and late in the afternoon was strengthened by Martin's battery of 12-pounders and a detachment of the 3d Pennsylvania cavalry under Lieutenant Frank W. Hess.

On the west side of Malvern Hill, overlooking Warren, were some thirty-six guns, some of long range, having full sweep up the valley and over the cleared lands north of the River road. These batteries comprised Captain S. H. Weed's Battery I, 5th U. S. Artillery, Captain John Edwards's Batteries L and M, 3rd U. S. Artillery, J. H. Carlisle's Battery E, 2d U. S. Artillery, John R. Snead's Battery K, 5th U. S. Artillery, and Adolph Voegelee's, Battery B, 1st N. Y. Artillery Battalion, with others in reserve. To these, later in the day, were added the siege-guns of the 1st Connecticut Artillery, under Colonel Robert O. Tyler, which were placed on elevated ground immediately to the left of the Malvern house, so as to fire over our front line at any attacking force, and to sweep the low meadow on the left.

To General (then Colonel) Hunt, the accomplished and energetic chief of artillery, was due the excellent posting of these batteries on June 30th, and the rearrangement of all the artillery along the whole line on Tuesday (July 1st), together with the management of the reserve artillery on that day.

Major Charles S. Lovell, commanding Colonel William Chapman's brigade of Sykes's division, supported some of these batteries, and, with the brigade of Buchanan on his right, in a clump of pines, extended the line northward, near the Crew (sometimes called the Mellert) house.

Morell, prolonging Sykes's line on Crew's Hill, with headquarters at Crew's house, occupied the right of the line extending to the Quaker road. To his left front, facing west, was the 14th New York Volunteers, under Colonel McQuade, with a section of Captain W. B. Weeden's Battery C, 1st Rhode Island Artillery, both watching the Richmond road and the valley and protecting our left. On their right, under cover of a narrow strip of woods, skirting the Quaker road, were the brigades of Martindale and Butterfield, while in front of these, facing north, was Griffin's brigade. All were supporting batteries of Morell's division, commanded by Captain Weeden and others, under the general supervision of Griffin, a brave and skilled artillery officer.

About 3 o'clock on Monday the enemy was seen approaching along the River road, and Warren Hunt made all necessary dispositions to receive them. About 4 o'clock the enemy advanced and opened fire from their artillery upon Warren and Sykes and on the extreme left of Morell, causing a few casualties in Morell's division. In return for this intrusion the concentrated rapid fire of the artillery was opened upon them, soon smashing one battery to pieces, silencing another, and driving back their infantry and cavalry in rapid retreat, much to the satisfaction of thousands of men watching the result. The enemy left behind in possession of Warren a few prisoners, two guns and six caissons, the horses of which had been killed. The battery which had disturbed Morell was also silenced by this fire of artillery. On this occasion the gun-boats in the James made apparent their welcome presence and gave good support by bringing their heavy guns to bear upon the enemy. Though their fire caused a few casualties among our men, and inflicted but little, if any, injury upon the enemy, their large shells, bursting amid the enemy's troops far beyond the attacking force, carried great moral influence with them, and naturally tended, in addition to the effect of our artillery, to prevent any renewed attempt to cross the open valley on our left. This attacking force formed a small part of Wise's brigade of Holmes's division. They were all raw troops, which accounts for their apparently demoralized retreat. This affair is known as the action of Turkey Bridge or Malvern Cliff.

Our forces lay on their arms during the night, in substantially the positions I have described, patiently awaiting the attack expected on the following day.

McCall's division of Pennsylvania Reserves, now under General Truman Seymour, arrived during the night and was posted just in front of the Malvern house, and was held in reserve, to be called upon for service only in case of absolute necessity.

Early on Tuesday our lines were re-formed and slightly advanced to take full advantage of the formation of the ground, the artillery of the front line being re-posted in commanding positions, and placed under General Griffin's command, but under Captain Weeden's care, just behind the crest of the hill. The infantry was arranged between the artillery to protect and be protected by its neighbors, and prepared to be thrown forward, if at any time advisable, so as not to interfere with the artillery fire.

The corps of Heintzelman and Sumner had arrived during the night and taken position in the order named to the right and rear of Couch's division, protecting that flank effectively toward Western Run. They did not expect to be seriously engaged, but were ready to resist attack and to give assistance to the center and left, if circumstances should require it. At an early hour in the day Sumner kindly sent me Caldwell's brigade, as he thought I might need help. This brigade I placed near Butterfield, who was directed to send it forward wherever it should be needed or called for. He sent it to Couch at an opportune moment early in the day.

General McClellan, accompanied by his staff, visited our lines at an early hour, and approved my measures and those of General Couch, or changed them where it was deemed advisable. Though he left me in charge of that part of the field occupied by Couch, I at no time undertook to control that general, or even indicated a desire to do so, but with full confidence in his ability, which was justified by the result of his action, left him free to act in accordance

with his own judgment. I coöperated with him fully, however, having Morell's batteries, under Weeden, posted so as to protect his front, and sending him help when I saw he needed it. The division of Couch, though it suffered severely in the battle of Fair Oaks, had seen less service and met with fewer losses in these "Seven Days' battles" than any one of my three, and was prepared with full ranks to receive an attack, seeming impatient and eager for the fight. Its conduct soon confirmed this impression. Batteries of Hunt's Artillery Reserve were sent to him when needed—and also Caldwell's brigade, voluntarily sent to me early in the day by Sumner, and Sickles's brigade, borrowed of Heintzelman for the purpose.

About 10 A.M. the enemy's skirmishers and artillery began feeling for us along our line; they kept up a desultory fire until about 12 o'clock, with no severe injury to our infantry, who were well masked, and who revealed but little of our strength or position by retaliatory firing or exposure.

Up to this time and until nearly 1 o'clock our infantry were resting upon their arms and waiting the moment, certain to come, when the columns of the enemy rashly advancing would render it necessary to expose themselves. Our desire was to hold the enemy where our artillery would be most destructive, and to reserve our infantry ammunition for close quarters to repel the more determined assaults of our obstinate and untiring foe. Attacks by brigade were made upon Morell, both on his left front and on his right, and also upon Couch; but our artillery, admirably handled, without exception, was generally sufficient to repel all such efforts and to drive back the assailants in confusion, and with great loss.

While the enemy's artillery was firing upon us General Sumner withdrew part of his corps to the slope of Malvern Hill, to the right of the Malvern house, which descended into the valley of Western Run. Then, deeming it advisable to withdraw all our troops to that line, he ordered me to fall back to the Malvern house; but I protested that such a movement would be disastrous, and declined to obey the order until I could confer with General McClellan, who had approved of the disposition of our troops. Fortunately Sumner did not insist upon my complying with the order, and, as we were soon vigorously attacked, he advanced his troops to a point where he was but little disturbed by the enemy, but from which he could quickly render aid in response to calls for help or where need for help was apparent.

The spasmodic, though sometimes formidable attacks of our antagonists, at different points along our whole front, up to about 4 o'clock, were presumably demonstrations or feelers, to ascertain our strength, preparatory to their engaging in more serious work. An ominous silence, similar to that which had preceded the attack in force along our whole line at Gaines's Mill, now intervened, until, at about 5:30 o'clock, the enemy opened upon both Morell and Couch with artillery from nearly the whole of his front, and soon afterward pressed forward his columns of infantry, first on one and then on the other, or on both. As if moved by a reckless disregard of life, equal to that displayed at Gaines's Mill, with a determination to capture our army, or destroy it by driving us into the river, regiment after regiment, and brigade after brigade, rushed at our batteries; but the artillery of both Morell and Couch mowed them down with shrapnel, grape, and canister; while our infantry, withholding their fire until the enemy were within short range, scattered the remnants of their columns, sometimes following them up and capturing prisoners and colors.

As column after column advanced, only to meet the same disastrous repulse, the sight became one of the most interesting imaginable. The havoc made by the rapidly bursting shells from guns arranged so as to sweep any position far and near, and in any direction, was fearful to behold. Pressed to the extreme as they were, the courage of our men was fully tried. The safety of our army—the life of the Union—was felt to be at stake. In one case the brigades of Howe, Abercrombie, and Palmer, of Couch's division, under impulse, gallantly pushed after the retreating foe, captured colors, and advantageously advanced the right of the line, but at considerable loss and great risk. The brigades of Morell, cool, well-disciplined, and easily controlled, let the enemy return after each repulse, but permitted few to escape their fire. Colonel McQuade, on Morell's left, with the 14th New York, against orders and at the risk of defeat and disaster, yielding to impulse, gallantly dashed forward and repulsed an attacking party. Assisted by Buchanan of Sykes's division, Colonel Rice, with the 44th New York Volunteers, likewise drove a portion of the enemy from the field, taking a flag bearing the inscription "Seven Pines." Colonel Hunt, directing the artillery, was twice dismounted by having his horse shot under him, but though constantly exposed continued his labors until after dark. General Couch, who was also dismounted in like manner, took advantage of every opportunity to make his opponents feel his blows.

It is not to be supposed that our men, though concealed by the irregularities of the ground, were not sufferers from the enemy's fire. The fact is that before they exposed themselves by pursuing the enemy, the ground was literally covered with the killed and wounded from dropping bullets and bursting shells and their contents; but they bravely bore the severe trial of having to remain inactive under a damaging fire.

As Morell's front ranks became thinned out and the ammunition was exhausted, other regiments eagerly advanced; all were stimulated by the hope of a brilliant and permanent success, and nerved by the approving shouts of their commrades and the cry of "Revenge, boys!" "Remember McLane!" "Remember Black!" "Remember Gove!" or "Remember Cass!" [Colonels] Black and McLane and Gove had been killed at Gaines's Mill; [Colonels] Woodbury and Cass were then lying before them. Colonel Mc-Quade was the only regimental commander of Griffin's brigade who escaped death during the Seven Days, and he was constantly exposed.

During that ominous silence of which I have spoken, I determined that our opponents should reap no advantage, even if our lines yielded to attack, and therefore posted batteries, as in Gaines's Mill, to secure against the disaster of a break in our lines, should such a misfortune be ours. For this purpose I sent Weed, Carlisle, and Smead, with their batteries, to the gorge of the roads on Crew's Hill, from which the enemy must emerge in pursuit if he should break our lines; instructing them to join in the fight if necessary, but not to permit the advance of the foe, even if it must be arrested at the risk of firing upon friends. To these Colonel Hunt added three batteries of horse artillery. Though they were all thus posted and their guns loaded with double canister, "they were," as Captain Smead reported, "very happy to find their services not needed on that occasion."

It was at this time, in answer to my call for aid, that Sumner sent me Meagher, and Heintzelman sent Sickles, both of whom reached me in the height of battle, when, if ever, fresh troops would renew our confidence and insure our success. While riding rapidly forward to meet Meagher, who was approaching at a "double-quick" step, my horse fell, throwing me over his head, much to my discomfort both of body and mind. On rising and remounting I was greeted with hearty cheers, which alleviated my chagrin. This incident gave rise to the report, spread through the country, that I was wounded. Fearing that I might fall into the hands of the enemy, and if so that my diary and dispatch-book of the campaign, then on my person, would meet with the same fate and reveal information to the injury of our cause, I tore it up, scattering the pieces to the winds, as I rode rapidly forward, leading Meagher into action. I have always regretted my act as destroying interesting and valuable memoranda of our campaign.

Advancing with Meagher's brigade, accompanied by my staff, I soon found that our forces had successfully driven back their assailants. Determined, if possible, satisfactorily to finish the contest, regardless of the risk of being fired upon by our artillery in case of defeat, I pushed on beyond our lines into the woods held by the enemy. About fifty yards in front of us, a large force of the enemy suddenly rose and opened with fearful volleys upon our advancing line. I turned to the brigade, which thus far had kept pace with my horse, and found it standing "like a stonewall," and returning a fire more destructive than it received and from which the enemy fled. The brigade was planted. My presence ws no longer needed, and I sought General Sickles, whom I found giving aid to Couch. I had the satisfaction of learning that night that a Confederate detachment, undertaking to turn Meagher's left, was met by a portion of the 69th New York Regiment, which, advancing, repelled the attack and captured many prisoners.

After seeing that General Sickles was in a proper position, I returned to my own corps, where I was

Union sharpshooters of Morell's Division skirmish in wheat field.

joined by Colonel Hunt with some 32-pounder howitzers. Taking those howitzers, we rode forward beyond our lines, and, in parting salutation to our opponents, Colonel Hunt sent a few shells, as a warning of what would be ready to welcome them on the morrow if they undertook to disturb us.

Almost at the crisis of the battle—just before the advance of Meagher and Sickles—the gun-boats on the James River opened their fire with the good intent of aiding us, but either mistook our batteries at the Malvern house for those of the enemy, or were unable to throw their projectiles beyond us. If the former was the case, their range was well estimated, for all their shot landed in or close by Tyler's battery, killing and wounding a few of his men. Fortunately members of our excellent signal-service corps were present as usual on such occasions, and the message signaled to the boats, "For God's sake, stop firing," promptly relieved us from further damage and the demoralization of a "fire in the rear." Reference is occasionally seen in Confederate accounts of this battle to the fearful sounds of the projectiles from those gunboats. But that afternoon not one of their projectiles passed beyond my headquarters; and I have always believed and said, as has General Hunt, that the enemy mistook the explosions of shells from Tyler's siege-guns and Kusserow's 32-pounder howitzers, which Hunt had carried forward, for shells from the gun-boats.

While Colonel Hunt and I were returning from the front, about 9 o'clock, we were joined by Colonel A. V. Colburn, of McClellan's staff. We all rejoiced over the day's success. By these officers I sent messages to the commanding general, expressing the hope that our withdrawal had ended and that we should hold the ground we now occupied, even if we did not assume the offensive. From my standpoint I thought we could maintain our position, and perhaps in a few days could improve it by advancing. But I knew only the circumstances before me, and these were limited by controlling influences. It was now after 9 o'clock at night. Within an hour of the time that Colonels Hunt and Colburn left me, and before they could have reached the commanding general, I received orders from him to withdraw, and to direct Generals Sumner and Heintzelman to move at specified hours to Harrison's Landing and General Couch to rejoin his corps, which was then under way to the same point.[1]

These orders were immediately sent to the proper officers, and by daybreak, July 2d, our troops, preceded by their trains, were well on their way to their destination, which they reached that day, greatly wearied after a hard march over muddy roads, in the midst of a heavy rain. That night, freed from care and oblivious of danger, all slept a long sleep; and they awoke the next morning with the clear sun, a happier, brighter, and stronger body of men than that which all the day before, depressed and fatigued, had shivered in the rain.

The conduct of the rear-guard was intrusted to Colonel Averell, commander of the 3d Pennsylvania

Union supply depot

Cavalry, sustained by Colonel Buchanan, with his brigade of regulars, and the 67th New York Regiment. No trying trust was ever better bestowed or more satisfactorily fulfilled. At daybreak Colonel Averell found himself accidentally without artillery to protect his command in its difficult task of preventing an attack before our rear was well out of range. He at once arranged his cavalry in bodies to represent horse-batteries, and, manœuvring them to create the impression that they were artillery ready for action, he secured himself from attack until the rest of the army and trains had passed sufficiently to the rear to permit him to retire rapidly without

molestation. His stratagem was successful, and without loss he rejoined the main body of the army that night. Thus ended the memorable "Seven Days' battles," which, for severity and for stubborn resistance and endurance of hardships by the contestants, were not surpassed during the war. Each antagonist accomplished the result for which he aimed: one insuring the temporary relief of Richmond; the other gaining security on the north bank of the James, where the Union army, if our civil and military authorities were disposed, could be promptly reënforced, and from whence only, as subsequent events proved, it could renew the contest suc-

1. The order referred to read as follows:
"HEADQUARTERS ARMY OF THE POTOMAC, 9 P.M., JULY 1ST, 1862; BRIGADIER-GENERAL F. J. PORTER, COMMANDING FIFTH PROVISIONAL CORPS.—GENERAL: The General Commanding desires you to move your command at once, the artillery reserve moving first to Harrison's Bar. In case you should find it impossible to move your heavy artillery, you are to spike the guns and destroy the carriages. Couch's command will move under your orders. Communicate these instructions to him at once. The corps of Heintzelman and Sumner will move next. Please communicate to General Heintzelman the time of your moving. Additional gun-boats, supplies, and reënforcements will be met at Harrison's Bar. Stimulate your men by informing them that reënforcements, etc., have arrived at our new base. By command of MAJOR GENERAL MCCELLAN, JAMES A. HARDIE, LIEUTENANT-COLONEL, A.D.C., A.A.A.G."

cessfully. Preparations were commenced and dispositions were at once made under every prospect, if not direct promise, of large reënforcements for a renewal of the struggle on the south side of the James, and in the same manner as subsequently brought a successful termination of the war.

In the Fifth Corps, however, mourning was mingled with rejoicing. Greatly injured by the mishap of a cavalry blunder at Gaines's Mill, it had at Malvern, with the brave and gallant help of Couch and the generous and chivalric assistance of Heintzelman and Sumner, successfully repulsed the foe in every quarter, and was ready to renew the contest at an opportune moment. Our killed and wounded were numbered by thousands; the loss of the Confederates may be imagined.

While taking Meagher's brigade to the front, I crossed a portion of the ground over which a large column had advanced to attack us, and had a fair opportunity of judging of the effect of our fire upon the ranks of the enemy. It was something fearful and sad to contemplate; few steps could be taken without trampling upon the body of a dead or wounded soldier, or without hearing a piteous cry, begging our party to be careful. In some places the bodies were in continuous lines and in heaps. In Mexico I had seen fields of battle on which our armies had been victorious, and had listened to pitiful appeals; but the pleaders were not of my countrymen then, and did not, as now, cause me to deplore the effects of a fratricidal war.

Sadder still were the trying scenes I met in and around the Malvern house, which at an early hour that day had been given up to the wounded, and was soon filled with our unfortunate men, suffering from all kinds of wounds. At night, after issuing orders for the withdrawal of our troops, I passed through the building and the adjoining hospitals with my senior medical officer, Colonel George H. Lyman. Our object was to inspect the actual condition of the men, to arrange for their care and comfort, and to cheer them as best we could. Here, as usual, were found men mortally wounded, by necessity left unattended by the surgeons, so that prompt and proper care might be given to those in whom there was hope of recovery.

While passing through this improvised hospital I heard of many sad cases. One was that of the major of the 12th New York Volunteers, a brave and gallant officer, highly esteemed, who was believed to be mortally wounded. While breathing his last, as was supposed, a friend asked him if he had any message to leave. He replied, "Tell my wife that in my last thoughts were blended herself, my boy, and my flag." Then he asked how the battle had gone and when told that we had been successful he said, "God bless the old fla————" and fell back apparently dead. For a long time he was mourned as dead, and it was believed that he had expired with the prayer left unfinished on his closing lips. Though still an invalid, suffering from the wound that he received, that officer recovered to renew his career in the war.

On the occasion of this visit we frequently witnessed scenes which would melt the stoutest heart: bearded men piteously begging to be sent home, others requesting that a widowed mother or orphan sisters might be cared for; more sending messages to wife or children, or to others near and dear to them. We saw the amputated limbs and the bodies of the dead hurried out of the room for burial. On every side we heard the appeals of the unattended, the moans of the dying, and the shrieks of those under the knife of the surgeon. We gave what cheer we could, and left with heavy hearts.

At noon on the 4th of July the usual national salute was fired, and the different corps were reviewed. General McClellan, as opportunity offered, made a few remarks full of hope and encouragement, thanking the men in most feeling terms for their uniform bravery, fortitude, and good conduct, but intimating that this was not the last of the campaign.

Contrary, however, to his expectations, the Peninsular campaign of the Army of the Potomac for 1862 virtually ended on the 4th of July. From that date to August 14th, when the army at sundown took up its march for Fort Monroe, its commander was engaged in the struggle to retain it on the James, as against the determination of the Secretary of War to withdraw it to the line of the Rappahannock, there to act in conjunction with the Army of Virginia.

Although General McClellan was assured, in writing, that he was to have command of both armies after their junction, he preferred, as a speedy and the only practicable mode of taking Richmond, to remain on the James, and renew the contest from the south bank, for which he had commenced operations. During this period he omitted nothing which would insure the removal of the army without loss of men and material. The withdrawal of the army changed the issue from the capture of Richmond to the security of Washington, transferred to the Federals the anxiety of the Confederates for their capital, and sounded an alarm throughout the Northern States.

JACKSON'S VALLEY CAMPAIGN

ONE OF THE MOST BRILLIANT CAMPAIGNS IN THE CIVIL WAR—INDEED IN THE HISTORY of war—was that conducted against a greatly superior foe in Virginia's Shenandoah Valley during May and June of 1862 by Confederate Maj. Gen. Thomas J. Jackson (1824–1863), better known as "Stonewall." The campaign had several purposes. It was necessary in order to prevent Union forces from overrunning the valley, which was a fertile agricultural storehouse and which, in the wrong hands, provided a back door into Virginia. In addition, the campaign served an important strategic function, for Jackson was able to pin down rather enormous Union forces, forces which might well have proven more useful elsewhere. Jackson accomplished his mission with such skill and panache that by its end he had not only defeated Union forces several times the size of his own, but had virtually paralyzed Federal movements in northern Virginia, and managed to bring his own forces into action alongside Lee against McClellan during the Seven Days. His campaign has ever since been considered a classic example of what can be accomplished by a small, well led force against a larger, less capably commanded one.

Stonewall Jackson

★★★

JOHN D. IMBODEN
Stonewall Jackson in the Shenandoah

John D. Imboden (1823–1895) was a Virginia lawyer and politician who organized an artillery battery for Confederate service on the outbreak of the war. After serving at Harper's Ferry and First Bull Run he was named commander of the 1st Partisan Rangers, a regiment of irregular cavalry, which he led during Jackson's Valley Campaign. Later made a brigadier general, he led a brigade of irregulars until illness forced him to assume an administrative post in 1864. After the war he had a busy career, for he resumed the practice of law, was involved in land development, and did some writing. He was married five times. Imboden's account of the Valley Campaign is taken from Battles and Leaders of the Civil War, *one of five articles which he contributed to that work.*

Soon after the battle of Bull Run Stonewall Jackson was promoted to major-general, and the Confederate Government having on the 21st of October, 1861, organized the Department of Northern Virginia, under command of General Joseph E. Johnston, it was divided into the Valley District, the Potomac District, and Aquia District, to be commanded respectively by Major-Generals Jackson, Beauregard, and Holmes. On October 28th General Johnston ordered Jackson to Winchester to assume command of his district, and on the 6th of November the War Department ordered his old "Stonewall" brigade and six thousand troops under command of Brigadier-General W. W. Loring to report to him. These, together with Turner Ashby's cavalry, gave him a force of about ten thousand men all told.

His only movement of note in the winter of 1861–62 was an expedition at the end of December to Bath and Rommey, to destroy the Baltimore and Ohio railroad and a dam or two near Hancock on the Chesapeake and Ohio canal. The weather set in to be very inclement about New Year's, with snow, rain, sleet, high winds, and intense cold. Many in Jackson's command were opposed to the expedition, and as it resulted in nothing of much military importance, but was attended with great suffering on the part of his troops, nothing but the confidence he had won by his previous services saved him from personal ruin. He and his second in command, General Loring, had a serious disagreement. He ordered Loring to take up his quarters, in January, in the exposed and cheerless village of Romney, on the south branch of the upper Potomac. Loring objected to this, but Jackson was inexorable. Loring and his principal officers united in a petition to Mr. Benjamin, Secretary of War, to order them to Winchester, or at least away from Romney. This document was sent direct to the War Office, and the Secretary, in utter disregard of "good order and discipline," granted the request without consulting Jackson. As soon as informaton reached Jackson of what had been done, he indignantly resigned his commission. Governor Letcher [of Virginia] was astounded, and at once wrote Jackson a sympathetic letter, and then expostulated with Mr. Davis and his Secretary with such vigor that an apology was sent to Jackson for their obnoxious course. The orders were revoked and modified, and Jackson was induced to retain his command. This little episode gave the Confederate civil authorities an inkling of what manner of man "Stonewall" Jackson was.

In that terrible winter's march and exposure, Jackson endured all that any private was exposed to. One morning, near Bath, some of his men, having crawled out from under their snow-laden blankets, half-frozen, were cursing him as the cause of their sufferings. He lay close by under a tree, also snowed under, and heard all this; and, without noticing it, presently crawled out, too, and, shaking the snow off, made some jocular remark to the nearest men, who had no idea he had ridden up in the night and lain down amongst them. The incident ran through the little army in a few hours, and reconciled his followers to all the hardships of the expedition, and fully reëstablished his popularity.

In March Johnston withdrew from Manassas, and General McClellan collected his army of more than one hundred thousand men on the Peninsula. Johnston moved south to confront him. McClellan had planned and organized a masterly movement to capture, hold, and occupy the Valley and the Piedmont region; and if his subordinates had been equal to the task, and there had been no interference from Washington, it is probable the Confederate army would have been driven out of Virginia and Richmond captured by midsummer, 1862.

Jackson's little army in the Valley had been greatly reduced during the winter from various causes, so that at the beginning of March he did not have over 5000 men of all arms available for the defense of his district, which began to swarm with enemies all around its borders, aggregating more than ten times his own strength. Having retired up the Valley, he learned that the enemy had begun to withdraw and send troops to the east of the mountains to coöperate with McClellan. This he resolved to stop by an aggressive demonstration against Winchester, occupied by General Shields, of the Federal army, with a division of 8000 to 10,000 men.

A little after the middle of March, Jackson concentrated what troops he could, and on the 23d he occupied a ridge at the hamlet of Kernstown, four miles south of Winchester. Shields promptly attacked him, and a severe engagement of several hours ensued, ending in Jackson's repulse about dark, followed by an orderly retreat up the Valley to

near Swift Run Gap in Rockingham county. The pursuit was not vigorous nor persistent. Although Jackson retired before superior numbers, he had given a taste of his fighting qualities that stopped the withdrawal of the enemy's troops from the Valley.

The result was so pleasing to the Richmond government and General Johnston that it was decided to reënforce Jackson by sending General Ewell's division to him at Swift Run Gap, which reached him about the 1st of May, thus giving Jackson an aggregate force of from 13,000 to 15,000 men to open his campaign with. At the beginning of May the situation was broadly about as follows: Milroy, with about 4087 men, was on the Staunton and Parkersburg road at McDowell, less than forty miles from Staunton, with Schenck's brigade of about 2500 near Franklin. The rest of Frémont's army in the mountain department was then about 30,000 men, of whom 20,000 were concentrating at Franklin, fifty miles north-west of Staunton, and within supporting distance of Milroy. Banks, who had fortified Strasburg, seventy miles north-east of Staunton by the great Valley turnpike, to fall back upon in an emergency, had pushed forward a force of 20,000 men to Harrisonburg, including Shields's division, 10,000 strong. General McDowell, with 34,000 men, exclusive of Shields's division, was at points east of the Blue Ridge, so as to be able to move either to Fredericksburg or to the Luray Valley and thence to Staunton. Not counting Colonel Miles's, later Sax-

Jackson's Foot Cavalry

ton's command, at Harper's Ferry, which was rapidly increased to 7000 men, sent from Washington and other points north of the Potomac, before the end of May, Jackson had about 80,000 men to take into account (including all Union forces north of the Rappahannock and east of the Ohio) and to keep from a junction with McClellan in front of Richmond. Not less than 65,000[1] of these enemies were in some part of the Valley under their various commanders in May and June.

Besides Ewell's division already mentioned, General Johnston could give no further assistance to Jackson, for McClellan was right in his front with superior numbers, and menacing the capital of the Confederacy with almost immediate and certain capture. Its only salvation depended upon Jackson's ability to hold back Frémont, Banks, and McDowell long enough to let Johnston try doubtful conclusions with McClellan. If he failed in this, these three commanders of an aggregate force then reputed to be, and I believe in fact, over one hundred thousand[2] would converge and move down upon Richmond from the west as McClellan advanced from the east, and the city and its defenders would fall an easy prey to nearly, if not quite, a quarter of a million of the best-armed and best-equipped men ever put into the field by any government.

Early in May, Jackson was near Port Republic contemplating his surroundings and maturing his plans. What these latter were no one but himself knew.

Suddenly the appalling news spread through the Valley that he had fled to the east side of the Blue Ridge through Brown's and Swift Run Gaps. Only Ashby remained behind with about one thousand cavalry, scattered and moving day and night in the vicinity of McDowell, Franklin, Strasburg, Front Royal, and Luray, and reporting to Jackson every movement of the enemy. Despair was fast settling upon the minds of the people of the Valley. Jackson made no concealment of his flight, the news of which soon reached his enemies. Milroy advanced two regiments to the top of the Shenandoah Mountain, only twenty-two miles from Staunton, and was preparing to move his entire force to Staunton, to be followed by Frémont.

Jackson had collected, from Charlottesville and other stations on the Virginia Central Railroad, enough railway trains to transport all of his little army. That it was to be taken to Richmond when the troops were all embarked no one doubted. It was Sunday, and many of his sturdy soldiers were Valley men. With sad and gloomy hearts they boarded the trains at Mechum's River Station. When all were on, lo! they took a westward course, and a little after noon the first train rolled into Staunton.

News of Jackson's arrival spread like wild-fire, and crowds flocked to the station to see the soldiers and learn what it all meant. No one knew.

As soon as the troops could be put in motion they took the road leading toward McDowell, the general having sent forward cavalry to Buffalo Gap and beyond to arrest all persons going that way. General

Edward Johnson, with one of Jackson's Valley brigades, was already at Buffalo Gap. The next morning, by a circuitous mountain-path, he tried to send a brigade of infantry to the rear of Milroy's two regiments on Shenandoah Mountain, but they were improperly guided and failed to reach the position in time, so that when attacked in front both regiments escaped. Jackson followed as rapidly as possible, and the following day, May 8th, on top of the Bull Pasture Mountain, three miles east of McDowell, encountered Milroy reënforced by Schenck, who commanded by virtue of seniority of commission. The conflict lasted four hours, and was severe and bloody. It was fought mainly with small-arms, the ground forbidding much use of artillery. Schenck and Milroy fled precipitately toward Franklin, to unite with Frémont. The route lay along a narrow valley hedged up by high mountains, perfectly protecting the flanks of the retreating army from Ashby's pursuing cavalry, led by Captain Sheetz. Jackson ordered him to pursue as vigorously as possible, and to guard completely all avenues of approach from the direction of McDowell or Staunton till relieved of this duty. Jackson buried the dead and rested his army, and then fell back to the Valley on the Warm Springs and Harrisonburg road.

The morning after the battle of McDowell I called very early on Jackson at the residence of Colonel George W. Hull of that village, where he had his headquarters, to ask if could be of any service to him, as I had to go to Staunton, forty miles distant, to look after some companies that were to join my command. He asked me to wait a few moments, as he wished to prepare a telegram to be sent to President Davis from Staunton, the nearest office to McDowell. He took a seat at a table and wrote nearly half a page of foolscap; he rose and stood before the fireplace pondering it some minutes; then he tore it in pieces and wrote again, but much less, and again destroyed what he had written, and paced the room several times. He suddenly stopped, seated himself, and dashed off two or three lines, folded the paper, and said, "Send that off as soon as you reach Staunton." As I bade him "good-bye," he remarked: "I may have other telegrams to-day or to-morrow, and will send them to you for transmission. I wish you to have two or three well-mounted couriers ready to bring me the replies promptly."

I read the message he had given me. It was dated "McDowell," and read about thus: "Providence blessed our arms with victory at McDowell yesterday." That was all. A few days after I got to Staunton a courier arrived with a message to be telegraphed to the Secretary of War. I read it, sent it off, and ordered a courier to be ready with his horse, while I waited at the telegraph office for the reply. The message was to this effect: "I think I ought to attack Banks, but under my orders I do not feel at liberty to do so." In less than an hour a reply came, but not from the Secretary of War. It was from General Joseph E. Johnston, to whom I supposed the Secretary had referred General Jackson's message. I have a distinct recollection of its substance, as follows: "If you think you can beat Banks, attack him. I only intended by my orders to caution you against attacking fortifications." Banks was understood to have fortified himself strongly at Strasburg and Cedar Creek, and he had fallen back there. I started the courier with this reply, as I supposed, to McDowell, but, lo! it met Jackson only twelve miles from Staunton, to which point on the Harrisonburg and Warm Springs turnpike he had marched his little army, except part of Ashby's cavalry, which, under an intrepid leader, Captain Sheetz, he had sent from McDowell to menace Frémont, who was concentrating at Franklin in Pendleton County, where he remained in blissful ignorance that Jackson had left McDowell, till he learned by telegraph some days later that Jackson had fallen upon Banks at Front Royal and driven him through Winchester and across the Potomac.

Two hours after receiving this telegram from General Johnston, Jackson was en route for Harrisonburg, where he came upon the great Valley turnpike. By forced marches he reached New Market in two days. Detachments of cavalry guarded every road beyond him, so that Banks remained in total ignorance of his approach. This Federal commander had the larger part of his force well fortified at and near Strasburg, but he kept a strong detachment at Front Royal, about eight miles distant and facing the Luray or Page Valley.

From New Market Jackson disappeared so suddenly that the people of the Valley were again mystified. He crossed the Massanutten Mountain, and, passing Luray, hurried toward Front Royal. He sometimes made thirty miles in twenty-four hours with his entire army, thus gaining for his infantry the sobriquet of "Jackson's foot cavalry." Very early in the afternoon of May 23d he struck Front Royal. The surprise was complete and disastrous to the enemy, who were commanded by Colonel John R. Kenly. After a fruitless resistance they fled toward Winchester, twenty miles distant, with Jackson at their heels. A large number were captured within four miles by a splendid cavalry dash of Colonel Flournoy and Lieutenant-Colonel Watts.

News of this disaster reached Banks ot Strasburg, by which he learned that Jackson was rapidly gaining his rear toward Newtown. The works Banks had constructed had not been made for defense in that direction, so he abandoned them and set out with all haste for Winchester; but, en route, near Newtown (May 24th), Jackson struck his flank, inflicting heavy loss, and making large captures of property, consisting of wagons, teams, camp-equipage, provisions, ammunition, and over nine thousand stand of arms, all new and in perfect order, besides a large number of prisoners.

Jackson now chased Banks's fleeing army to Winchester, where the latter made a stand, but after a sharp engagement with Ewell's division on the 25th he fled again, not halting till he had crossed the Potomac, congratulating himself and his Govern-

General Richard Ewell

ment in a dispatch that his army was at last safe in Maryland. General Saxton, with some 7000 men, held Harper's Ferry, 32 miles from Winchester. Jackson paid his respects to this fortified post, by marching a large part of his forces close to it, threatening an assault, long enough to allow all the captured property at Winchester to be sent away toward Staunton, and then returned to Winchester. His problem now was to escape the clutches of Frémont, knowing that that officer would be promptly advised by wire of what had befallen Banks. He could go back the way he came, by the Luray Valley, but that would expose Staunton (the most important depot in the valley) to capture by Frémont, and he had made his plans to save it.

I had been left at Staunton organizing my recruits. On his way to attack Banks, Jackson sent me an order from New Market to throw as many men as I could arm, and as quickly as possible, into Brock's Gap, west of Harrisonburg, and into any other mountain-pass through which Frémont could reach the valley at or south of Harrisonburg. I knew that

---

1. Imboden is here overestimating Union strength, which was actually about 45,000, still impressively greater than Jackson's.—A.A.N.
2. Probably 80,000.—A.A.N.

Pennsylvania volunteers play the national anthem.

within four miles of Franklin, on the main road leading to Harrisonburg, there was a narrow defile hemmed in on both sides by nearly perpendicular cliffs, over five hundred feet high. I sent about fifty men, well armed with long-range guns, to occupy these cliffs, and defend the passage to the last extremity.

On the 25th of May, as soon as Frémont learned of Banks's defeat and retreat to the Potomac, he put his army of about 14,000 in motion from Franklin to cut off Jackson's retreat up the valley. Ashby's men were still in his front toward McDowell, with an unknown force; so Frémont did not attempt that route, but sent his cavalry to feel the way toward Brock's Gap, on the direct road to Harrisonburg. The men I had sent to the cliffs let the head of the column get well into the defile or gorge, when, from a position of perfect safety to themselves, they poured a deadly volley into the close column. The attack being unexpected, and coming from a foe of unknown strength, the Federal column halted and hesitated to advance. Another volley and the "rebel yell" from the cliffs

turned them back, never to appear again. Frémont took the road to Moorefield, and thence to Strasburg, though he had been peremptorily ordered on May 24th by President Lincoln to proceed direct to Harrisonburg. It shows how close had been Jackson's calculation of chances, to state that as his rear-guard marched up Fisher's Hill, two miles fron Strasburg, Frémont's advance came in sight on the mountainside on the road from Moorefield, and a sharp skirmish took place. Jackson continued to Harrisonburg, hotly pursued by Frémont, but avoiding a conflict.

The news of Banks's defeat created consternation at Washington, and Shields was ordered to return from east of the Blue Ridge to the Luray Valley in all haste to coöperate with Frémont. Jackson was advised of Shields's approach, and his aim was to prevent a junction of their forces till he reached a point where he could strike them in quick succession. He therefore sent cavalry detachments along the Shenandoah to burn the bridges as far as Port Republic, the river being at that time too full for fording. At

General Frémont's division marches through Shenandoah woods.

Harrisonburg he took the road leading to Port Republic, and ordered me from Staunton, with a mixed battery and battalion of cavalry, to the bridge over North River near Mount Crawford, to prevent a cavalry force passing to his rear.

At Cross Keys, about six miles from Harrisonburg, he delivered battle to Frémont, on June 8th, and, after a long and bloody conflict, as night closed in he was master of the field. Leaving one division—Ewell's—on the ground, to resist Frémont if he should return next day, he that night marched the rest of his army to Port Republic, which lies in the forks of the river, and made his arrangements to attack the troops of Shields's command next morning on the Lewis farm, just below the town.

On the day of the conflict at Cross Keys I held the bridge across North River at Mount Crawford with a battalion of cavalry, four howitzers, and a Parrott gun, to prevent a cavalry flank movement on Jackson's trains at Port Republic. About 10 o'clock at night I received a note from Jackson, written in pencil on the blank margin of a newspaper, directing me to report with my command at Port Republic before daybreak. On the same slip, and as a postscript, he wrote, "Poor Ashby is dead. He fell gloriously. . . . I know you will join with me in mourning the loss of our friend, one of the noblest men and soldiers in the Confederate army." I carried that slip of paper till it was literally worn to tatters.

It was early, Sunday, June 8th, when Jackson and his staff reached the bridge at Port Republic. General E. B. Tyler, who, with two brigades of Shields's division, was near by on the east side of the river, had sent two guns and a few men under a green and inefficient officer to the bridge. They arrived about the same time as Jackson, but, his troops soon coming up, the Federal officer and his supports made great haste back to the Lewis farm, losing a gun at the bridge.

I reached Port Republic an hour before daybreak of June 9th, and sought the house occupied by Jackson; but not wishing to disturb him so early, I asked the sentinel what room was occupied by "Sandy" Pendleton, Jackson's adjutant-general. "Upstairs, first

Roughrider John Charles Frémont leads the troops into battle.

room on the right," he replied.

Supposing he meant our right as we faced the house, I went up, softly opened the door, and discovered General Jackson lying on his face across the bed, fully dressed, with sword, sash, and boots all on. The low-burnt tallow candle on the table shed a dim light, yet enough by which to recognize him. I endeavored to withdraw without waking him. He turned over, sat up on the bed, and called out, "Who is that?"

He checked my apology with "That is all right. It's time to be up. I am glad to see you. Were the men all up as you came through camp?"

"Yes, General, and cooking."

"That's right. We move at daybreak. Sit down. I want to talk to you."

I had learned never to ask him questions about his plans, for he would never answer such to any one. I therefore waited for him to speak first. He referred very feelingly to Ashby's death, and spoke of it as an irreparable loss. When he paused, I said, "General, you made a glorious winding-up of your four weeks' work yesterday."

He replied, "Yes, God blessed our army again yesterday, and I hope with his protection and blessing we shall do still better to-day."

Then seating himself, for the first time in all my intercourse with him, he outlined the day's proposed operations. I remember perfectly his conversation. He said: "Charley Winder [brigadier-general commanding his old 'Stonewall' brigade] will cross the river at daybreak and attack Shields on the Lewis farm [two miles below]. I shall support him with all the other troops as fast as they can be put in line. General 'Dick' Taylor will move through the woods on the side of the mountain with his Louisiana brigade, and rush upon their left flank by the time the action becomes general. By 10 o'clock we shall get them on the run, and I'll now tell you what I want with you. Send the big new rifle-gun you have [a 12-pounder Parrott] to Poague [commander of the Rockbridge artillery] and let your mounted men report to the cavalry. I want you in person to take your mountain howitzers to the field, in some safe position in rear of the line, keeping everything packed on the mules, ready at any moment to take to the mountain-side. Three miles below Lewis's there is a defile on the Luray road. Shields may rally and make a stand there. If he does, I can't reach him with the field-batteries on account of the woods. You can carry your 12-pounder howitzers on the mules up the mountain-side, and at some good place unpack and shell the enemy out of the defile, and the cavalry will do the rest."

This plan of battle was carried out to the letter. I took position in a ravine about two hundred yards in rear of Poague's battery in the center of the line. General Tyler, who had two brigades of Shields's division, made a very stubborn fight, and by 9 o'clock matters began to look very serious for us. Dick Taylor had not yet come down out of the woods on Tyler's left flank.

Meanwhile I was having a remarkable time with our mules in the ravine. Some of the shot aimed at Poague came bounding over our heads, and occasionally a shell would burst there. The mules became frantic. They kicked, plunged, and squealed. It was impossible to quiet them, and it took three or four men to hold one mule from breaking away. Each mule had about three hundred pounds weight on him, so securely fastened that the load could not be dislodged by any of his capers. Several of them lay down and tried to wallow their loads off. The men held these down, and that suggested the idea of throwing them all on the ground and holding them there. The ravine sheltered us so that we were in no danger from the shot or shell which passed over us.

Just about the time our mule "circus" was at its height, news came up the line from the left that Winder's brigade near the river was giving way. Jackson rode down in that direction to see what it meant. As he passed on the brink of our ravine, his eye caught the scene, and reining up a moment, he accosted me with, "Colonel, you seem to have trouble down there." I made some reply which drew forth a hearty laugh, and he said, "Get your mules to the mountain as soon as you can, and be ready to move."

Then he dashed on. He found his old brigade had yielded slightly to overwhelming pressure. Galloping up, he was received with a cheer; and, calling out at the top of his voice, "The 'Stonewall' brigade never retreats; follow me!" led them back to their original line. Taylor soon made his appearance, and the flank attack settled the work of the day. A wild retreat began. The pursuit was vigorous. No stand was made in the defile. We pursued them eight miles. I rode back with Jackson, and at sunset we were on the battlefield at the Lewis mansion.

Jackson accosted a medical officer, and said, "Have you brought off all the wounded?" "Yes, all of ours, but not all of the enemy's." "Why not?" "Because we were shelled from across the river." "Had you your hospital flag on the field?" "Yes." "And they shelled that?" "Yes." "Well, take your men to their quarters; I would rather let them all die than have one of my men shot intentionally under the yellow flag when trying to save their wounded."

Frémont, hearing the noise of the battle, had hurried out from near Harrisonburg to help Tyler; but Jackson had burnt the bridge at Port Republic, after Ewell had held Frémont in check some time on the west side of the river and escaped, so that when Frémont came in sight of Tyler's battle-field, the latter's troops had been routed and the river could not be crossed.

The next day I returned to Staunton, and found General W. H. C. Whiting, my old commander after the fall of General Bee at Bull Run, arriving with a division of troops to reënforce Jackson. Taking him and his staff to my house as guests, General Whiting left soon after breakfast with a guide to call on Jackson at Swift Run Gap, near Port Republic, where he was resting his troops. The distance from Staunton was about twenty miles, but Whiting returned after midnight. He was in a towering passion, and declared that Jackson had treated him outrageously. I asked, "How is that possible, General, for he is very polite to every one?"

"Oh! hang him, he was polite enough. But he didn't say one word about his plans. I finally asked him for orders, telling him what troops I had. He simply told me to go back to Staunton, and he would send me orders to-morrow. I haven't the slightest idea what they will be. I believe he hasn't any more sense than my horse."

Seeing his frame of mind, and he being a guest in my house, I said little. Just after breakfast, next morning, a courier arrived with a terse order to embark his troops on the railroad trains and move to Gordonsville at once, where he would receive further orders. This brought on a new explosion of wrath. "Didn't I tell you he was a fool, and doesn't this prove it? Why, I just came through Gordonsville day before yesterday."

However, he obeyed the order; and when he reached Gordonsville he found Jackson there, and his little Valley army coming after him; a few days later McClellan was astounded to learn that Jackson was on his right flank on the Chickahominy. Shortly after the seven days' battle around Richmond, I met Whiting again, and he then said: "I didn't know Jackson when I was at your house. I have found out now what his plans were, and they were worthy of a Napoleon. But I still think he ought to have told me his plans; for if he had died McClellan would have captured Richmond. I wouldn't have known what he was driving at, and might have made a mess of it. But I take back all I said about his being a fool."

From the date of Jackson's arrival at Staunton till the battle of Port Republic was thirty-five days. He marched from Staunton to McDowell, 40 miles, from McDowell to Front Royal, about 110, from Front Royal to Winchester, 20 miles, Winchester to Port Republic, 75 miles, a total of 245 miles, fighting in the meantime 4 desperate battles, and winning them all.

On the 17th of June, leaving only his cavalry, under Brigadier-General B. H. Robertson, and Chew's battery, and the little force I was enlisting in the valley (which was no longer threatened by the enemy), Jackson moved all his troops south-east, and on the 25th arrived at Ashland, seventeen miles from Richmond. This withdrawal from the valley was so skillfully managed that his absence from the scene of his late triumphs was unsuspected at Washington. On the contrary, something like a panic prevailed there, and the Government was afraid to permit McDowell to unite his forces with McClellan's lest it should uncover and expose the capital to Jackson's supposed movement on it.

Jackson's military operations were always unexpected and mysterious. In my personal intercourse with him in the early part of the war, before he had become famous, he often said there were two things never to be lost sight of by a military commander: "Always mystify, mislead, and surprise the enemy, if possible; and when you strike and overcome him, never let up in the pursuit so long as your men have strength to follow; for an army routed, if hotly pursued, becomes panic-stricken, and can be destroyed by half their number. The other rule is, never fight against heavy odds, if by any possible manœuvring you can hurl your own force on only a part, and that the weakest part, of your enemy and crush it. Such tactics will win every time, and a small army may thus destroy a large one in detail, and repeated victory will make it invincible."

His celerity of movement was a simple matter. He never broke down his men by too-long continued marching. He rested the whole column very often, but only for a few minutes at a time. I remember that he liked to see the men lie down flat on the ground to rest, and would say, "A man rests all over when he lies down."

★★★

RICHARD TAYLOR
With Jackson in the Valley

Dick Taylor (1826–1879), the son of Mexican War hero and President Zachary Taylor, received an extraordinary education (Edinburg, Harvard, Yale, and a French university), before settling down to become a Louisiana planter. A member of the Louisiana secession convention, he received a commission at the start of the war

and was promoted brigadier general in late 1861, subsequently commanding the famous Louisiana Brigade in the Valley and during the Seven Days, during which he was quite ill and led his troops from an ambulance. Promoted major general, he was sent to the trans-Mississippi theater, where he distinguished himself in a number of actions, until relieved in 1864 in a dispute with his commanding officer, E. Kirby Smith, whom he called "stupid, pig-headed, and obstinate." Taylor, one of the best amateur soldiers of the war, ended the conflict war as a lieutenant general commanding in East Louisiana, Mississippi, and Alabama, and was among the last Confederate generals to sur- *render. After the war he recovered his fortunes, became a close friend to Ulysses S. Grant, and wrote* Destruction and Reconstruction: Personal Experiences of the Late War *(New York, 1879), one of the finest memoirs of the war, from which the accompanying account of the capture of Winchester, with its fine portrait of Jackson, is taken.*

. . . I sought Jackson, whom I had never met. . . . The mounted officer who had been sent on in advance pointed out a figure perched on the topmost rail of a fence overlooking the road and field, and said it was Jackson. Approaching, I saluted and declared my name and rank, then waited for a response. Before this came I had time to see a pair of cavalry boots covering feet of gigantic size, a mangy cap with visor drawn low, a heavy, dark beard, and weary eyes—eyes I afterward saw filled with intense but never brilliant light. A low, gentle voice inquired the road and distance marched that day.

"Keazletown road, six and twenty miles."

"You seem to have no stragglers."

"Never allow straggling."

"You must teach my people; they straggle badly." A bow in reply. Just then my creoles started their band and a waltz. After a contemplative suck at a lemon, "Thoughtless fellows for serious work" came forth. I expressed a hope that the work would not be less well done because of the gayety. A return to the lemon gave me the opportunity to retire. Where Jackson got his lemons "no fellow could find out," but he was rarely without one. To have lived twelve miles from that fruit would have disturbed him as much as it did the witty Dean.

Quite late that night General Jackson came to my camp fire, where he stayed some hours. He said we would move at dawn, asked a few questions about the marching of my men, which seemed to have impressed him, and then remained silent. If silence be golden, he was a "bonanza." He sucked lemons, ate hard-tack, and drank water, and praying and fighting appeared to be his idea of the "whole duty of man."

In the gray of the morning, as I was forming my column on the pike, Jackson appeared and gave the route—north—which, from the situation of its camp, put my brigade in advance of the army. After moving a short distance in this direction, the head of the column was turned to the east and took the road over Massanutten gap to Luray. Scarce a word was spoken on the march, as Jackson rode with me. From time to time a courier would gallop up, report, and return toward Luray. An ungraceful horseman, mounted on a sorry chestnut with a shambling gait, his huge feet with out-turned toes thrust into his stirrups, and such parts of his countenance as the low visor of his shocking cap failed to conceal wearing a wooden look, our new commander was not prepossessing. That night we crossed the east branch

of the Shenandoah by a bridge, and camped on the stream, near Luray. Here, after three long marches, we were but a short distance below Conrad's store, a point we had left several days before, I began to think that Jackson was an unconscious poet, and, as an ardent lover of nature, desired to give strangers an opportunity to admire the beauties of his Valley. It seemed hard lines to be wandering like sentimental travelers about the country, instead of gaining "kudos" on the Peninsula.

Off the next morning, my command still in advance, and Jackson riding with me. The road led north between the east bank of the river and the western base of the Blue Ridge. Rain had fallen and softened it, so as to delay the wagon trains in rear. Past midday we reached a wood extending from the mountain to the river, when a mounted officer from the rear called Jackson's attention, who rode back with him. A moment later, there rushed out of the wood to meet us a young, rather well-looking woman, afterward widely known as Belle Boyd. Breathless with speed and agitation, some time elapsed before she found her voice. Then, with much volubility, she said we were near Front Royal, beyond the wood; that the town was filled with Federals, whose camp was on the west side of the river, where they had guns in position to cover the wagon bridge, but none bearing on the railway bridge below the former; that they believed Jackson to be west of Massanutten, near Harrisonburg; that General Banks, the Federal commander, was at Winchester, twenty miles northwest of Front Royal, where he was slowly concentrating his widely scattered forces to meet Jackson's advance, which was expected some days later.

All this she told with the precision of a staff officer making a report, and it was true to the letter. Jackson was possessed of these facts before he left Newmarket, and based his movements upon them, but, as he never told anything, it was news to me, and gave me an idea of the strategic value of Massanutten—pointed out, indeed by Washington before the Revolution. There also dawned on me quite another view of our leader than the one from which I had been regarding him for two days past.

Convinced of the correctness of the woman's statements, I hurried forward at "a double," hoping to surprise the enemy's idlers in the town, or swarm over the wagon bridge with them and secure it. Doubtless this was rash, but I felt immensely "cocky" about my brigade, and believed that it

Mississippi Wildcats regiment passes along Main Street, Winchester, on way to Bunker Hill, Virginia.

would prove equal to any demand. Before we had cleared the wood Jackson came galloping from the rear, followed by a company of horse. He ordered me to deploy my leading regiment as skirmishers on both sides of the road and continue the advance, then passed on. We speedily came in sight of Front Royal, but the enemy had taken the alarm, and his men were scurrying over the bridge to their camp, where troops could be seen forming.

The situation of the village is surpassingly beautiful. It lies near the east bank of the Shenandoah, which just below unites all its waters, and looks directly on the northern peaks of Massanutten. The Blue Ridge, with Manassas Gap, through which passes the railway, overhangs it on the east; distant Alleghany bounds the horizon to the west; and down the Shenandoah, the eye ranges over a fertile, well-farmed country. Two bridges spanned the river—a wagon bridge above, a railway bridge some yards lower. A good pike led to Winchester, twenty miles, and another followed the river north, whence many cross-roads united with the Valley pike near Winchester. The river, swollen by rain, was deep and turbulent, with strong current. The Federals were posted on the west bank, here somewhat higher than the opposite, and a short distance above the junction of waters, with batteries bearing more especially on the upper bridge.

Under instructions, my brigade was drawn up in line, a little retired from the river, but overlooking it—the Federals and their guns in full view. So far, not a shot had been fired. I rode down to the river's brink to get a better look at the enemy through a field-glass, when my horse, heated by the march, stepped into the water to drink. Instantly a brisk fire was opened on me, bullets striking all around and raising a little shower-bath. Like many a foolish fellow, I found it easier to get into than out of a difficulty. I had not yet led my command into action, and, remembering that one must "strut" one's little part to the best advantage, sat my horse with all the composure I could muster. A provident camel, on the eve of a desert journey, would not have laid in a greater supply of water than did my thoughtless beast. At last he raised his head, looked placidly around, turned, and walked up the bank.

This little incident was not without value, for my men welcomed me with a cheer; upon which, as if in response, the enemy's guns opened, and, having the range, inflicted some loss on my line. We had no guns to reply, and, in advance as has been mentioned, had outmarched the troops behind us. Motionless as a statue, Jackson sat his horse some few yards away, and seemed lost in thought. Perhaps the circumstances mentioned some pages back had obscured his star; but if so, a few short hours swept away the cloud, and it blazed, Sirius-like, over the land. I approached him with the suggestion that the railway bridge might be passed by stepping on the cross-ties, as the enemy's guns bore less directly on it than on the upper bridge. He nodded approval.

The 8th regiment was on the right of my line, near at hand; and dismounting, Colonel Kelly led it across under a sharp musketry fire. Several men fell to disappear in the dark water beneath; but the movement continued with great rapidity, considering the difficulty of walking on ties, and Kelly with his leading files gained the opposite shore. Thereupon the enemy fired combustibles previously placed near the center of the wagon bridge. The loss of this structure would have seriously delayed us, as the railway bridge was not floored, and I looked at Jackson, who, near by, was watching Kelly's progress. Again he nodded, and my command rushed at the bridge. Concealed by the cloud of smoke, the suddenness of the movement saved us from much loss; but it was rather a near thing. My horse and clothing were scorched, and many men burned their hands severely while throwing brands into the river. We were soon over, and the enemy in full flight to Winchester, with loss of camp, guns, and prisoners.

Just as I emerged from flames and smoke, Jackson was by my side. How he got there was a mystery, as the bridge was thronged with my men going at full speed; but smoke and fire had decidedly freshened up his costume. . . .

Late in the night Jackson came out of the darkness and seated himself by my camp fire. He mentioned that I would move with him in the morning, then relapsed into silence. I fancied he looked at me kindly, and interpreted it into an approval of the conduct of the brigade. The events of the day, anticipations of the morrow, . . . drove away sleep, and I watched Jackson. For hours he sat silent and motionless, with eyes fixed on the fire. I took up the idea that he was inwardly praying, and he remained through the night.

Off in the morning, Jackson leading the way, my brigade, a small body of horse, and a section of the Rockbridge (Virginia) artillery forming the column. Major Wheat, with his battalion of "Tigers," was directed to keep close to the guns. Sturdy marchers, they trotted along with the horse and artillery at Jackson's heels, and after several hours were some distance in advance of the brigade, with which I remained.

A volley in front, followed by wild cheers, stirred us up to a "double," and we speedily came upon a moving spectacle. Jackson had struck the Valley pike at Middletown, twelve miles south of Winchester, along which a large body of Federal horse, with many wagons, was hastening north. He had attacked at once with his handful of men, overwhelmed resistance, and captured prisoners and wagons. The gentle Tigers were looting right merrily, diving in and out of wagons with the activity of rabbits in a warren; but this occupation was abandoned on my approach, and in a moment they were in line, looking as solemn and virtuous as deacons at a funeral. . . .

At dusk we overtook Jackson, pushing the enemy with his little mounted force, himself in advance of all. I rode with him, and we kept on through the darkness. There was not resistance enough to deploy infantry. A flash, a report, and a whistling bullet from some covert met us, but there were few casualties. I quite remember thinking at the time that Jackson was invulnerable, and that persons near him shared that quality. An officer, riding hard, overtook us, who proved to the the chief quartermaster of the army. He reported the wagon trains far behind, impeded by a bad road in Luray Valley.

"The ammunition wagons?" sternly.

"All right, sir. They were in advance, and I doubled teams on them and brought them through."

"Ah!" in a tone of relief.

To give countenance to this quartermaster, if such can be given of a dark night, I remarked jocosely: "Never mind the wagons. There are quantities of store in Winchester, and the General has invited me to breakfast there to-morrow."

Jackson, who had no more capacity for jests than a Scotchman, took this seriously, and reached out to touch me on the arm. In fact, he was of Scotch-Irish descent, and his unconsciousness of jokes was *de race*. Without physical wants himself, he forgot that others were differently constituted, and paid little heed to commissariat; but woe to the man who failed to bring up ammunition! In advance, his trains were left far behind. In retreat, he would fight for a wheelbarrow.

Some time after midnight, by roads more direct from Front Royal, other troops came on the pike, and I halted my jaded people by the roadside, where they built fires and took a turn at their haversacks.

Moving with the first light of morning, we came to Kernstown, three miles from Winchester, and the place of Jackson's fight with Shields. Here heavy and sustained firing, artillery and small arms, was heard. A staff officer approached at full speed to summon me to Jackson's presence and move up my command. A gallop of a mile or more brought me to him. Winchester was in sight, a mile to the north. To the east Ewell with a large part of the army was fighting briskly and driving the enemy on to the town. On the west a high ridge, overlooking the country to the south and southeast, was occupied by a heavy mass of Federals with guns in position. Jackson was on the pike, and near him were several regiments lying down for shelter, as the fire from the ridge was heavy and searching. A Virginian battery, Rockbridge artillery, was fighting at a great disadvantage, and already much cut up. Poetic authority asserts that "Old Virginny never tires," and the conduct of this battery justified the assertion of the muses. With scarce a leg or wheel for man and horse, gun or caisson, to stand on, it continued to hammer away at the crushing fire above.

Jackson, impassive as ever, pointed to the ridge and said, "You must carry it." I replied that my command would be up by the time I could inspect the ground, and rode to the left for that purpose. A small stream, Abraham's creek, flowed from the

west through the little vale at the southern base of the ridge, the ascent of which was steep, though nowhere abrupt. At one point a broad, shallow, trough-like depression broke the surface, which was further interrupted by some low copse, outcropping stone, and two fences. On the summit the Federal lines were posted behind a stone wall, along a road coming west from the pike. Worn somewhat into the soil, this road served as a countersink and strengthened the position. Further west, there was a break in the ridge, which was occupied by a body of horse, the extreme right of the enemy's line.

There was scarce time to mark these features before the head of my column appeared, when it was filed to the left, close to the base of the ridge, for protection from the plunging fire. Meanwhile, the Rockbridge battery held on manfully and engaged the enemy's attention. Riding on the flank of my column, between it and the hostile line, I saw Jackson beside me. This was not the place for the commander of the army, and I ventured to tell him so; but he paid no attention to the remark. We reached the shallow depression spoken of, where the enemy could depress his guns, and his fire became close and fatal. Many men fell, and the whistling of shot and shell occasioned much ducking of heads in the column. This annoyed me no little, as it was but child's play to the work immediately in hand. Always an admirer of delightful "Uncle Toby," I had contracted the most villainous habit of his beloved army in Flanders, and, forgetting Jackson's presence, ripped out, "What the h— are you dodging for? If there is any more of it, you will be halted under this fire for an hour."

The sharp tones of a familiar voice produced the desired effect, and the men looked as if they had swallowed ramrods; but I shall never forget the reproachful surprise expressed in Jackson's face. He placed his hand on my shoulder, said in a gentle voice, "I am afraid you are a wicked fellow," turned, and rode back to the pike.

The proper ground gained, the column faced to the front and began the ascent. At the moment the sun rose over the Blue Ridge, without cloud or mist to obscure his rays. It was a lovely Sabbath morning, the 25th of May, 1862. The clear, pure atmosphere brought the Blue Ridge and Alleghany and Massanutten almost overhead. Even the cloud of murderous smoke from the guns above made beautiful spirals in the air, and the broad fields of luxuriant wheat glistened with dew. . . .

As we mounted we came in full view of both armies, whose efforts in other quarters had been slackened to await the result of our movement. I felt an anxiety amounting to pain for the brigade to acquit itself handsomely; and this feeling was shared by every man in it. About half way up, the enemy's horse from his right charged; and to meet it, I directed Lieutenant-Colonel Nicholls, whose regiment, the 8th, was on the left, to withhold slightly his two flank companies. By one volley, which emptied some saddles, Nicholls drove off the horse, but was soon after severely wounded. Progress was not stayed by this incident. Closing the many gaps made by the fierce fire, steadied the rather by it, and preserving an alignment that would have been creditable on parade, the brigade, with cadenced step and eyes on the foe, swept grandly over copse and ledge and fence, to crown the heights from which the enemy had melted away. Loud cheers went up from our army, prolonged to the east, where warm-hearted Ewell cheered himself hoarse, and led forward his men with renewed energy. In truth, it was a gallant

Frémont's wounded and ragged soldiers retreat out of the Shenandoah Valley.

fear of arms, worthy of the pen of him who immortalized the charge of the "Buffs" at Albuera.

Breaking into column, we pursued closely. Jackson came up and grasped my hand, worth a thousand words from another, and we were soon in the streets of Winchester, a quaint old town of some five thousand inhabitants. There was a little fighting in the streets, but the people were all abroad—certainly all the women and babies. They were frantic with delight, only regretting that so may "Yankees" had escaped, and seriously impeded our movements.

A buxom, comely dame of some five and thirty

summers, with bright eyes and tight ankles, and conscious of these advantages, was especially demonstrative, exclaiming, "Oh! you are too late—too late!"

Whereupon, a tall creole from the Teche sprang from the ranks of the 8th regiment just passing, clasped her in his arms and imprinted a sounding kiss on her ripe lips, with *"Madame! je n'arrive jamais trop tard."* A loud laugh followed, and the dame, with a rosy face but merry twinkle in her eye, escaped.

Jackson's strategic genius in the Shenandoah Valley led to the Union defeat and retreat from the Peninsula.

IV

THE SECOND BULL RUN CAMPAIGN

FOR THE UNION THE DISASTROUS CONCLUSION OF THE PENINSULAR CAMPAIGN WAS A heavy blow. But even as the Peninsular Campaign ran its course Lincoln began to concentrate strong forces in Northern Virginia, in order to pose an additional threat to Richmond. As McClellan fell back from the Confederate capital under Lee's repeated blows during the Seven Days, Union Maj. Gen. John Pope, fresh from some minor successes in the Upper Mississippi Valley, was assigned to command this Army of Virginia, nearly 50,000 men gathered from the Union veterans of the Valley and the garrison of Washington. Reinforced by troops brought by sea from the Peninsula, Pope's army began to advance southwards in early July. What followed—a series of actions known collectively as the Second Bull Run Campaign—was one of the most brilliant operations of the Civil War, in which Lee showed himself a master of maneuver.

E. P. ALEXANDER

From the Peninsula to Cedar Mountain

Edward Porter Alexander (1835–1910), a native Georgian and West Point graduate (1857), had a brief career in the Old Army before resigning to enter Confederate service in 1861. Commissioned a captain of Engineers, he served on Beauregard's staff during the First Bull Campaign. He was soon promoted major and made Chief of Ordance for the Army of Northern Virginia. Late in 1862 he commanded an artillery battalion in Longstreet's corps. In early 1863 he became Longstreet's chief of artillery, a post which he held for the rest of the war. An able officer, Alexander, who directed the Con-federate preliminary bombardment on the third day at Gettysburg, ended the struggle as a brigadier general. After the war he held public office, taught engineering, was active in the oil and railroad business, and did some farming. Alexander was a careful, analytic observer and an excellent critic of military affairs, as can be seen from his account of the strategic situation after the Peninsular Campaign and the early phases of the Second Bull Run Campaign, taken from his excellent Mililtary Memoirs of a Confederate *(New York, 1907).*

The close of the Seven Days found both armies greatly in need of rest. Lincoln called upon the governors of the Northern States for 300,000 more men, and bounties, State and Federal, were offered to secure them rapidly. They were easily obtained, but a mistake was made in putting the recruits in the field. They were organized into entirely new regiments, which were generally hurried to the field after but little drilling and training. President Davis also called for conscripts,—all that could be gotten. No great number were obtained, for those arriving at the age of conscription usually volunteered in some selected regiment. Those who were conscripted were also distributed among veteran regiments to repair the losses of the campaign, and this was done as rapidly as the men could be gotten to the front. Although this method allowed no time for drill or training, yet it was far more effective in maintaining the strength of the army than the method pursued by the Federals.

During the short intermission from active operations, something was accomplished, too, to improve our organizations, though leaving us still greatly behind the example long before set us by the enemy. Longstreet and Jackson were still but major-generals commanding divisions, but each now habitually commanded other divisions besides his own, called a Wing, and the old divisions became known by the names of new commanders. Thus, Jackson's old division now became Taliaferro's, and Longstreet's division became Pickett's, while Longstreet and Jackson each commanded a Wing, so called.

It was not until another brief rest in October, after the battle of Sharpsburg, that Longstreet and Jackson were made lieutenant-generals, and the whole army was definitely organized into corps. Some improvement was also made in our armament by the guns and rifled muskets captured during the Seven Days, and my reserve ordnance train was enlarged. Lines of light earthworks were constructed, protecting Chaffin's Bluff batteries on the James River, and stretching across the peninsula to connect with the lines already built from the Chickahominy to the head of White Oak Swamp.

Gen. D. H. Hill also constructed lines on the south side of the James, protecting Drury's Bluff and Richmond from an advance in that quarter; and Gen. French at Petersburg, as already mentioned, threw lines around that city, from the river below to the river above.

Just at the beginning of the Seven Days' Battles, President Lincoln had called from the West Maj.-Gen. John Pope, and placed him in command of the three separate armies of Frémont and Banks, in the Valley of Virginia, and McDowell near Fredericksburg. The union of the three into one was a wise measure, but the selection of a commander was as eminently unwise. One from the army in Virginia, other things being equal, would have possessed many advantages, and there was no lack of men of far sounder reputation than Pope had borne among his comrades in the old U. S. Army. He had spent some years in Texas boring for artesian water on the Staked Plains, and making oversanguine reports of his prospects of success. An army song had summed up his reputation in a brief parody of some well-known lines, "Hope told a flattering tale," as follows:—

Pope told a flattering tale,
  Which proved to be bravado,
About the streams which spout like ale
  On the Llano Estacado.

Pope arrived early in July and began to concentrate and organize his army. A characteristic "flattering tale" is told in an address to his troops, July 14, dated "Headquarters in the Saddle":—

Let us understand each other. I come to you from the West where we have always seen the backs of our enemies; from an army whose business it has been to seek the adversary, and beat him when he was found; whose policy has been attack and not defence. . . . I presume I have been called here to pursue the same system, and to lead you against the enemy. . . . Meantime, I desire you to dismiss from your minds certain phrases, which I am sorry to find so much in vogue amongst you. I hear constantly of 'taking strong positions and holding them'; of 'lines of retreat,' and of 'bases of supplies.' Let us discard such ideas. . . . Let us study the probable lines of retreat of our opponents and leave our own to take care of themselves. . . . Success and glory are in the advance. Disaster and shame lurk in the rear. . . .

The arrogance of this address was not calculated to impress favorably officers of greater experience in actual warfare, who were now overslaughed by his promotion. McDowell would have been the fittest selection, but he and Banks, both seniors to Pope, submitted without a word; as did also Sumner, Franklin, Porter, Heintzelman, and all the major-generals of McClellan's army. But Frémont protested, asked to be relieved, and practically retired from active service.

Meanwhile, after the discomfiture of McClellan, Mr. Lincoln felt the want of a military advisor, and, on July 11, appointed Gen. Halleck commander-in-chief of all the armies of the United States, and summoned him to Washington City. Pope's *Story of the Civil War* thus comments upon this appointment:—

It is easy to see how this unfortunate selection came to be made: Halleck was at that time the most successful general in the Federal service; it was perfectly natural that he should be the choice of the President and Secretary of War, to whom his serious defects as a military man could not have become known. His appointment was also satisfactory to the public, for, as so much had been effected under his command in the West, he was generally credited with great strategic ability. . . . But both the people and the President were before long to find out how slender

was Halleck's intellectual capacity, how entirely unmilitary was the cast of his mind, and how repugnant to his whole character was the assumption of any personal and direct control of an army in the field.

Halleck arrived in Washington and took charge on July 22. He found, awaiting for his decision, a grave problem. It was whether McClellan's army, now intrenched at Westover on the James, should be heavily reënforced and allowed to enter upon another active campaign from that point as a base, or whether it should abandon the James River entirely, and be brought back, by water, to unite with the army now under Pope, in front of Washington.

McClellan earnestly begged for reënforcements, and confidently predicted success if they were given him. He had begun to appreciate the strategic advantages of his position, and he was even proposing as his first movement the capture of Petersburg by a *coup-de-main*. This would not have been, at that time, a difficult operation. McClellan had 90,000 men available, for he could have even abandoned his position on the north side and used his whole force. As to its effect, it would probably have finally compelled the evacuation of Richmond, as it did in 1865. Had McClellan possessed enterprise and audacity, he would have waited neither for permission nor reënforcements, but have made the dash on his own responsibility as soon as he found that there was serious thought of recalling his army. All of this time, however, McClellan was still representing to his government that Lee had 200,000 men. If he really believed this, it is not strange that he kept closely within his intrenchments; but Mr. Ropes, the most careful historian of the war, asserts that neither McClellan nor Halleck believed this "preposterous story." McClellan told it, and stuck to is, trying to scare the administration into giving him unlimited reënforcements: but his real belief, Mr. Ropes thinks, is apparent in his offer to undertake the new campaign with only 20,000 reënforcements, raising his force to only 110,000. Mr. Ropes says that Halleck saw and appreciated McClellan's insincerity, but, wishing to have the army brought back, he affected to believe in the 200,000 men, and easily confounded McClellan's arguments by pointing out what such a force might do under such generals as Lee and Jackson.

Halleck had visited McClellan on the James soon after his arrival in Washington, and the matter was argued, pro and con, in correspondence afterward for some weeks.

McClellan ended with a strong appeal, pointing out that he could deliver his battle within 10 miles of Richmond, which was the heart of the Confederacy, while a victory 70 miles off might count for little. Halleck answered that it was unsafe to have a divided army in the face of Lee's force; that the location on the James River was very unhealthy in the fall months, and that most of McClellan's leading generals favored the withdrawal of the army. So orders were given, and the Federal army, on Aug. 14, began the evacuation of the only position from which it could soon have forced the evacuation of Richmond. They were only to find it again after two years' fighting, and the loss of over 100,000 men; and they would find it then, only by being defeated upon every other possible line of advance. The army was marched to Fortress Monroe, whence, as rapidly as boats could be furnished, it was carried up the Poto-

Rebel troops march to fight Pope's army at Second Bull Run.

mac to Acquia Creek or Alexandria. Thence, each corps, as fast as it arrived, was marched to join Pope's army, it being designed to concentrate everything behind the Rappahannock.

Now let us turn to Lee, and see how he met the difficulties of his situation, and what fortune attended his efforts. He realized that the immediate danger was that McClellan should be reenforced and renew his campaign from his new base. The first solicitude was to have McClellan's army recalled.

Some early efforts were made to demoralize the transport vessels, on the James, by which the army was supplied. Light guns were sent to various points along the river, whence they could, as it were, ambush passing vessels and fire upon them. But the Federal gunboats had soon learned the danger points and how to protect transports passing them, and no serious result could be accomplished. There were, however, persistent rumors that the Confederates were constructing one or more ironclads at Richmond, which would soon come down the James and destroy the whole Federal fleet. The uneasiness caused in Washington by these rumors may have contributed to the result finally reached. But Lee could not afford to wait at Richmond for the enemy to make up his mind slowly. His only chance was to strike Pope's army before it could be joined by McClellan's. As early, therefore, as July 13, he had ordered Jackson, with Taliaferro's and Ewell's divisions, to Gordonsville, to oppose reported advances of Pope. The latter had, on July 14, ordered Gen. Hatch to seize Gordonsville, then held by only about 200 infantry and a few cavalry. Hatch, however, lost time by listening to false reports that the Confederates were near at hand, and by waiting to take infantry, artillery, and a wagon-train, along with the considerable cavalry force which Pope had intended should alone be used. It alone would have been ample, as Jackson's troops did not reach Gordonsville until July 19. Hatch's expedition, therefore, was a failure.

Jackson, on his arrival, was anxious to undertake some aggressive operation against Pope, but found his force—only about 12,000 men—inadequate to accomplish anything against Pope's 47,000; so he appealed to Lee for reënforcement. Not yet assured that McClellan would not soon resume the offensive, Lee hesitated; but, on July 27, ordered A. P. Hill's division, about 12,000 strong, to Gordonsville. Hill joined Jackson on Aug. 2. Meanwhile, Pope had received instructions from Halleck to make demonstrations toward Gordonsville, with the view of occupying Lee's attention, and preventing his interference with the contemplated withdrawal of McClellan's force from the Peninsula.

On Aug. 6 Pope began to cross his infantry over the Rappahannock to concentrate about Culpeper. With swift appreciation of the opportunity, Jackson, on the 7th, put his whole force in motion to fall upon that portion of the enemy which first reached Culpeper. Could he defeat one of Pope's three corps, and occupy that central position in time, he might deal with the other two in succession, as he had dealt with Shields and Frémont at Port Republic. His strategy was excellent, but it was defeated by his own logistics. On the 7th the march was but eight miles, having only been begun in the afternoon. On the 8th there were 20 miles to go to reach Culpeper, with the Rapidan and Robertson rivers to ford, the latter being held by the Federal cavalry, about 12 miles in front of the town. The weather was intensely hot, and it could hardly be expected that the

Confederates would make the march in time to give battle on the same day. It would have been, however, only an easy march to reach a point, so close to the enemy, that battle could be delivered at an early hour on the 9th, allowing time to reap the fruits of victory, if successful. But on the 8th, some little blunders and omissions in giving the orders to the three divisions utterly confounded the march, and the head of the column only made eight miles, and the rear of it but two.

In the first place, each division was allowed to take its own wagon-train behind it on the road, instead of concentrating all three into one train behind the whole force. In the next place, Ewell's division, which was to lead and be followed by Hill's, had its route changed without Hill's being informed. This led to delay on Hill's part; and to Jackson's division (now commanded by Winder) getting ahead. Winder presently found his line of march intersected by Ewell's. It was also charged that Hill showed little zeal, being offended that Jackson, with his usual reticence, had given him no information of his plans.

Lee, indeed, in a recent letter had given Jackson a hint that his reticence might be carried too far. He had said:—

> A. P. Hill you will, I think, find a good officer, with whom you can consult, and, by advising with your division commanders as to your movements, much trouble will be saved you in arranging details, and they can aid more intelligently.

The whole incident shows that our staff service was poorly organized, and not efficient in its operations. The result of all this delay was that it was about 3 P.M. on the 9th before Ewell's division on the right, and Winder's on the left, had formed line in front of Banks's corps, which had been encountered at Cedar Mountain, some seven miles south of Culpeper. Lawton's large brigade of Ewell's division and Gregg's of Hill's division, had been left behind to guard the wagon-trains against the enemy's superior force of cavalry. The remainder of Hill's division was not yet up, and, while waiting their arrival, 26 rifled guns were brought up by Jackson and opened up the enemy's lines and batteries.

The left of Winder's division rested along the front edge of a considerable body of wood, which had not been thoroughly examined. Pope, in his report, asserts that Banks had been ordered to take a strong position and hold it, awaiting reënforcements, which were rapidly coming up. This should have been his play; but Pope had used expressions in orders, sent by his Chief of Cavalry, which Banks understood as permission to attack if the enemy were not in great force. Being, personally, both brave and aggressive, Banks thought the opportunity had arrived, and before Jackson was ready to advance, between 5 and 6 P.M., he attacked with his whole force. The right of his line overlapped the left of Winder's division, and taking it in flank and pressing vigorously, it entirely routed the left brigade under Garnett, and threw the whole division into much confusion. Winder himself had been killed by a cannon-shot in the preliminary artillery fighting.

Just at this juncture, however, Hill's division arrived upon the field, and not only restored the battle, but drove the enemy from the field and across Cedar Creek, a short distance in rear. By this time it was about dark, but Jackson was determined to lose no possible chance. Favored by a moon but little past the full, he brought forward two fresh brigades,—Field's and Stafford's, and Pegram's battery,—crossed the creek, and continued the pursuit.

Banks's corps, however, had, in its retreat, met Ricketts's division of McDowell's corps, accompanied by Pope in person, and followed also by the leading troops of Sigel's corps. About one and a half miles beyond Cedar Creek the Confederate advance found itself close in front of a strong line of battle, composed of Rickett's four brigades, with four batteries of artillery. Pegram's four guns were pushed to the front, and, at close canister range, opened upon the enemy. They were replied to by a dozen guns, but continued the action until they were practically cut to pieces. It was now nearly midnight, and Jackson, having learned from the cavalry of the capture of prisoners from Sigel's corps, was constrained to halt for the night. By morning he found that the greater part of Pope's army was now united in his front, and that his opportunity to attack the enemy in detail had passed,—lost by the bad marching on the 8th. He still, however, felt able to defeat them if they could be induced to attack him in position, as Pope was pledged to do in his order 75, so he withdrew his line across the creek, and occupied himself in gleaning the battle-field of arms. Pope showed too much wisdom to accept the gage of further battle. Heavy reënforcements were coming to him, and it was as clearly his game to await their arrival as it had been Jackson's to anticipate it. So, on the 11th, he sent in a flag of truce asking permission to bury his dead of the 9th, which were still within Jackson's lines. It was granted, until noon, and then extended until sundown.

On the 12th, finding that Pope would not be tempted to attack him there, he tried another ruse. He fell back from the battlefield, not only to the south side of the Rapidan, where he might easily have halted and maintained himself, but he continued his retreat through Orange C.H. [Court House] and on to Gordonsville. He hoped that Pope would construe the move as a confession of weakness and would be inspired by it and his own boastings to follow. This strategy was very nearly successful. On Aug. 12, Pope, having heard that the reënforcements under Burnside would soon join him, wired Halleck that, on their arrival, he would cross the Rapidan and advance upon Louisa C. H. This would have given the Confederates the very opportunity desired. On Aug. 13, Lee had ordered Longstreet and Hood, with 12 brigades, to proceed by raid to Gordonsville, and, on the 14th, he also

John Pope

ordered up Anderson's division of infantry, three brigades, and Stuart's cavalry. On the 15th he went up in person and took the command.

The casualties at Cedar Mountain had been as follows:—

	killed	wounded	missing	total
Confederate:	229	1047	31	1307
Federal:	314	1445	622	2381

The Confederate losses were distributed among nine brigades of infantry and one of cavalry, and were greatest in Garnett's and Taliaferro's, of Jackson's division, slightly over 300 in each. The Federal losses were in eight brigades of infantry and one of cavalry. Crawford's brigade lost 857, Geary's 465, Prince's 452, and Gordon's 344. The fighting upon Jackson's left, where Garnett's and Taliaferro's brigades were broken by the charge of Crawford's and Gordon's brigades, and the line reëstablished, by

Crawford's and Gordan's brigades drive the Rebel
forces from the woods at Cedar Mountain.

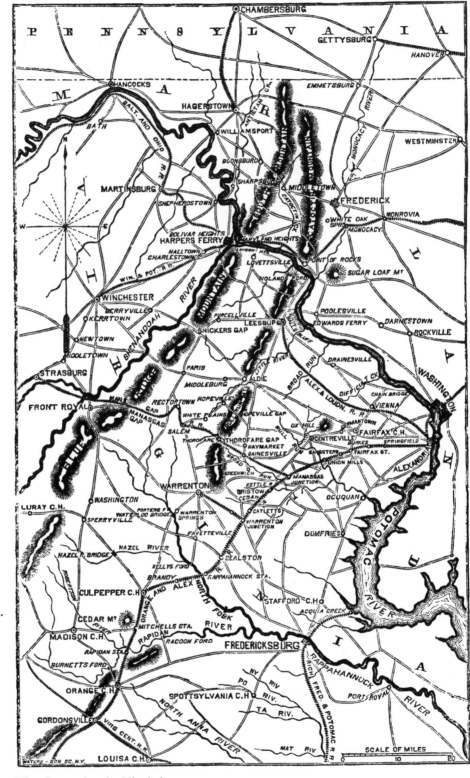

The Campaign in Virginia

Branch's, Archer's, and Winder's brigades, was very desperate, as is shown by the casualties of some of the Federal regiments.

An incident of the battle was a charge upon Taliaferro's brigade by two squadrons of the 1st Pa. Cav., under Maj. Falls, when the brigade, in some disorder, was pressing hard upon the retreat of the Federal infantry. The charge successfully rode through the Confederate skirmish-line, but was driven back by the fire of the line of battle with the loss of 93 men out of 164.

JOHN GIBBON
Second Bull Run

John Gibbon (1827–1896), a native of Philadelphia who was raised in North Carolina, graduated from West Point in 1847 and had an impressive career as a junior officer in the Old Army, serving in the Mexican and Seminole Wars and as an instructor at West Point, while finding time to write The Artillerist's Manual, *a basic text for garrison and field service. At the outbreak of the war, which found him on a remote frontier post, he threw in his lot with the Union despite having three brothers in Confederate service. His wartime career was a distinguished one. He led the famed Black Hat brigade during the Second Bull Run and Antietam, commanded a division at Fredericksburg, where he was badly wounded, and at Chancel-lorsville, and was acting commander of II Corps at Gettysburg, where he was again seriously wounded while receiving Pickett's Charge. He subsequently commanded a division and then a corps in the Virginia Campaigns of 1864 and 1865, and was one of the commissioners who received the surrender of the Army of Northern Virginia. In later years he served on the frontier, retiring as a regular army brigadier general. Gibbon's clear and stylish account of the Second Battle of Bull Run, drawn from his* Personal Recollections of the Civil War *(New York, 1928), opens as Irwin McDowell's III Corps of Pope's army prepared to march south across the Rappahannock.*

. . . Our Division moved under orders on the tenth up the river, crossed at Kelly's Ford and pushed forward for two days in the direction of Culpeper Court House under an intensely hot sun, being repeatedly hurried by despatches from General McDowell. We reached the vicinity of the battlefield of Cedar Mountain at 9 o'clock at night, and the next morning being close to the Headquarters of Generals Pope and McDowell learned that Jackson with his force had retreated, and General John Buford with his cavalry had been sent in pursuit. I rode at once out to the battlefield and as Buford moved to the front, I caught sight of the enemy's rear guard (cavalry) as it disappeared over the distant hills. A view of the field of battle disclosed evidence of a severe struggle, but from what I could learn it was not a very decisive one, only a small portion of Pope's army being engaged, and Jackson retired behind the Rapidan only because he found himself in the presence of a superior force.

On the 16th, just a week from the battle, we made an advance of a few miles, our division being camped on the field where the stench of the dead horses and men was intolerable. Here Reno's division of Burnside's Corps joined us from Fredericksburg, and was placed in position on our left. Rumors now reached us that the whole Army of the Potomac was leaving the Peninsula, but this was promptly denied by our newspapers. If this were true then the military question would simply resolve itself into this:—Which army would be the first to be concentrated and made ready for battle. The location would be determined by the time and manner in which this concentration took place. If it occurred out here then the advantage would probably be with the enemy, for his lines of communication were shorter. If closer to Washington the advantage might be on our side depending a good deal on the decision and skill of our generals, or rather our general, for under the critical position of affairs one general, even a poor one, would be worth much more than several good ones.

The question at issue was soon now to solve itself and our first move in the game of war was the right one. Two days after our advance we received orders to retreat (Aug. 18th). A retreat is always a much more severe test of discipline than any other movement especially if made in the presence of the enemy. Green troops will advance in much better order although confident of going into danger, than they will retreat, which is supposed to be an escape from danger. Hence with undisciplined troops commanders frequently prefer to run the risk of an engagement than to convert their retreating troops into a stampeded mob, liable at any moment to take counsel of their fears and yield to the thousand and one rumors always sure to be set afloat in such a force.

The orders were for the troops to commence falling back at 10 o'clock at night and as soon as it was dark, our long wagon trains began moving to the rear. The troops could not move of course until these were out of the way and it was 10 o'clock the next morning, 12 hours after the hour designated for the march, before they were able to take the road. This was a bad beginning, for our tired, sleepy men were in poor condition for the long, hot, dusty march which followed. We soon overtook the rear of our wagon train, and all day long slowly plodded along behind it. Long after darkness had closed around us our Division reached the vicinity of the railroad crossing the Rappahannock River. Here we found the road in front of us to be solidly blocked up with troops and wagons in which no movement took place for hours. No orders came and so far as we could see those who ought to have given them had disappeared. At a late hour I sent out orders to my Brigade to bivouac alongside the road, that tired and hungry as the men were, they might get what rest they could. The next morning early (20th) we were in motion and crossing the Rappahannock on the bridge. We found everything on the other side in the utmost confusion. Wagon-trains, Divisions, Brigades, and Regiments were all mixed up, apparently in the most inextricable confusion, nobody seeming to know where to go or where anybody else was, and there was such a total absence of all order and authority as to produce a most painful impression on the mind. But as the day advanced matters began to assume better shape; commands were got together, and something like military order began to prevail as the troops were ordered into position along the river, with an evident intention of disputing its passage.

The enemy did not allow the grass to grow under his feet but soon confronted us on the other side of the Rappahannock and for several days an active duel was kept up between the batteries with now and then an effort to cross with infantry or cavalry. These were successfully resisted and our troops began to get used to the constant roar of artillery and the occasional dropping of a shell amongst them. One of these killed an officer of the 7th Wisconsin of my Brigade.

We remained in position along the river for three days or rather moving along it from place to place as efforts were made by the enemy to cross and on the 23rd of August we were startled by the information that Stuart and his cavalry had crossed the river above, and moving around our right flank, had struck our line of communication at Catlett's station, captured a large train lying there with an insufficient guard and destroyed it. A part of the train

Confederate troops under Jackson advance to attack on Pope.

belonged to General Pope's Headquarters but it was only patially plundered, not destroyed, on account of a heavy rain which was falling. Stuart escaped by the way of Warrenton. About the same time information reached General Pope that a part of the enemy's forces having crossed at Sulphur Springs had been cut off by a rise in the river. With the view of capturing this detached force, a large number of troops were at once pushed up towards Sulphur Springs. But the enemy becoming aware of the danger, built a bridge and retired across the river to the main body. This movement on our part was extended and our division with other troops marched to Warrenton which place we reached on the 23rd. On the 26th the division moved out to Sulphur Springs where our artillery exchanged some shots with the enemy across the river. Whilst lying here, General John F. Reynolds was sent out to take command of the position, our division commander having a few days before been stricken with a severe attack of illness from which he was still suffering. Reynolds and his Division Commander McCall had both been taken prisoners, and Meade, a Brigade Commander in the

same division, wounded during the operations on the Peninsula. Reynolds and Meade, only partly recovered from his wound, had just rejoined their commands. These were both fine soldiers and I was much struck with a remark made to me in a conversation held with Meade whilst we were in the vicinity of Warrenton. We were discussing the condition of military affairs and Meade told me of a conversation he had just had with Pope, asking him very pointedly, "What are you doing out here? This is no place for this army. It should at once fall back so as to meet the rest of the Army of the Potomac coming up and by superior forces overwhelm Lee." This enunciation of a sound strategic principle was met by Pope with the remark that he had "orders from Washington to hold the Rappahannock as long as possible and that he should be well reinforced in 48 hours," and Pope querulously added that more than that number of hours had passed and the reinforcements had not arrived. This defence of Pope's, which was undoubtedly true, left the painful impression that although Halleck (a military man) was in Washington the pernicious practice of attempting

to command an army in the field far from the scenes of its operations was still kept up in spite of the severe experience we had gone through only two months before. It was also demonstrated that General Pope was lacking in that sort of independence of character which not only prompts but enables an army commander to do on the spot that which he knows the exigencies require, independent of orders received from superiors at a distance and ignorant of the situation.

On the 27th, we received orders to fall back from Sulphur Springs and taking the road we marched through Warrenton late in the afternoon. As my men were becoming very short of provisions, I sent staff officers forward with directions to have provisions placed along the sidewalks so the men could pick them up and supply themselves as we marched through the town. When we arrived the streets were packed with troops, and trains slowly making their way forward, but everything else seemed to be hurried and confused. General McDowell, standing on the porch of the hotel—Warren Green—was rapidly giving orders to hurry the troops forward and on seeing my brigade halt to get the provisions prepared for them, sent me orders to push forward at once. I explained to him in person that my men were much in want of the provisions and it would take but a few minutes to make the issue, but he reiterated his orders to push forward the march and much to our regret, we were obliged to turn our backs on and abandon the much-needed food. This was all the more to be regretted since scarcely had we cleared the town than the road was found so blocked up in front that our progress was very slow and after marching till long after dark we bivouacked for the night only five miles beyond Warrenton.

As I passed through the town I could not help recalling our former visit there in the preceeding June, reflecting that what was now going on was a consequence of the faulty principles of military strategy, followed then. Whilst standing on the porch of the hotel, I had a conversation with General McDowell on the subject. He complained bitterly of the conduct of Mr. Stanton toward him just after the abortive pursuit of Jackson was ended and contrasted it with his hearing just before that pursuit began. It was well known in the army that McDowell had at the time urged upon the Washington authorities a different movement from the one dictated by them and McDowell seemed to think that as he had yielded his military judgment to them, they should not have held him responsible for the resultant failure. He evidently did not relish my assertion that under such circumstances a soldier had but one course to pursue, which was to tender his resignation from the army. He did not do this and was superseded, thus losing not only his command but his reputation also.

During these movements all sorts of rumors were afloat as to what was taking place, and amidst much that was wild talk it seemed to be pretty well understood that Jackson, with a part of Lee's army, was marching around us to the north intending to strike our line of communication. He had, in fact, at this very time (night of the 27th) actually struck it and destroyed our supplies at Manassas Junction.

General McDowell had by an order from General Pope been placed in command of Sigel's Corps as well as his own and that corps preceded ours on the march. We resumed the march early the next morning pushing along the turnpike towards Gainesville, being delayed occasionally by some wagons in our front. Passing through Gainesville, a cluster of two or three houses where the Manassas Gap railroad crosses the turnpike, we made a halt just beyond and whilst resting there General John Buford, accompanied by Colonel Charles H. Tompkins and a cavalry force, passed us to the rear on the way to make a reconnoissance back in the direction of Warrenton or Thoroughfare Gap. To the latter point General McDowell had sent Ricketts' division to take possession of and hold the Gap against Lee's main army which, it had been ascertained, was marching to pass through there.

When we resumed the march we came to a country road a few miles beyond Gainesville which branched off from the pike obliquely to the right. Taking this we marched a mile or two farther and then halted. Orders were given for us to form a line

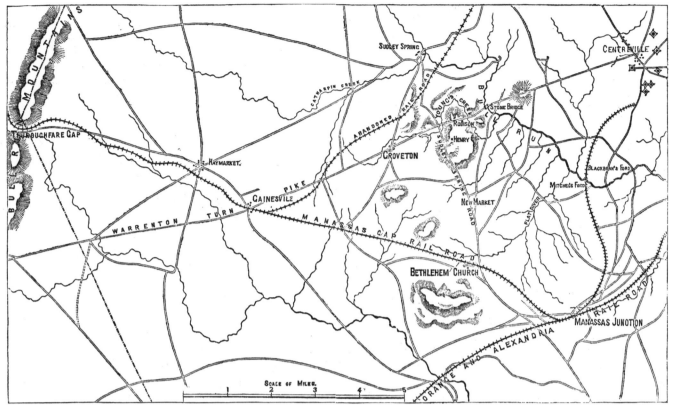

Thoroughfare Gap   **Gainesville Area**

of battle and then countermanded. We remained halted in this position for many hours, and everybody was busy speculating as to what was going on and what was to be done. During this halt I rode to the front to a prominent hill where McDowell and several others were using their glasses, looking over the country to the north and east. In that direction heavy clouds of dust could be seen rising above the treetops indicating the movement of columns of troops; and I began to think that McDowell's prediction of the night before that "something was bound to break" to-day was about to be verified. During or just preceding this halt the report of several guns had been heard to our left and front and we learned afterwards that the enemy had fired upon Reynolds' Division, which was leading, killing and wounding several of his men. Still we did not move and as the day wore on our men began to get hungry. We had but few provisions along, except beef on the hoof, and some of the Regimental officers asked permission, if we were to be here long enough, to kill some of the cattle and cook the beef. I could obtain no definite information in regard to our probable stay, and after hesitating some time I gave orders to have the beef killed and cooked. This was done and the beef was eaten before any orders came. It was quite late in the afternoon before we resumed the march on a road which led back to the turnpike. This was now the condition of affairs in McDowell's command,—Sigel's Corps had disappeared in the woods

Troop Positions, at sunset, August 29

in front of us, so also had Reynolds' Division, Ricketts' Division was on its way back towards Thoroughfare Gap, so that King's Division was alone and, it seems, had orders to march to Centreville. Hatch's Brigade led in the march; mine followed, Doubleday's next and Patrick's brought up the rear, one battery being with each brigade. When I reached the pike with the head of my brigade, Hatch's Brigade, recognizing the gray dress of the 14th Brooklyn, was seen to be deployed on the high ground to the north of the pike, engaged evidently, in making a reconnoissance. After some delay it passed quietly over the brow of the hill and out of sight.

At a little pool of water near the turnpike, General King was seated with some of his staff eating lunch. I reported to him and asked if I should follow Hatch along the turnpike. Receiving an affirmative answer my brigade moved off followed by my own battery under command of Bvt. Capt. J. B. Campbell. The turnpike, straight as an arrow, passed in our front, through a strip of heavy timber which extended across the pike. On emerging into the open ground beyond, I could see no troops, Hatch's Brigade having disappeared behind another piece of woods in our front. Riding just ahead of my leading regiment I reached a gentle rise on the north of the pike and paused to look around me. Not a moving thing was in sight, but on casting my eyes to the left there suddenly appeared, coming out of the timber, a short mile away, a number of horses. I had scarcely had time to think whether they belonged to friend or enemy, or whether we might have any cavalry in that direction, when I was struck by the fact that the horses presented their flanks to view. My experience as an artillery officer, told me at once what this meant; guns coming into "battery"! I despatched a staff officer to the rear to bring up my battery at a gallop and he had scarcely left me when several shells came screaming over our heads. There was no longer any question of our being in the presence of an enemy. The battery was located within a short distance of the very place where only a little while before Hatch's Brigade had been in position. Campbell's pieces came up on the gallop, the fences along the pike being torn down to let them pass into the field. With shells bursting about them they were placed in position and began to reply rapidly from the knoll where I had first caught sight of the enemy's guns. Never was there a more complete surprise and from troops, too, which had been in that vicinity since early morning, and with which some of our troops had been in conflict only a few hours before.

As soon as our guns opened fire I moved off to the left and front of the battery in the woods to witness the effect of the fire. Whilst in this position I heard, off to the left, in the direction of the Douglas House, the sound of a cannon which I supposed to be firing towards the rear of our column. Still unaware of the proximity of any of the enemy's infantry, I sent hastily back to the turnpike an order to bring up one of my regiments and then, started through the woods to meet it. In the timber I met the 2nd Wisconsin and conducted it by a wood road through the timber to the open ground beyond, explaining to Colonel O'Connor as we rode along what I wanted him to do. Outside of the wood the regiment was formed into line and silently moved up the gentle slope in front. As soon as it reached the brow of the hill, a few shots were fired, a line of skirmishers was quickly thrown forward, the enemy's skirmishers driven in and the regiment advanced to the plateau beyond. As the picket firing opened, the guns which up to this time had continued to fire, became silent and the 2nd Wisconsin had not advanced much farther before a very heavy musketry fire was opened upon it. It at once replied vigorously and finding that the regiment had become badly involved I ordered the rest of the brigade rapidly up to its support. They moved up and promptly formed in line with the 2nd Wisconsin, the 19th Indiana on its left, the 7th Wisconsin on its right whilst the 6th Wisconsin took position still farther to the right and then for over an hour the most terrific musketry fire I have ever listened to rolled along those two lines of battle. It was a regular stand up fight during which neither side yielded a foot. My command exhibited in the highest degree the effects of discipline and drill, officers and men standing up to their work like old soldiers. Going over the ground the following year I could plainly trace out the line of battle they had occupied by the half-buried bodies and the cartridge papers. The left of my line rested at the Douglas House, and from that point, as darkness came on, I could see the enemy's line extending far to my left. Should the enemy get possession of this house, and yard full of trees, he would entirely flank my line and enfilade it. As the darkness increased and the fire on both sides slackened I gave orders to the left of the 19th Indiana to fall back obliquely to the rear so as to protect the flank. To do this, the men ceased firing and before we had formed in the new position the enemy threw forward some men into the yard of the Douglas House and in the darkness opened fire upon us. Here some confusion took place but the men readily responded to the voices of their officers and formed line again on the edge of the woods behind them and everything except the groans of the wounded quieted down. The fight was over. During this short hour and a half I sent repeated and urgent requests for assistance, both to the Division commander and to General Patrick whose brigade I knew was behind mine (to my left and rear) and from which I had not heard a shot fired.

After establishing the left of my line in the timber, I found General King and reported to him. He was sitting with the members of his staff in a fence corner alongside the turnpike near the point where we first received the fire of the enemy's guns. I must, I think, have been in a very bad temper and expressed myself very freely in regard to the way in which I thought I had been left to do the fighting with my Brigade alone and it then transpired that two regiments from Doubleday's brigade *had* been sent to my assistance, but as they went to a different part of the field from where I was I had not seen them.

This fight was the "baptism of fire" of my brigade and we paid for it a heavy penalty. Out of 1,800 men I took into action, about one third were killed or wounded in the space of one hour and a half. O'Connor, Colonel of the 2nd, was killed, Cutler, Colonel of the 6th, wounded, Colonel Robinson, Lieut. Col. Hamilton and Major Bill, all of the 7th, wounded besides many other commissioned officers in all the regiments, killed or wounded. I was exceedingly proud of the way my command had behaved in the presence of what was evidently a much superior force, but this feeling was saddened by my very heavy losses, which were rendered apparent when the regiments were collected that night. I found Generals Hatch and Doubleday with General King. The former as soon as he heard the sound of my firing, had turned back with his brigade and marched to the sound of the guns, but the whole thing was soon over that he had not had time to get into action. Soon after the rear brigade was ordered up, General Patrick joining us, we discussed the situation, and the question naturally arose, what under the circumstances, was to be done. General King said his orders were to march to Centreville. "From whom were these orders received?" was asked. "From General McDowell." "Where was General McDowell?" Nobody seemed to know. I was under the impression that I had seen him present with Hatch's Brigade when it made its reconnoissance in the afternoon, but this turned out afterwards to be a mistake. I objected that we could not now carry out the order to go to Centreville, for the enemy appeared to be between us and that point, and "Besides, why go to Centreville when the enemy we were looking for was here?"

In the meantime, while this discussion was going on some few prisoners who had wandered into our picket line on the battle ground were questioned and from them we learned that Jackson's main force was in our front. No one seemed to know where any other portion of our forces were and so far as we could see, this division, one of its Brigades very badly crippled, stood alone in the presence of Jackson's right wing. I was the junior general officer present, but none of the other officers expressed any opinion except General King and he seemed disposed to attempt to obey the orders he had received, to march to Centreville. I strongly opposed this because I did not think it practicable to do it in the darkness, and as a better plan, proposed we should take the road to Manassas Junction with the hope

that we might meet troops coming from there to support us. Still no one else expressing any opinion, either for or against the proposition, I took a piece of paper and by the light of a candle wrote out what I proposed and showed it to the other generals, finally handing it to General King. They all agreed that it was the best thing to do under the circumstances and General King, after adding something in his own handwriting, signed it as a despatch to General McDowell, one of whose staff officers being present volunteered to carry it, although he confessed he did not know where General McDowell was. Long afterwards General John F. Reynolds told me of his experience on that night. His division, as I have already stated, had passed to the front and disappeared in the woods. Just before sundown he heard my firing and, with a staff officer, rode towards it. He came on the ground in the midst of the fight, and meeting General Doubleday on the turnpike, asked him who was engaged. Being told it was my Brigade he asked why the troops were not sent up to my assistance and received the reply that "some have been sent." "But why," he asked, "don't you push all these troops up?" He afterwards saw General King and told him that his division was not far off and that if he (King) would hold his position till daylight, he would by that time bring his division to his support. I did not see General Reynolds, did not know he had been on the ground, and knew nothing of his proposition to support us. His offer fully demonstrated that this fine soldier duly appreciated the importance of our position. On reaching the ground the next morning, he found we had vacated it.

After collecting our wounded at points in the woods, south of the turnpike where they received such surgical attention as could be given them, we loaded those that could be moved, into ambulances and at 1 o'clock in the morning left the pike and commenced the march towards Manassas Junction.

It was a sad, tedious march, but contrary to expectations we met nobody on the road and reached the vicinity of the Junction just as day was breaking. Here a halt was made, our poor tired men lying down alongside the road for much-needed rest, whilst steps were at once taken to supply them with food and ammunition. Although very tired, I could not sleep for thinking, and mounting my horse again, I rode up to the Junction hoping to find General Pope there that I might inform him what had happened to us the night before.

The Junction was a scene of desolation and ruin, long trains of cars which had been filled with supplies for our army were now a smouldering mass of ashes, the rebel troops, first supplying themselves, having set the balance on fire two nights before (27th). After riding about for some time I failed to find General Pope, but met a staff officer who said he had left him on Bull Run at Blackburn's ford. I urged him to go to General Pope and give him my report but he declined as he was then carrying an order. I finally concluded to go myself leaving my staff officers to provide for the wants of the brigade.

Running low on ammunition, Confederate troops throw stones at advancing Federals.

On reaching Bull Run, however, I learned General Pope had left for Centreville, so I determined to ride on there where I found him with his staff in a house at Centreville and told him what had happened.

One of the first questions he asked was: "Where is McDowell?" I told him I did not know; that he was not present when the fight took place.

He said with passion, "G——— damn McDowell, he is never where he ought to be!" The remark struck me with surprise for it was generally supposed in the army that Pope liked, trusted and leaned upon McDowell very much. I then proceeded to explain that my object in coming to see him, was to call his attention to the fact that our abandon-

ment of the turnpike left no troops interposed between Jackson's and Lee's main army and consequently the two forces could join without opposition, presuming that if he had any forces available, he would at once throw them forward into the opening. At first he did not seem to appreciate the importance of this, and spoke with great confidence of the result of his operations against Jackson's forces, saying his troops were now in contact with Jackson's and pressing them but he finally turned to his Adjutant (Ruggles) and said, "Write a note to General Porter and direct him to move out with his corps on Gainesville road and take King's Division with him," adding, "Give it to General Gibbon and let him take it to General Porter at Manassas Junction." My own horse was much broken down and I was fearful I should not be able to carry the order rapidly enough. On making this statement to General Pope he ordered a fresh horse to be given me. Mounting again, I started back as rapidly as possible, but I found my fresh horse but little faster than my tired one, and was glad on passing our train near Bull Run to exchange him for another, of my own, and on him I rode rapidly back to the Junction. Here I found quite a large body of troops, and seeking out General Porter, gave him the order which read as follows:

Hd. Qrs. Army of Virginia,
Centreville, Aug. 29, 1862.

Push forward with your corps and King's Division which you will take with you, to Gainesville. I am following the enemy down the Warrenton pike. Be expeditious or we shall lose much.

JOHN POPE,
Maj. Gen. Comdg.

Whilst I was talking with Porter, General McDowell came up and the order was shown to him. He expressed some dissatisfaction at that part of the order referring to King's Division. Talking to Porter, I heard him say, "General Porter, when you form your line, I wish you would place King on your right so that I can have my command together." Porter then made some enquiry of me as to the location of the road he was to follow and I volunteered to pilot his leading Division into it. He gave his order and riding with General Morell, I conducted him to the road. When we reached the point where our division was lying, I left him and joined my brigade.

As soon as the 5th Corps had passed we took the road in its rear and began to retrace our steps over the same route we had followed only a few hours before. But we were not destined to retrace many of them for we had not gone very far, perhaps not over a mile or two, when there came a halt in the column which turned out to be one of considerable length, during which, all, of course, were speculating as to "what was up." At last we were brought to our feet by orders and moved on again. Somewhat to our surprise, a part of our column turned off to the right and followed McDowell along what turned out to be the Sudley Spring road leading by the Henry House. On this road we marched till late in the afternoon, halting every now and then for a considerable time, part of the troops leaving the road and going off to the north, from which direction the sound of cannon reached us as we marched along. Late in the afternoon, approaching the Henry House ahead of my brigade, I met General McDowell with his staff and mounted escort around him. He came forward to meet me, appearing to be laboring under great excitement and exclaiming—"Hurry forward, hurry forward you are just in the nick of time!" I explained that my tired men were coming as fast as possible, but that was not very fast as they had been marching

all the night before and all day and were very much tired out. He repeated his admonition "to hurry" and as the head of the column appeared I asked him what orders he had. He said, "Go right up that road," pointing to the continuation of the road we were on as it climbs the hill on the other side of the Warrenton pike leading to Sudley Spring. "To whom shall I report?" I asked. "Go right up that road," he replied, "I shall be here."

I followed his direction and crossing the pike reached the top of the hill beyond, where I stopped to look around me. Some few troops were in sight and down about a mile in front was a strip of timber from which came the sounds of conflict, musketry, cannon shots and cheers. Whilst enquiring "who was in command" and wondering whether I was expected blindly to throw myself and command into the conflict below, a staff officer of General Pope, General W. L. Elliot, rode up, giving me General Pope's order to go into position on the hill where I then was and support several batteries standing there. It then appeared that I was entirely separated from all other parts of the division, how, when, or where it was difficult to decide. Not only separated from the Division but from our Corps also for Reynolds' Division was somewhere out to the front and Rickett's Division on the march from Thoroughfare Gap via Bristow station and the Junction.

The conflict in the woods in front continued all the rest of the afternoon and towards sundown General Pope rode up on the hill near my position where I was seated on my horse looking on. He listened to the conflict for awhile and then turning to his Adjutant General, Ruggles, said, "Colonel Ruggles, telegraph to Washington that we have had a severe battle and have lost ten thousand men." Adding as if to himself, "I think we have lost ten thousand." All these details are impressed on my mind as vividly as if they had happened only a few years ago.

As night approached the fight died down but about dark another one broke out on the south side of the pike and to the south of Groveton, the shouts of the combatants and the sounds of musketry continuing till long after nightfall and then quiet reigned over the field of slaughter.

The following morning (30th) was comparatively quiet for many hours and every one seemed to be asking the question "What next?" As the morning wore on I paid a visit to General Pope's Headquarters, nothing more than a position on the line just in rear of where I was. There were no tents, nothing to mark the spot except a cracker box or two for seats. General Pope talked very freely to the few officers around him and I recollect his complaining bitterly of what he termed "the inaction of General Fitz-John Porter," saying he had done nothing whilst the rest of the army was fighting, adding, personally addressing me, "That is not the way for an officer to act, Gibbon." I knew Porter's reputation as a soldier well and felt confident that he was not a man to stand by and do nothing when he ought to fight, but I knew little or nothing of the military situation and said

Confederate soldiers loot the supply depot at Manassas Junction.

nothing.

The morning wore on and all seemed to be waiting on events. Reports were constantly coming from the field to General Pope and late in the day I was surprised to hear him announce that the enemy was retreating. Everybody was now on the alert, and later some general officer rode up (I think either McDowell or Heintzelman) and before he could utter more than a word or two, General Pope interrupted him with, "I know what you are going to say, the enemy is retreating."

Orders were at once issued for the pursuit. McDowell was placed in charge and Porter in direct command of the pursuing forces. He had arrived on the field that morning pursuant to an order sent him by General Pope the night before. His troops were moved out to the front on the right of the turnpike and our division under Hatch was posted on his right, my brigade in the rear supporting. We moved to the front, formed line of battle and entered the woods just to the left of where the fighting had taken place the afternoon previous and soon the roar of battle commenced. The underbrush was thick and impassable for horses, so all mounted officers had to go on foot, leaving their horses behind, and it was with difficulty that any alignment could be preserved. Bullets came thick from the front and very

soon shells were bursting among us, coming from the left. Still, we moved forward, unable to see far through the thick underbrush which broke up our line separating the regiments, until I found myself standing in the rear of the only one in sight (the 6th Wisconsin). Men were falling thick and fast and neither enemy nor friends, except those immediately about me, were to be seen. The fire slackened and rumour came that our troops had been repulsed and were falling back. I waited for orders and then receiving positive information that all other troops had retired, we withdrew from the woods. On reaching the open ground, I found my Brigade Quartermaster, Captain Mason, waiting with my horse. The faithful officer, in his search for me, had run into the enemy's advancing picket line on our left and had received a bullet in the hip. He confirmed the statement that all our troops had gone to the rear. I mounted my horse, threw a line of pickets to the rear and marched in line of battle to the hill behind us near the Dogan House where several batteries were in position, my own amongst the number, and the other Regiments of the Brigade close by. The Brigade was now formed on the hill around the Dogan House in support of the batteries and we awaited the advance of the enemy. Soon from the very point of the woods we had left, troops came out in line of battle. I was so sure that they were the remnant of our troops coming back that I rode into the batteries and ordered them not to fire, but it soon became evident that they were the enemy's, and our guns opened upon them. The battle recommenced, not only in our front, but away off to our left to the south of the pike where we could see the masses of the enemy moving forward. As they approached a bald hill in front of the Henry House, a severe conflict took place and for some time it remained doubtful which would win. At last our troops began to give way, leaving some guns behind them. But they were reinforced and again advanced, driving the enemy before them. All this we had time to observe before we ourselves attacked. But our fire checked the enemy's advance and in the midst of the firing, an officer who announced himself as on the staff of General Hooker, brought me an order to "retreat." General Hooker was almost a stranger to me and belonged to a different corps. I called the attention of the officer, bringing the order, to the importance of the position we held, especially in view of the fact that our troops appeared to have retaken possession of the hill near the Henry House and that if we fell back, the whole line would have to do so and requested him to so state to General Hooker. He left and almost immediately returned to say that I must fall back as General Pope had ordered a general retreat.

We then fell back across a valley and up on a hill behind passing, as we did so, a great pile of knapsacks and other equipment, lying in a piece of timber where they had probably been left when their owners had gone into action. As the troops moved back I caught sight of General Hooker on a spur just behind our former position, looking on at the battle. I rode up to him to make some explanation regarding my hesitancy in obeying the order he had sent me but he interrupted me saying, "That is all right," and added some complimentary remark about the way which we had held our position, which at once excited my pride and attracted me to him. I then left him and climbing the opposite slope, encountered General McDowell. He met me with unusual cordiality and shaking hands, said he was glad to see me, as General Porter had told him I was killed. I spoke with enthusiasm of the way in which my brigade, just then passing, had behaved, and shall not soon forget his reply. "If you have such troops as that," he said, "you shall act as rear guard and be the last, except myself, to pass Bull Run!" I must admit that up to this time I had not got it through my head, that there was such a thing as a retreat or that we were to have a rear guard.

My brigade was now placed in position on the ridge alongside the Pike where it climbed the hill near the Robinson House, the pieces of Battery "B" being unlimbered, were prepared for action. The sun was now just disappearing and the atmosphere so thick with smoke the eye could not reach to any great distance. We could not see any of the enemy's movements but the sound of cannon was still heard both to our right and our left.

Whilst waiting in position I heard some one inquire in a short quick tone: "Whose command is this?" and turning to look, I recognized General Phil Kearny. I walked up to him and told him I was directed to act as rear guard. He was a soldierly looking figure as he sat, straight as an arrow, on his horse, his empty sleeve pinned to his breast.

Turning towards me, he said in his curt way: "You must wait for my command, sir." "Yes," I replied, "I will wait for all our troops to pass to the rear. Where is your command, General?" "Off on the right, don't you hear my guns? You must wait for Reno, too." "Where is he?" "On the left—you hear his guns? He is keeping up the fight and I am doing all I can to help."

Then in a short bitter tone he broke out with: "I suppose you appreciate the condition of affairs here, sir?"

I did not understand the remark and only looked inquiringly at him. He repeated:

"I suppose you appreciate the condition of affairs? It's another Bull Run, sir, it's another Bull Run!"

"Oh!" I said, "I hope not quite as bad as that General."

"Perhaps not. Reno is keeping up the fight. He is not stampeded. I am not stampeded, you are not stampeded. That is about all, sir, my God that's about all!"

It is impossible to describe the extreme bitterness and vehemence with which he uttered these words as he rode away towards his command. Two days afterwards, September 1st, General Kearny was killed at Chantilly. I have seen one of the last letters he ever wrote, dated the 31st, in which he thus alludes to the Battle of Bull Run: "The army ran like sheep, all but a General Reno and a General Gibbon," and in a letter dated the next day (since published) he says: "On the 30th nine-tenths of the troops disgracefully fled. I held the entire right until 10 P.M., as Reno did the left, and Gibbon the main road."

As darkness closed in, the guns ceased to fire and silence settled over the field, except that we could hear down in the valley below, the sound of the rebel officers as they halted and formed their troops, evidently to discontinue the pursuit. Hearing nothing from the troops on my left, I rode off in that direction and with many fears of running into the enemy's lines in the darkness, I slowly felt my way

Union troops retreat from Bull Run again over the stone bridge.

along and finally reached a body of men which I was much relieved to find were friends. It was a brigade of Reno's command and a Regular battery with it whose captian—Graham—I knew but they had heard nothing from Reno, and did not know where he was.

The Brigade and Battery Commanders urged me to order them back, but I was averse to doing this in the absence of their proper commanders. After waiting and watching for some time, I concluded that Reno must have retired and finally gave the order to retire, acting myself as pilot to the column. But the fear of running into the enemy's lines still prevailed so I bore off too far to the right, finally reaching the turnpike a mile or more in rear of where my brigade was. Starting back I reached my command to learn that Kearny's troops had gone to the rear and I was just about to direct my brigade to retire, when someone came riding up from the left and a cheery voice called out of the darkness:

"What the devil are you ordering my troops off the field for, Gibbon?" and to my infinite relief, I recognized the short stumpy figure of General Reno. I explained the circumstances to him and he replied, "All right, all right. All my troops have gone back, and now you can leave as soon as you please." It will be seen that Kearny says he held his ground till 10 o'clock, but I think it scarcely could have been so late as that when my command finally withdrew and took the road back to Bull Run.

On reaching the Stone Bridge over Bull Run, I began to realize the truth of what Kearny had said that it was a "second Bull Run." Overturned wagons were lying alongside the road, and from their contents my hungry men eagerly supplied themselves with the much-needed hard bread. Crossing the bridge we formed on the other side, the road being blocked up with a mingled mass of stragglers, wagons, artillery, ambulances, and wounded, some of whom were in hand litters as they had left the field. As I crossed the bridge an officer came up to me and introduced himself as Colonel Kane of the Pennsylvania Bucktails who said he had a party of his men with him and offered his services to blow up the bridge after we had passed but I told him I had orders to act as rear guard only as far as Bull Run and called his attention to the fact that the whole 11th Corps had apparently halted on a hill west of the stream, had built large fires and were evidently making coffee and cooking rations. Leaving them there we pursued our march, slowly following the moving mass in front of us, until having passed Cub Run, some sort of organization began to appear and it became evident that the whole army had not gone to pieces. Leaving orders with the staff officers to select a position and put the brigade into camp, and without attempting to find the rest of the Division, I rode on to Centreville. Finding General McDowell at General Pope's Headquarters in a house in the town. I reported to him that his orders had been obeyed.

I was kindly invited by General Pope to remain, get a cup of coffee and sleep at his Headquarters for the night, and tired as I was, I was only too glad to accept his hospitality. The next morning we were awakened early by the entrance of Col. J. H. Taylor, Gen. Sumner's Adjutant General, who announced the arrival of the 2nd Corps. As Franklin with the 6th Corps had arrived the day before, the long deferred consolidation with the Army of the Potomac had now been effected, but, unfortunately, not until the conflict between our divided forces and the enemy had taken place and been decided against us. Again had faulty strategy defeated us, and again the folly of attempting to command armies in the field from a distance had been demonstrated.

The 31st was very quiet, scattered commands were got together, placed in position and the whole force present concentrated in and around Centreville; our division being just back of the town and the trains sent to the rear.

The 1st of September found us still in position but reports reached us that the enemy was moving around by our right flank. In the afternoon some cannon shots were heard in our rear and that afternoon a retrograde movement to Fairfax Court House began. Our Division was placed in position near Germantown, the junction of the Little River turnpike with the pike from Centreville. From this position we could hear the sounds of a heavy conflict taking place in our front in the direction of Chantilly. It was a battle between a flanking force of the enemy and a portion of our troops and was fought in the midst of a terrific thunderstorm. During the fight Generals Phil Kearny and T. J. Stevens were killed and the next day, whilst riding along the pike, I met an ambulance bringing in General Kearny's body. It had been sent in from the enemy's line under a flag of truce. The retreat was continued and on the 2nd our wearied, footsore, and hungry troops were once more within the fortifications of Washington, this time with the enemy at their heels.

Our portion of the army marched by the way of Falls Church and as we approached our old campgrounds near Munson's Hill, an officer, I think of the Division staff, met me and announced that General McClellan was in command of the army. The soldiers had had such a report amongst them whilst the battle was going on, on the 30th, how or by whom started, no one seemed to know and I, therefore, supposed this was a repetition of the same rumor. But the officer assured me that he knew the report to be true and that he had seen General McClellan only a few moments before, giving orders to some of the troops. I knew then that it must be so. Facing about, I rode towards the head of my brigade which was slowly approaching, and on reaching the leading regiment, called out, "Men, General McClellan is in command of the army!" The announcement was all that was necessary. Up went caps in the air and a cheer broke out which, as the news travelled, was taken up and carried to the rear of the column and the weary fagged men went into camp, cheering and happy to talk over their rough experience of the past three weeks and speculate as to what was ahead.

Philip Kerny is shot dead after accidentally running into Confederate line.

Ambulance crew attends to the wounded.

V

THE ANTIETAM CAMPAIGN

LEE'S SUCCESS IN THE SECOND BULL RUN CAMPAIGN, COMING HARD UPON THE HEELS of his victory in the Peninsular Campaign, prompted him to go over to the offensive, to carry the war into the north. Screened by J. E. B. Stuart's fine cavalry division, on 4 September Lee began crossing the Potomac about 40 miles upstream from Washington, just a day after the last elements of Pope's defeated army had gained the security of the defenses of the city. By the 7th the Army of Northern Virginia was concentrated about Frederick. Over the next few days Lee's Army of Northern Virginia spread out over western Maryland, foraging and laying contributions on the towns. Meanwhile George B. McClellan—newly restored to overall command amid enthusiastic rejoicing by the troops—had undertaken a rapid reorganization of the Union forces, and begun a cautious advance, trying to locate Lee while keeping Washington covered. Although the ensuing campaign lasted only a few days, it produced the single bloodiest day of the war, when the Army of the Potomac came up against the Army of Northern Virginia along Antietam Creek on 17 September.

GEORGE B. McCLELLAN
The Antietam Campaign

In 1885, at the request of the editors of The Century Magazine, *George B. McClellan was working on an account of the war from the close of the Peninsular Campaign to the Battle of Antietam. His death found the project barely started, a mere rough sketch essay being all that was on paper. Although incomplete and un-polished, McClellan's account is nevertheless of considerable value, for it illustrates McClellan's understanding of the situation, as he recalled it. In addition, it reveals the basic flaws of* character *which made McClellan a less than great commander, his mistrust of his political superiors, his arrogance, his lack of truth-fulness, his willingness to spread around the blame, his glory seeking, and his lack of intes-tinal fortitude. The incomplete essay was published in* The Century *and subsequently included in* Battles and Leaders of the Civil War, *from which the following excerpt has been taken.*

On the 1st of September I met General Halleck at his office in Washington, who by verbal order di-rected me to take charge of Washington and its de-fenses, but expressly prohibited me from exercising any control over the active troops under General Pope.

At this interview I informed General Halleck that from information received through one of my aides I was satisfied that affairs were not progressing favor-ably at the front, and urged him to go out in person to ascertain the exact state of the case. He declined doing this, but finally sent Colonel Kelton, his adju-tant-general.

Next morning while at breakfast at an early hour I received a call from the President, accompanied by General Halleck.

The President informed me that Colonel Kelton had returned and represented the condition of affairs as much worse than I had stated to Halleck on the previous day; that there were thirty thousand strag-glers on the roads; that the army was entirely de-feated and falling back to Washington in confusion. He then said that he regarded Washington as lost, and asked me if I would, under the circumstances, consent to accept command of all the forces. With-out one moment's hesitation and without making any conditions whatever, I at once said that I would accept the command and would stake my life that I would save the city. Both the President and Halleck again asserted that it was impossible to save the city, and I repeated my firm conviction that I could and would save it. They then left, the President verbally placing me in entire command of the city and of the troops falling back upon it from the front.

I at once sent for my staff-officers and dispatched them on various duties; some to the front with or-ders for the disposition of such corps as they met, others to see to the prompt forwarding of ammuni-tion and supplies to meet the retreating troops. In a

very short time I had made all the requisite preparations and was about to start to the front in person to assume command as far out as possible, when a message came to me from General Halleck informing me that it was the President's order that I should not assume command until the troops had reached the immediate vicinity of the fortifications. I therefore waited until the afternoon, when I rode out to Upton's Hill, the most advanced of the detached works covering the capital.

Soon after arriving there the head of Hatch's command of infantry arrived, immediately followed by Generals Pope and McDowell escorted by a regiment, or part of a regiment, of cavalry. I obtained what information I could from General Pope and dispatched the few remaining aides with me to meet the troops on the roads leading in on the left, with final orders to them, when quite a heavy distant artillery firing broke out in the direction of the

Chantilly and Vienna road. Asking General Pope what that was, he replied it was probably an attack on Sumner, who commanded the rear-guard in that direction; in reply to another question he said that he thought it probably a serious affair. He and McDowell then asked if I had any objection to their proceeding to Washington. I said that they might do so, but that I was going to the firing. They then proceeded on with their escort while, with a single aide (Colonel Colburn) and three orderlies, I struck across country to intercept the column on our right by the shortest line. It was a little after dark when I reached the column.

I leave to others who were present the description of what then occurred: the frantic cheers of welcome that extended for miles along the column; the breaking of ranks and the wild appeals of the men that I should then and there take them back on the line of retreat and let them snatch victory out of defeat. Let

Confederates cross the Potomac.

it suffice to say that before the day broke the troops were all in position to repulse attack, and that Washington was safe.

On the 3d it was clear that the enemy intended an invasion of Maryland and Pennsylvania by crossing the Upper Potomac; I therefore moved the Second, Ninth, and Twelfth Corps to the Maryland side of the Potomac in position to meet any attack upon the city on that side.

As soon as this was done I reported the fact to General Halleck, who asked what general I had placed in command of those three corps; I replied that I had made no such detail, as I should take command in person if the enemy appeared in that direction. He then said that my command included only the defenses of Washington and did not extend to any active column that might be moved out beyond the line of works; that no decision had yet been made as to the commander of the active army. He repeated the same thing on more than one occasion before the final advance to South Mountain and Antietam took place.

I should here state that the only published order ever issued in regard to the extent of my command after my interview with the President on the morning of the 2d was the following:

War Department, Adjutant-General's Office
Washington, September 2, 1862

Major-General McClellan will have command of the fortifications of Washington and of all the troops for the defense of the capital.
By order of Major-General Halleck.
E. D. Townsend, Assistant Adjutant-General

A few days after this and before I went to the front, Secretary Seward came to my quarters one evening and asked my opinion of the condition of affairs at Harper's Ferry, remarking that he was not at ease on the subject. Harper's Ferry was not at that time in any sense under my control, but I told Mr. Seward that I regarded the arrangements there as exceedingly dangerous; that in my opinion the proper course was to abandon the position and unite the garrison (about ten thousand men) to the main army of operations, for the reason that its presence at Harper's Ferry would not hinder the enemy from crossing the Potomac; that if we were unsuccessful in the approaching battle, Harper's Ferry would be of no use to us and its garrison necessarily would be lost; that if we were successful we would immediately recover the post without any difficulty, while the addition of ten thousand men to the active army would be an important factor in securing success. I added that if it were determined to hold the position the existing arrangements were all wrong, as it would be easy for the enemy to surround and capture the garrison, and that the garrison ought, at least, to be withdrawn to the Maryland Heights, where they could resist attack until relieved.

The Secretary was much impressed by what I said,

and asked me to accompany him to General Halleck and repeat my statement to him. I acquiesced, and we went together to General Halleck's quarters, where we found that he had retired for the night. But he received us in his bedroom, when, after a preliminary explanation by the Secretary as to the interview being at his request, I said to Halleck precisely what I had stated to Mr. Seward.

Halleck received my statement with ill-concealed contempt—said that everything was all right as it was; that my views were entirely erroneous, etc., and soon bowed us out, leaving matters at Harper's Ferry precisely as they were.

On the 7th of September, in addition to the three corps already mentioned (the Second, Ninth, and Twelfth), the First and Sixth Corps, Sykes's division of the Fifth Corps, and Couch's division of the Fourth Corps, were also on the Maryland side of the river; the First and Ninth Corps at Leesboro; the Second and Twelfth in front of Rockville; the Sixth Corps at Rockville; Couch's division at Offutt's Cross Roads; Sykes's division at Tenallytown.

As the time had now arrived for the army to advance, and I had received no orders to take command of it, but had been expressly told that the assignment of a commander had not been decided, I determined to solve the question for myself, and when I moved out from Washington with my staff and personal escort I left my card with P. P. C. written upon it, at the White House, War Office, and secretary Seward's house, and went on my way.

I was afterward accused of assuming command without authority, for nefarious purposes, and in fact I fought the battles of South Mountain and Antietam with a halter around my neck, for if the Army of the Potomac had been defeated and I had survived I would, no doubt, have been tried for assuming authority without orders, and, in the state of feeling which so unjustly condemned the innocent and most meritorious General F. J. Porter, I would probably have been condemned to death. I was fully aware of the risk I ran, but the path of duty was clear and I tried to follow it. It was absolutely necessary that Lee's army should be met, and in the state of affairs I have briefly described there could be no hesitation on my part as to doing it promptly. Very few in the Army of the Potomac doubted the favorable result of the next collision with the Confederate army, but in other quarters not a little doubt prevailed, and the desire for very rapid movements, so loudly expressed after the result was gained, did not make itself heard during the movements preceding the battles; quite the contrary was the case, as I was more than once cautioned that I was moving too rashly and exposing the capital to an attack from the Virginia side.

As is well known, the result of General Pope's operations had not been favorable, and when I finally resumed command of the troops in and around Washington they were weary, disheartened, their organization impaired, their clothing, ammunition, and supplies in a pitiable condition.

Harper's Ferry Area

The Army of the Potomac was thoroughly exhausted and depleted by its desperate fighting and severe marches in the unhealthy regions of the Chickahominy and afterward, during the second Bull Run campaign; its trains, administration services and supplies were disorganized or lacking in consequence of the rapidity and manner of its removal from the Peninsula as well as from the nature of its operations during the second Bull Run campaign. In the departure from the Peninsula, trains, supplies, cavalry, and artillery in many instances had necessarily been left at Fort Monroe and Yorktown for lack of vessels, as the important point was to remove the infantry divisions rapidly to the support of General Pope. The divisions of thc Army of Virginia were also exhausted and weakened, and their trains were disorganized and their supplies deficient by reason of the movements in which they had been engaged.

Had General Lee remained in front of Washington it would have been the part of wisdom to hold our own army quiet until its pressing wants were fully supplied, its organization was restored, and its ranks were filled with recruits—in brief, until it was prepared for a campaign. But as the enemy maintained the offensive and crossed the Upper Potomac to threaten or invade Pennsylvania, it became necessary to meet him at any cost notwithstanding the condition of the troops, to put a stop to the invasion, save Baltimore and Washington, and throw him back across the Potomac. Nothing but sheer necessity justified the advance of the Army of the Potomac to South Mountain and Antietam in its then condition, and it is to the eternal honor of the brave men who composed it that under such adverse circumstances they gained those victories. The work of supply and reorganization was continued as best we might while on the march, and even after the close of the battles [September 14th–17th] so much remained to be done to place the army in condition for a campaign, that the delay which ensued was absolutely unavoidable, and the army could not have entered upon a new campaign one day earlier than it did. It must then be borne constantly in mind that the purpose of advancing from Washington was simply to meet the necessities of the moment by frustrating Lee's invasion of the Northern States, and, when that was accomplished, to push with the utmost rapidity the work of reorganization and supply so that a new campaign might be promptly inaugurated with the army in condition to prosecute it to a successful termination without intermission.

The advance from Washington was covered by the cavalry, under General Pleasonton, which was pushed as far to the front as possible, and was soon in constant contact with the enemy's cavalry, with whom several well-conducted and successful affairs occurred.

Partly in order to move men freely and rapidly, partly in consequence of the lack of accurate information as to the exact position and intention of Lee's army, the troops advanced by three main roads: that part near the Potomac by Offutt's Cross Roads and the mouth of the Seneca; that by Rockville to Frederick, and that by Brookville and Urbana to New Market. We were then in condition to act according to the development of the enemy's plans and to concentrate rapidly in any position. If Lee threatened our left flank by moving down the river road, or by crossing the Potomac at any of the fords from Coon's Ferry upward, there were enough troops on the river road to hold him in check until the rest of the army could move over to support them; if Lee took up a position behind the Seneca near Frederick the whole army could be rapidly concentrated in that direction to attack him in force; if he moved upon Baltimore the entire army could rapidly be thrown in his rear and his retreat would be cut off; if he moved by Gettysburg or Chambersburg upon York or Carlisle we were equally in position to throw ourselves in his rear.

The first requisite was to gain accurate information as to Lee's movements, and the second, to push the work of supply and reorganization as rapidly as possible.

General Lee and I knew each other well. In the days before the war we served together in Mexico, and we had commanded against each other in the Peninsula. I had the highest respect for his ability as a commander, and knew that he was a general not to be trifled with or carelessly afforded an opportunity of striking a fatal blow. Each of us naturally regarded his own army as the better, but each entertained the highest respect for the endurance, courage, and fighting qualities of the opposing army; and this feeling extended to the officers and men. It was perfectly natural under these circumstances that both of us should exercise a certain amount of caution,—I in my endeavors to ascertain Lee's strength, position, and intentions before I struck the fatal blow; he to abstain from any extended movements of invasion, and to hold his army well in hand until he could be satisfied as to the condition of the Army of the Potomac after its second Bull Run campaign, and as to the intentions of its commander.

DANIEL H. HILL

The Battle of South Mountain, or Boonsboro

McClellan's slow advance from Washington did not discomfit Lee overmuch. By 13 September he had fallen back from Frederick, but his Army of Northern Virginia was scattered over some

500 square miles of western Maryland and northern Virginia. Lee's forces were dangerously overstretched. Of his ten divisions, only two of infantry and one of cavalry were available to cover his open right flank, stretching nearly 40 miles between Harper's Ferry and Hagerstown, along South Mountain, a long ridgeline. At this point, the fortunes of war intervened. On the morning of 13 September a copy of Lee's Special Order No. 191 fell into McClellan's hands, detailing his plans and precarious dispositions. Although McClellan was slow to act, the situation for the Confederate forces became critical. Daniel H. Hill (1821–1889), a West Point (1842) graduate, had served in the Mexican War, but left the army in 1849 to teach mathematics, rising to the presidency of the North Carolina Military Institute. On the outbreak of the Civil War, Hill—his wife was the sister of Stonewall Jackson's second wife—entered Confederate service. Rising rapidly, he was made a major general and commander of a division on 26 March 1862. Hill had a distinguished and varied career, serving mostly in Virginia. In mid-1863 the argumentative Hill was appointed a lieutenant general, but ran afoul of Confederate President Jefferson Davis for recommending that one of Davis' pet generals be relieved and was never confirmed. Thereafter he was largely unemployed, though he was back in command of a division at the end of the war. After the war he returned to academe and was involved in publishing and writing, mostly in defense of his military reputation. The most controversial moment in Hill's career was South Mountain, where his performance left much to be desired. His own self-justifying account of the battle, and of the famous "lost order incident," appeared in Battles and Leaders of the Civil War.

Major General Daniel H. Hill

In the retirement of Lee's army from Frederick to Hagerstown and Boonsboro', my division constituted the rear-guard. It consisted of five brigades (Wise's brigade being left behind), and after the arrival at Boonsboro' was intrusted with guarding the wagon trains and parks of artillery belonging to the whole army. Longstreet's corps went to Hagerstown, thirteen miles from Boonsboro', and I was directed to distribute my five brigades so as not only to protect the wagons and guns, but also to watch all the roads leading from Harper's Ferry, in order to intercept the Federal forces that might make their escape before Jackson had completed the investment of that place. It required a considerable separation of my small command to accomplish these two objects, and my tent, which was pitched about the center of the five brigades, was not less than three miles from Turner's Gap on the National road crossing South Mountain.

During the forenoon of the 13th General Stuart, who was in an advance position at the gap in the Catoctin Mountain, east of Middletown, with our cavalry, sent a dispatch to me saying that he was followed by two brigades of Federal infantry, and asking me to send him a brigade to check the pursuit at South Mountain. I sent him the brigades of Colquitt and Garland, and the batteries of Bondurant and Lane, with four guns each. Pleasonton's Federal cavalry division came up to the mountain and pressed on till our infantry forces were displayed, when it returned without fighting. The Confederates, with more than half of Lee's army at Harper's Ferry, distant a march of two days, and with the remainder divided into two parts, thirteen miles from each other, were in good condition to be beaten in detail, scattered and captured. General Longstreet writes to me that he urged General Lee in the evening of the 13th to unite at Sharpsburg the troops which were then at Hagerstown and Boonsboro'. He said that he could effect more with one-third of his own corps, fresh and rested, than with the whole of it, when exhausted by a forced march to join their comrades. That night, finding that he could not rest, General Longstreet rose and wrote to his com-

Boonesboro was situated in Turner's Gap.

mander, presenting his views once more, favoring the abandonment of the defense of the mountain except by Stuart and the concentration at Sharpsburg.

I received a note about midnight of the 13th from General Lee saying that he was not satisfied with the condition of things on the turnpike or National road, and directing me to go in person to Turner's Gap the next morning and assist Stuart in its defense. In his official report General Lee says:

Learning that Harper's Ferry had not surrendered and that the enemy was advancing more rapidly than was convenient from Fredericktown, I determined to return with Longstreet's command to the Blue Ridge to strengthen D. H. Hill's and Stuart's divisions engaged in holding the passes of the mountain, lest the enemy should fall upon McLaws's rear, drive him from the Maryland Heights, and thus relieve the garrison at Harper's Ferry.

This report and the note to me show that General Lee expected General Stuart to remain and help defend the pass on the 14th. But on reaching the Mountain House between daylight and sunrise that morning, I received a message from Stuart that he had gone to Crampton's Gap. He was too gallant a soldier to leave his post when a battle was imminent, and doubtless he believed that there was but a small Federal force on the National road. I found Garland's brigade at the Mountain House and learned that Colquitt's was at the foot of the mountain on the east side. I found General Colquitt there without vedettes and without information of the Federals, but believing that they had retired. General Cox's Federal division was at that very time marching up the old Sharpsburg or Braddock's road, a mile to the south, seizing the heights on our right and establishing those heavy batteries which afterward commanded the pike and all the approaches to it. General Pleasonton, of the Federal cavalry, had learned the ground by the reconnoissance of the day

before, and to him was intrusted the posting of the advance troops of Reno's corps on the south side of the pike. He says:

> I directed Scammon's brigade to move up the mountain on the left-hand road, gain the crest, and then move to the right, to the turnpike in the enemy's rear. At the same time I placed Gibson's battery and the heavy batteries in position to the left, covering the road on that side and obtaining a direct fire on the enemy's position in the gap.

This shows that Pleasonton knew that the Confederate forces were at the foot of the mountain. However, I brought Colquitt's brigade back to a point near the summit and placed the 23d and 28th Georgia regiments on the north side of the pike behind a stone-wall, which afforded an excellent fire upon the pike. The other three regiments, the 6th and 27th Georgia and the 13th Alabama, were posted on the south side of the pike, a little in advance of the wall and well protected by a dense wood. This brigade did not lose an inch of ground that day. The skirmishers were driven in, but the line of battle on both sides of the road was the same at 10 o'clock at night as it was at 9 o'clock in the morning. After posting Colquitt's brigade I went with Major Ratchford of my staff on a reconnoissance to our right. About three-fourths of a mile from the Mountain House we discovered, by the voices of command and the rumbling of wheels, that the old road and heights above it were occupied, and took it for granted that the occupation was by Federal troops. We did not see them, and I suppose we were not seen by them. Colonel T. L. Rosser of the cavalry had been sent that morning with his regiment and Pelham's artillery, by order of General Stuart, to seize Fox's Gap on the Braddock road. Cox had got to the heights first and confronted Rosser with a portion of his command, while the remainder of it could be plainly seen at the foot of the mountain. General Rosser writes to me that he reported the situation of things to Stuart, who was passing by on the east side of the mountain on his way south. He, Rosser, was not directed to report to me, and I did not suspect his presence. I do not know to this hour whether Ratchford and myself came near stumbling upon him or upon the enemy.

Returning through the woods we came upon a cabin, the owner of which was in the yard, surrounded by his children, and evidently expectant of something. The morning being cool, Ratchford was wearing a blue cloak which he had found at Seven Pines. In questioning the mountaineer about the roads I discovered that he thought we were Federals.

"The road on which your battery is," said he, "comes into the valley road near the church." This satisfied me that the enemy was on our right, and I asked him: "Are there any rebels on the pike?" "Yes; there are some about the Mountain House." I asked: "Are there many?" "Well, there are several; I don't know how many." "Who is in command?" "I don't know."

Just then a shell came hurtling through the woods, and a little girl began crying. Having a little one at home of about the same age, I could not forbear stopping a moment to say a few soothing words to the frightened child, before hurrying off to the work of death.

The firing had aroused that prompt and gallant soldier, General Garland, and his men were under arms when I reached the pike. I explained the situation briefly to him, directed him to sweep through the woods, reach the road, and hold it at all hazards, as the safety of Lee's large train depended upon its being held. He went off in high spirits and I never saw him again. I never knew a truer, better, braver man. Had he lived, his talents, pluck, energy, and purity of character must have put him in the front rank of his profession, whether in civil or military life.

After passing through the first belt of woods Garland found Rosser, and, conferring with him, determined to make his stand close to the junction of the roads, near the summit of the mountain (Fox's Gap). He had with him five regiments of infantry and Bondurant's battery of artillery—his infantry force being a little less than one thousand men, all North Carolinians. The 5th regiment was placed on the right of the road, with the 12th as its support; the 23d was posted behind a low stone-wall on the left of the 5th; then came the 20th and 13th. From the nature of the ground and the duty to be performed, the regiments were not in contact with each other, and the 13th was 250 yards to the left of the 20th. Fifty skirmishers of the 5th North Carolina soon encountered the 23d Ohio, deployed as skirmishers under Lieutenant-Colonel R. B. Hayes, afterward President of the United States, and the action began at 9 A.M. between Cox's division and Garland's brigade.

I will delay an account of the fight to give the strength of the forces engaged. The Ninth Corps (Reno's) consisted of four divisions under Cox, Willcox, Sturgis, and Rodman; or eight brigades—Scammon and Crook (Cox); Christ and Welsh (Willcox); Nagle and Ferrero (Sturgis); and Fairchild and Harland (Rodman). It had 29 regiments of infantry, 3 companies of cavalry, and 8 batteries of artillery, 3 of them United States batteries of regulars under Benjamin, Clark, and Muhlenberg.

General Cox, who fought Garland, had six Ohio regiments under Brigadiers Scammon and Crook, and also the batteries of McMullin and Simmonds, and three companies of cavalry. The heavy batteries in position (20-pounder Parrotts) were of service to him also, in commanding the approaches to the scene of the conflict. The strength of the division is not given directly, but Scammon estimates his effectives at 1455. The other brigade was most likely equally strong, and I conclude that Cox's infantry, artillery, and cavalry reached three thousand. Garland's brigade is estimated at "scarce a thousand."

Scammon's brigade led the attack with great spirit. The 13th North Carolina, under Lieutenant-Colonel Ruffin, and the 20th, under Colonel Alfred Iverson, were furiously assailed on the left. Both regiments were under tried and true soldiers, and they received the assault calmly. Lieutenant Crome, of McMullin's battery, ran up a section of artillery by hand, and opened with effect upon the 20th North Carolina; but the skirmishers under Captain Atwell of that regiment killed the gallant officer while he was himself serving as a gunner. The section was abandoned, but the Confederates were unable to capture it. The effort seemed to be to turn the 13th; and Colonel Ruffin in vain urged General Garland to go to the other part of his line. But with Garland the post of danger was the post of honor. Judge Ruffin, in a recent letter to me, thus speaks of the fall of the hero:

> I said to him: "General, why do you stay here? you are in great danger."
> To which he replied: "I may as well be here as yourself." I said: "No, it is my duty to be here with my regiment, but you could better superintend your brigade from a safer position."
> "Just then I was shot in the hip, and as there was no field-officer then with the regiment, other than myself, I told him of my wound, and that it might disable me, and in that case I wished a field-officer to take my place. He turned and gave some order, which I have forgotten. In a moment I heard a groan, and looked and found him mortally wounded and writhing in pain. We continued to occupy this position for some time, when I sent my adjutant to the right to see what was going on (as the furious fighting had ceased in that direction). He returned and reported that the remainder of the brigade was gone and that the ground was occupied by the enemy. I then attempted to go to the left, hoping to come in contact with some portion of your command,

but was again confronted by the enemy. I next tried to retreat to the rear, but to my dismay found myself entirely surrounded. The enemy in front was pressing us, and I saw but one way out, and that was to charge those in my front, repel them, if possible, and then, before they could recover, make a dash at those in my rear and cut my way out. This plan was successfully executed. I shall never forget the feelings of relief which I experienced when I first caught sight of you. You rode up to me, and, shaking my hand, said that you had given us up for lost and did not see how it was possible for us to have escaped. You then attached us to G. B. Anderson's brigade, which had come up in the meantime. . . . I remember one remark which you made just after congratulating me upon cutting my way out that surprised me very much. You said that you were greatly gratified to find that McClellan's whole army was in your front. As I knew how small your force was, I could not understand how it could be a source of pleasure to you to find yourself assailed by twenty times your number. In a moment you made it plain to me by saying that you had feared at first that McClellan's attack upon you was but a feint, and that with his main army he would cross the mountain at some of the lower gaps and would thus cut in between Jackson's corps and the forces under Lee.

A little before this I had seen from the lookout station near the Mountain House the vast army of McClellan spread out before me. The marching columns extended back as far as eye could see in the distance; but many of the troops had already arrived and were in double lines of battle, and those advancing were taking up positions as fast as they arrived. It was a grand and glorious spectacle, and it was impossible to look at it without admiration. I had never seen so tremendous an army before, and I did not see one like it afterward. For though we confronted greater forces at Yorktown, Sharpsburg, Fredericksburg, and about Richmond under Grant, these were only partly seen, at most a corps at a time. But here four corps were in full view, one of which was on the mountain and almost within rifle-range. The sight inspired more satisfaction than discomfort; for though I knew that my little force could be brushed away as readily as the strong man can brush to one side the wasp or the hornet, I felt that General McClellan had made a mistake, and I hoped to be able to delay him until General Longstreet could come up and our trains could be extricated from their perilous position.

When two distinct roars of artillery were heard south of us that morning, I thought that the nearer one indicated that McClellan was forcing his way across some gap north of Harper's Ferry with a view of cutting Lee's army in two. I suppose that Stuart believed that this would be the movement of the enemy, and for this reason abandoned Turner's Gap and hastened to what he believed to be the point of danger. McClellan was too cautious a man for so daring a venture. Had he made it, Jackson could have escaped across the Potomac, but the force under Lee in person (Longstreet's corps and my division) must have been caught. My division was very small and was embarrassed with the wagon trains and artillery of the whole army, save such as Jackson had taken with him. It must be remembered that the army now before McClellan had been constantly marching and fighting since the 25th of June. It had fought McClellan's army from Richmond to the James, and then had turned about and fought Pope's army, reënforced by parts of McClellan's, from the Rapidan to the Potomac. The order excusing barefooted men from marching into Maryland had sent thousands to the rear. Divisions had become smaller than brigades were when the fighting first began; brigades had become smaller than regiments, and regiments had become smaller than companies.[1] Dabney, a careful statistician, in his "Life of Jackson," estimates Lee's forces at Sharpsburg (Antietam) at 33,000 men, including the three arms of service.[2] Three of Longstreet's twelve brigades had gone to Harper's Ferry with Jackson. He (Longstreet) puts the strength of his nine brigades at Hagerstown on the morning of the 14th of September at thirteen thousand men. Accepting the correctness of his estimate for the present (though I expect to prove it to be too large), I find that Lee had under his immediate command that morning but eighteen thousand men.

McClellan gives his force at Sharpsburg at 87,164. Had he made the movement which Stuart and myself thought he was making, it was hardly possible for the little force under Lee in person to have escaped, encumbered as it was with wagon trains and reserve artillery. Forming his infantry into a solid column of attack, Lee might have cut a way through the five-fold force of his antagonist, but all the trains must have been lost,—an irreparable loss to the South. Frederick the Great's campaign against the allies shows what he would have done had he been in command of the Federal army. But the American soldier preferred to do sure work rather than brilliant work, his natural caution being increased by the carping criticisms of his enemies.

Upon the fall of Garland, Colonel McRae, of the 5th North Carolina regiment, assumed command, and ordered the two regiments on the left to close in to the right. This order either was not received or it was found to be impossible of execution. The main attack was on the 23d North Carolina behind the stone-wall. The Federals had a plunging fire upon

---

1. Thus the 18th Virginia Regiment is put at 120 men; 56th Virginia Regiment at 80; 8th Virginia at 34; Hampton Legion at 77; 17th South Carolina Regiment at 59.—D.H.H.

2. According to Thomas White, Chief Clerk in the Adjutant-General's Office at Lee's headquarters, General Lee had 33,000 infantry at Sharpsburg, or 41,500 of all arms. Adding 2000 for the previous casualties (only partly given), the total Confederate force on the 14th would appear to be 43,500, of which 15,000 were at Harper's Ferry, on the Virginia side, and 28,500 in Maryland.—B&L

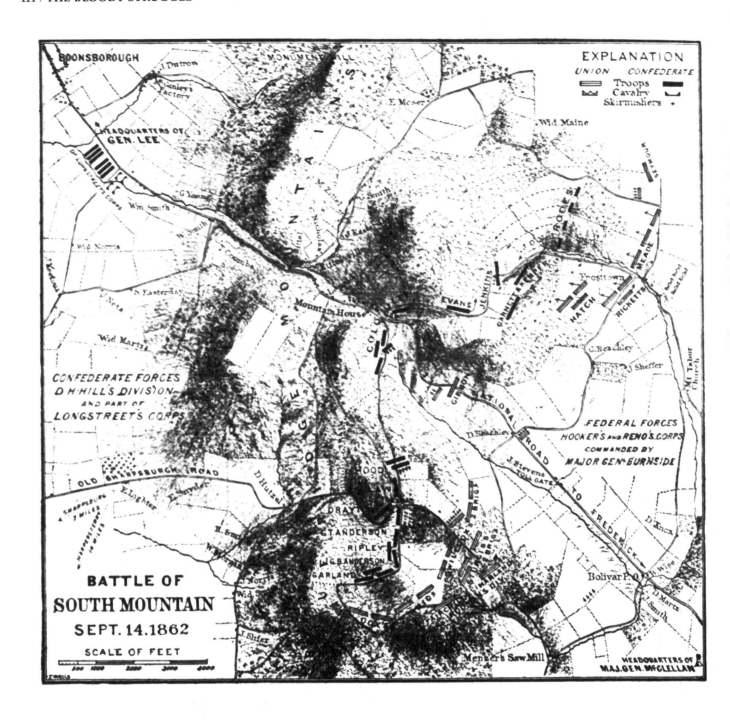

this regiment from the crest of a hill, higher than the wall, and only about fifty yards from it. The 12th North Carolina, a badly trained regiment, on that day under the command of a young captain, deserted the field. The 12th Ohio, actuated by a different impulse, made a charge upon Bondurant's battery and drove it off, failing, however, to capture it. The 30th Ohio advanced directly upon the stone-wall in their front, while a regiment moved upon the 23d North Carolina on each flank. Some of the 30th Ohio forced through a break in the wall, and bayonets and clubbed muskets were used freely for a few moments. Garland's brigade, demoralized by his death and by the furious assault on its center, now broke in confusion and retreated behind the moun-

tain, leaving some two hundred prisoners of the 5th, 23d, and 20th North Carolina in the hands of the enemy. The brigade was too roughly handled to be of any further use that day. Rosser retired in better order, not, however, without having some of his men captured, and took up a position from which he could still fire upon the old road, and which he held until 10 o'clock that night.

General Cox, having beaten the force in his front, now showed a disposition to carry out General Pleasonton's instructions, and advance to the Mountain House by the road running south from it on the summit of the mountain. There was nothing to oppose him. My other three brigades had not come up; Colquitt's could not be taken from the pike except in the last extremity. So two guns were run down from the Mountain House and opened a brisk fire on the advancing foe. A line of dismounted staff-officers, couriers, teamsters, and cooks was formed behind the guns to give the appearance of battery supports. I do not remember ever to have experienced a feeling of greater loneliness. It seemed as though we were deserted by "all the world and the rest of mankind." Some of the advancing Federals encountered Colquitt's skirmishers under Captain Arnold, and fell back to their former positions.

General Cox seems not to have suspected that the defeat of Garland had cleared his front of every foe. He says in his report: "The enemy withdrew their battery to a new position on a ridge more to the front and right, forming their infantry in support and moving columns toward both our flanks."

It was more than half an hour after the utter rout and dispersion of Garland's brigade when G. B. Anderson arrived at the head of his small but fine body of men. He made an effort to recover the ground lost by Garland, but failed and met a serious repulse. General Cox says of this attack: "The enemy made several attempts to retake the crest, advancing with great obstinacy and boldness."

Under the strange illusion that there was a large Confederate force on the mountain, the Federals withdrew to their first position in the morning to await the arrival of the other three divisions of Reno's corps. Willcox's arrived about noon, and Sturgis's and Rodman's between 3 and 4 o'clock, but there was no advance until 5 P.M. The falling back of Cox's division is alluded to by Colonel Ewing of Scammon's brigade and by Major Lyman J. Jackson of Crook's brigade. The former says: "We fell back to the original position until the general advance at 5 P.M." Major Jackson, after speaking of fighting the enemy behind a stone-wall with the coöperation of two other regiments, adds: "We then fell back to the hillside in the open fields, where we were out of reach of their guns, and remained here with the rest of our brigade until an advance was made against the enemy by the Pennsylvania and Rhode Island troops on our right."

After the arrival of his whole corps General Reno arranged his line of battle as follows: Cox's division on the left, resting on the batteries already in position; Willcox's on the right, supported by the division of Sturgis. Rodman's division was divided; Fairchild's brigade was sent to the extreme left to support the batteries, and Harland's was placed on the extreme right.

In the meantime Rodes and Ripley, of my division, reported to me for orders. Rodes was sent with his brigade of twelve hundred men to a commanding knoll north of the pike or National road. Ripley was directed to attach himself to G. B. Anderson's left. Anderson, being thus strengthened, and finding there was no enemy in his immediate front, sent out the 2d and 4th North Carolina regiments of his brigade on a reconnoissance to the front, right, and rear. Captain E. A. Osborne, commanding the skirmishers of the 4th North Carolina, discovered a brigade in an old field south of Fox's Gap, facing toward the turnpike and supporting a battery with its guns turned in the same direction. Captain Osborne hastened back to Colonel Grimes, commanding the regiment, and told him that they could deliver a flank fire upon the brigade before it could change its position to meet them. But a Federal scout had seen the captain, and the brigade was the first to open fire. The fight was, of course, brief, the regiment beating a hasty retreat. The brigade halted at the edge of the woods, probably believing that there was a concealed foe somewhere in the depths of the forest. This Federal brigade was, possibly, Benjamin C. Christ's of Willcox's division—the same which had made the successful flank movement in the previous fight.

About 3:30 P.M. the advance of Longstreet's command arrived and reported to me—one brigade under Colonel G. T. Anderson and one under General Drayton. They were attached to Ripley's left, and a forward movement was ordered. In half an hour or more I received a note from Ripley saying that he was progressing finely; so he was, to the rear of the mountain on the west side. Before he returned the fighting was over, and his brigade did not fire a shot that day. The Federal commander intrusted to General Burnside the management of the fight, but under his own eyes; Burnside ordered a general advance on both sides of the pike. The First Corps, under Hooker, was to attack on the north side of the National road, while the Ninth Corps, under Reno, was to move forward, as before, on the south side. Hooker's corps consisted of 3 divisions, 10 brigades, or 42 regiments, with 10 batteries of artillery and a battalion of cavalry. General Meade, a division commander, had under him the brigades of Seymour, Magilton, and Gallagher, containing 13 regiments with 4 batteries attached. General Hatch, division commander, had under him the brigades of Doubleday, Phelps, Patrick, and Gibbon—17 regiments and 4 batteries. General Ricketts, division commander, had under him the brigades of Duryée, Christian, and Hartsuff—12 regiments and 2 batteries. From the nature of the ground, none of the artillery of Hooker's corps could be used, except that which went directly up the pike with Gibbon's brigade and one battery (Cooper's) on the enemy's right.

The hour for the general advance is not specified in the reports. Some of the Federal officers, as we have seen, speak of the general advance at 5 P.M. General Sturgis says that he became engaged on the south side of the pike at 3:30 P.M. General Meade, on the north side, says that he moved toward the right at 2 P.M., while General Ricketts, who took part in the same movement, says that he did not arrive at the foot of the mountain until 5 P.M. If General Meade was not mistaken as to the time of his starting, he must have been long delayed in the thick woods through which the first part of his march was made.

Here is probably the best place to explain the

Union troops charge Rebel positions on South Mountain.

extraordinary caution of the Federals, which seemed so mysterious to us on that 14th of September. An order of General Lee, made while at Frederick, directing Jackson to capture Harper's Ferry, and Longstreet and myself to go to Boonsboro', had fallen into the hands of the Federals, and had been carried to General McClellan. This order (known at the South as the Lost Dispatch) was addressed to me, but I proved twenty years ago that it could not have been lost through my neglect or carelessness. The Federal commander gained two facts from the order, one of which was needless and the other misleading. He learned that Jackson had gone to Harper's Ferry—a truth that he must have learned from his own scouts and spies and the roar of artillery in his own ears: the cannonading could be distinctly heard at Frederick, and it told that some one was beleaguering Harper's Ferry. The misleading report was that Longstreet was at Boonsboro'. The map of the battle-field of South Mountain, prepared in 1872, ten years after the fight, by the United States Bureau of Engineers, represents ten regiments and one battalion under Longstreet at the foot of the mountain on the morning of the 14th of September, 1862. But Longstreet was then an ordinary day's march from that point. In fact, after the removal of Colquitt's brigade, about 7 A.M., there was not a Southern soldier at the foot of the mountain until 3 P.M., when Captain Park of the 12th Alabama Regiment was sent there with forty men. General McClellan in his report says: "It is believed that the force opposed to us at Turner's Gap consisted of D. H. Hill's corps (fifteen thousand) and a part if not the whole of Longstreet's, and perhaps a portion of Jackson's,—probably thirty thousand men in all." ("Official Records," Volume XIX, Pt. I, p. 53) The mistake of the Federal commander in regard to General Longstreet was natural, since he was misled by the Lost Dispatch. But it seems strange that the United States Engineers should repeat the blunder, with the light of history thrown for ten years upon all the incidents of the battle. It was incomprehensible to us of the losing side that the men who charged us so boldly and repulsed our attacks so successfully should let slip the fruits of victory and fall back as though defeated. The prisoners taken were from my division, but the victors seemed to think that Longstreet's men lay hidden somewhere in the depths of those mysterious forests. Thus it was that a thin line of men extending for miles along the crest of the mountain could afford protection for so many hours

to Lee's trains and artillery and could delay the Federal advance until Longstreet's command did come up, and, joining with mine, saved the two wings of the army from being cut in two. But for the mistake about the position of our forces, McClellan could have captured Lee's trains and artillery and interposed between Jackson and Longstreet before noon on that 14th of September. The losing of the dispatch was the saving of Lee's army.

About 4 P.M. I saw what appeared to be two Federal brigades emerge from the woods south of Colquitt's position and form in an open field nearly at right angles to each other—one brigade facing toward the pike, and the other facing the general direction of the mountain. This inverted V-like formation was similar to that of the 1st Mississippi Regiment at Buena Vista. If it was made anywhere else during the Civil War, I never heard of it. The V afforded a fine target from the pike, and I directed Captain Lane to open on it with his battery. His firing was wild, not a shot hitting the mark. The heavy batteries promptly replied, showing such excellent practice that Lane's guns were soon silenced. A small force in the edge of the woods on the west side of the old field opened fire upon the V. The

Federals changed their formation, and, advancing in line of battle, brushed away their assailants and plunged into the woods, when heavy firing began which lasted possibly half an hour.

I suppose that the Federal force which I saw was the division of General Sturgis, and that he left behind Harland's brigade of Rodman's division to guard his flank in his advance, since Harland reports that he had no casualties. General Sturgis claims that he swept everything before him. So do his comrades who fought on his left. On the other hand, General Hood, who came up a short time before this advance, with the brigades of Wofford and Law, claims that he checked and drove back the Federals. G. T. Anderson reports that only his skirmishers were engaged. The surviving officers under G. B. Anderson (who was killed at Sharpsburg, and left no report) say that the same thing was true of their brigade in the afternoon. Ripley's brigade was not engaged at all. About dusk the 2d and 13th North Carolina Regiments attacked Fairchild's brigade and the batteries protected by it on the extreme Federal left, and were repulsed disastrously. Generals Burnside and Willcox say that the fight continued until 10 o'clock at night. Hood was mistaken, then, in thinking that he had driven back the Federal advance. The opposing lines were close together at nightfall, and the firing between the skirmishers was kept up till a late hour. Equally erroneous is the claim that any Confederates were driven except Drayton's small brigade. We held the crest of the mountain, on the National road and the old Sharpsburg road, until Lee's order for withdrawal was given. General Reno, the Federal corps commander on our right, was killed at 7 P.M., in Wise's field, where the fight began at 9 o'clock in the morning. But on our left a commanding hill was lost before night. Batteries placed upon it next morning, acting in concert with the heavy batteries placed on our right by General Pleasonton before we were aware of his presence, would have made any position untenable on the pike or the crest of the mountain. I made that statement to General Lee about 9 P.M., when he consulted with Longstreet and myself in regard to renewing the fight the next morning. Longstreet concurred in this view, remarking that I knew the ground and the situation better than he did.

General Hooker detached Gibbon's brigade, consisting of three Wisconsin regiments and one Indiana regiment, from Hatch's division, and directed it to move directly up the pike with a section of artillery. Then the divisions of Meade and Hatch were formed on the north side of the pike, with the division of Ricketts in supporting distance in rear. A belt of woods had to be passed through, and then it was open field all the way to the summit, and the two detached peaks were in full view upon which the devoted little band of Rodes was posted—the 12th Alabama Regiment on one, and the 3d, 5th, 6th, and 26th Alabama regiments on the other. Under the illusion that there were ten regiments and one battalion of Longstreet's command in those woods, the progress through them was slow, but, when once cleared, the advance was steady and made almost with the precision of movement of a parade day. Captain Robert E. Park, of Macon, Georgia, who commanded the forty skirmishers in the woods, thinks that he delayed the Federal advance for a long time.

It is not more improbable that a few active skirmishers north of the pike should prove an obstacle to progress through the forest there, than that a division on the south side should hesitate to penetrate a forest from which their foes had been completely driven. The success of the Federals on the north side was due to the fact that after getting through the belt of woods at the foot of the mountain, they saw exactly what was before them. The lack of complete success south of the pike was owing to the thick woods on that side, which were supposed to be full of hidden enemies. In the battle of South Mountain the imaginary foes of the Lost Dispatch were worth more to us than ten thousand men.

The advance of Hatch's division in three lines, a brigade in each, was as grand and imposing as that of Meade's division. Hatch's general and field officers were on horseback, his colors were all flying, and the alignment of his men seemed to be perfectly preserved. General Hooker, looking at the steady and precise movement from the foot of the mountain, describes it as a beautiful sight. From the top of the mountain the sight was grand and sublime, but the elements of the pretty and the picturesque did not enter into it. Doubtless the Hebrew poet whose idea of the awe-inspiring is expressed by the phrase, "terrible as an army with banners," had his view of the enemy from the top of a mountain.

There was not a single Confederate soldier to oppose the advance of General Hatch. I got some guns from the reserve artillery of Colonel Cutts to fire at the three lines; but owing to the little practice of the gunners and to the large angles of depression, the cannonade was as harmless as blank-cartridge salutes in honor of a militia general. While these ineffective missiles were flying, which the enemy did not honor by so much as a dodge, Longstreet came up in person with three small brigades, and assumed direction of affairs. He sent the brigade of Evans under Colonel Stevens to the aid of Rodes's men, sorely pressed and well-nigh exhausted. The brigade of Pickett (under Garnett) and that of Kemper were hurried forward to meet and check Hatch, advancing, hitherto, without opposition.

General Meade had moved the brigade of Seymour to the right to take Rodes's position in reverse, while the brigades of Magilton and Gallagher went straight to the front. Meade was one of our most dreaded foes; he was always in deadly earnest, and he eschewed all trifling. He had under him brigade commanders, officers, and soldiers worthy of his leadership. In his onward sweep the peak upon which the 12th Alabama was posted was passed, the gallant Colonel Gayle was killed, and his regiment was routed and dispersed. The four other regiments of Rodes made such heroic resistance that Meade, believing his division about to be flanked, sent for and obtained Duryée's brigade of Ricketts's division. It was pitiable to see the gallant but hopeless struggle of those Alabamians against such mighty odds. Rodes claimed to have fought for three hours without support; but an over-estimate of time under such circumstances is usual and natural. He lost 61 killed, 157 wounded, and 204 missing (captured), or more than one-third of his brigade. His supports [Evans's brigade] fought gallantly and saved him from being entirely surrounded, but they got on the ground too late to effect anything else. Evans's brigade under Stevens had been wasted by two campaigns and was small when it left Hagerstown that morning, and many had fallen out on the hot and dusty forced march. Of the four regiments in the brigade, we find in Volume XIX. of the "Official Records" only the report of one, the 17th South Carolina regiment under Colonel McMaster. That says that 141 men entered the fight on South Mountain, and of these 7 are reported killed, 37 wounded, and 17 missing (captured). Colonel McMaster writes to me that his was the largest regiment in the brigade; so the brigade must have been about 550 strong. General Meade says in his report that he lost 397 men, or ten per cent. of his division. As he received the support of Duryée before or about the time that Rodes got the aid of Stevens, he fought Rodes with the advantage all the while of three to one.

When Ripley came up, as before described, the pressure was all at Fox's Gap. He was sent in there and his brigade was uselessly employed by him in marching and counter-marching. Had it been sent to strengthen Rodes the key of the position might not have been lost. But the vainest of all speculations and regrets are about "the might have been."

Meade encamped that night on the commanding eminence which he had won.

The strength of the two brigades sent to check General Hatch did not exceed eight hundred men, as I will show presently. They must have performed prodigies of valor, and their praises can best be spoken in the words of their enemies. General Patrick, commanding the leading Federal brigade, tells of a race between his men and a strong force of the enemy for the possession of a fence. Patrick won the race and delivered his fire from the fence, picking off the cannoneers at some of our guns. General Hatch was wounded at this fence, and the command devolved on General Doubleday. The latter speaks of lying down behind the fence and allowing the enemy to charge up to within fifteen paces, whereupon he opened a deadly fire. Colonel Wainwright, who succeeded Doubleday in command of his brigade, was also wounded here, and Colonel Hofmann assumed command of it. Colonel Hofmann tells us that the ammunition of the brigade was just giving out when Ricketts relieved Doubleday. Several of the reports speak of the "superior force of the enemy." General Ricketts says that "he relieved Doubleday hard-pressed and nearly out of ammunition." Before Ricketts came in person with Hartsuff's brigade, he had sent Christian's brigade to the assistance of Doubleday. The brigades of Kemper and Pickett (the latter under Garnett) must have fought valiantly, else such results could not have been achieved. General Doubleday's report contains this curious story: "I learned from a wounded prisoner that we were engaged with four to five thousand under the immediate command of General Pickett, with heavy masses in their vicinity. He stated also that Longstreet in vain tried to rally the men, calling them his pets and using every effort to induce them to renew the attack." Of course, the old rebel knew that Pickett was not there in person and that there were no heavy masses in the vicinity. The astonishing thing is that General Doubleday should believe that there were 4000 or 5000 men before him under the immediate command of Pickett. But Doubleday's belief of the story is a tribute to the efficiency of the 800 men who fought a division of 3500 men (the number reported by Hatch after Gibbon had been detached), and fought it so vigorously that two brigades were sent to its assistance.

Jenkins's brigade, under Walker, came up at dusk, too late to be in the fight; but it went in on the right of Garnett and took part in the irregular firing which was kept up till a late hour. Colonel Walker's report shows a loss of 3 killed and 29 wounded, which proves that he was but slightly engaged. The tired men of both sides lay down at last to rest within a hundred yards of each other. But now Gibbon was putting in earnest work on the pike. He had a choice brigade, strong in numbers and strong in the pluck of his men, all from the North-west, where habitually good fighters are reared. He had pushed forward cautiously in the afternoon with the 7th Wisconsin regiment, followed by the 6th on the north side of the pike and the 19th Indiana, supported by the 2d Wisconsin, on the south side. The ten imaginary regiments of the Lost Dispatch retarded his progress through the woods; and at one time, believing that the 7th Wisconsin was about to be turned on its right flank, he sent the 6th to its assistance. There were only a few skirmishers on his right, but the Lost Dispatch made him believe otherwise. About 9 P.M. the stone-wall was reached, and several gallant efforts were made in vain to carry it. When each repulse was followed by the "rebel" yells, the young men on my staff would cry out: "Hurrah for Georgia! Georgia is having a free fight." The Western men had met in the 23d and 28th Georgia regiments men as brave as themselves and far more advantageously posted. Colonel Bragg, of the 6th Wisconsin, says in his report: "We sat down in the dark to wait another attack, but the enemy was no more seen." At midnight Gorman's brigade of Sumner's corps relieved Gibbon's.

General Gibbon reports officially 318 men killed and wounded—a loss sustained almost entirely, I think, at the stone-wall. The colonel of the 7th Wisconsin reports a loss of 147 men in killed and wounded out of 375 muskets carried into action. This shows that he had brave men and that he encountered brave men. From his report we infer that Gibbon had fifteen hundred men. On our side Colquitt had 1100 men, and lost less than 100, owing to the admirable position in which he had been placed.

★★★

JACOB D. COX
The Battle of Antietam

*South Mountain alerted Lee to his danger and
he began to concentrate his army around the
town of Sharpsburg, behind Antietam Creek.
There, on 17 September, occurred the battle
known in the North as Antietam and in the
South as Sharpsburg, and the bloodiest day of
the war. Jacob D. Cox (1828–1900), an Ohio
lawyer, polymath, and militia officer, had a
distinguished career during the Civil War, rising rapidly to division command. At South
Mountain he assumed control of IX Corps on
the death of Jesse L. Reno, leading it ably over
the next few days. Promoted to major general,
he commanded various departments, divisions,
and corps in West Virginia, Tennessee, and the
Carolinas. After the war he served as governor
of Ohio, Secretary of the Interior, and member of
Congress, while finding time to pursue a successful business career and write several
volumes of memoirs and military history. His
account of Antietam is taken from* Battles and
Leaders of the Civil War.

It was not till some time past noon of the 15th of
September that, the way being clear for the Ninth
Corps at South Mountain, we marched through
Fox's gap to the Boonsboro' and Sharpsburg turnpike, and along this road till we came up in rear of
Sumner's command. Hooker's corps, which was part
of the right wing (Burnside's), had been in the advance, and had moved off from the turnpike to the
right near Keedysville. I was with the Kanawha Division, assuming that my temporary command of the
corps ended with the battle on the mountain. When
we approached the line of hills bordering the Antietam, we received orders to turn off the road to the
left, and halted our battalions closed in mass. It was
now about 3 o'clock in the afternoon. McClellan, as
it seemed, had just reached the field, and was surrounded by a group of his principal officers, most of
whom I had never seen before. I rode up with General Burnside, dismounted, and was very cordially
greeted by General McClellan. He and Burnside
were evidently on terms of most intimate friendship
and familiarity. He introduced me to the officers I
had not known before, referring pleasantly to my
service with him in Ohio and West Virginia, putting
me upon an easy footing with them in a very agreea-
ble and genial way.

We walked up the slope of the ridge before us, and looking westward from its crest the whole field of the coming battle was before us. Immediately in front the Antietam wound through the hollow, the hills rising gently on both sides. In the background on our left was the village of Sharpsburg, with fields inclosed by stone fences in front of it. At its right was a bit of wood (since known as the West Wood), with the little Dunker Church standing out white and sharp against it. Farther to the right and left the scene was closed in by wooded ridges with open farm lands between, the whole making as pleasing and prosperous a landscape as can easily be imagined. We made a large group as we stood upon the hill, and it was not long before we attracted the enemy's attention. A puff of white smoke from a knoll on the right of the Sharpsburg road was followed by the screaming of a shell over our heads. McClellan directed that all but one or two should retire behind the ridge, while he continued the rec-

McClellan gets an enthusiastic reception in Maryland as he pursues the Rebel army.

onnoissance, walking slowly to the right. I noted with satisfaction the cool and business-like air with which he made his examination under fire. The Confederate artillery was answered by a battery, and a lively cannonade ensued on both sides, though without any noticeable effect. The enemy's position was revealed, and he was evidently in force on both sides of the turnpike in front of Sharpsburg, covered by the undulations of the rolling ground which hid his infantry from our sight.

The examination of the enemy's position and the discussion of it continued till near the close of the day. Orders were then given for the Ninth Corps to move to the left, keeping off the road, which was occupied by other troops. We moved through fields and farm lands, an hour's march in the dusk of the evening, going into bivouac about a mile south of the Sharpsburg bridge, and in rear of the hills bordering the Antietam.

On Tuesday, September 16th, we confidently expected a battle, and I kept with my division. In the afternoon I saw General Burnside, and learned from him that McClellan had determined to let Hooker make a movement on our extreme right to turn Lee's position. Burnside's manner in speaking of this implied that he thought it was done at Hooker's solicitation and through his desire, openly evinced, to be independent in command.

I urged Burnside to assume the immediate command of the corps and allow me to lead only my own division. He objected that as he had been announced as commander of the right wing of the army composed of two corps (his own and Hooker's), he was unwilling to waive his precedence or to assume that Hooker was detached for anything more than a temporary purpose. I pointed out that Reno's staff had been granted leave of absence to take the body of their chief to Washington, and that my division staff was too small for corps duty; but he met this by saying that he would use his staff for this purpose and help me in every way he could, till the crisis of the campaign should be over.

The 16th passed without serious fighting, though there was desultory cannonading and picket firing. It was hard to restrain our men from showing themselves on the crest of the long ridge in front of us, and whenever they did so they drew the fire from some of the enemy's batteries, to which ours would respond. In the afternoon McClellan reconnoitered the line of the Antietam near us, Burnside being with him. As the results of this we were ordered to change our positions at nightfall, staff-officers being sent to guide each division to its new camp. Rodman's division went half a mile to the left, where a country road led to a ford in a great bend in the Antietam curving deeply into the enemy's side of the stream. Sturgis's division was placed on the sides of the road leading to the stone bridge, since known as Burnside's Bridge (below the Sharpsburg bridge). Willcox's was put in reserve in rear of Sturgis. My own division was divided, Scammon's brigade going with Rodman, and Crook's going with Sturgis.

Crook was ordered to take the advance in crossing the bridge, in case we should be ordered to attack. This selection was made by Burnside himself, as a compliment to the division for the vigor of its assault at South Mountain. While we were moving, we heard Hooker's guns far off on the right and front, and the cannonade continued an hour or more after it became dark.

The morning of Wednesday, the 17th, broke fresh and fair. The men were astir at dawn, getting breakfast and preparing for a day of battle. The artillery opened on both sides as soon as it was fairly light, and the positions which had been assigned us in the dusk of the evening were found to be exposed in some places to the direct fire of the Confederate guns, Rodman's division suffering more than the others. Fairchild's brigade alone reported thirty-six casualties before they could find cover. It was not till 7 o'clock that orders came to advance toward the creek as far as could be done without exposing the men to unnecessary loss. Rodman was directed to acquaint himself with the situation of the ford in front of him, and Sturgis to seek the best means of approach to the stone bridge. All were then to remain in readiness to obey further orders.

When these arrangements had been made, I rode to the position Burnside had selected for himself, which was upon a high knoll north-east of the Burnside Bridge, near a hay-stack which was a prominent landmark. Near by was Benjamin's battery of 20-pounder Parrotts, and a little farther still to the right, on the same ridge, General Sturgis had sent in Durell's battery. These were exchanging shots with the enemy's guns opposite, and had the advantage in range and weight of metal.

Whatever the reason, McClellan had adopted a plan of battle which practically reduced Sumner and Burnside to the command of one corps each, while Hooker had been sent far off on the right front, followed later by Mansfield, but without organizing the right wing as a unit so that one commander could give his whole attention to handling it with vigor. In his preliminary report, made before he was relieved from command, McClellan says:

> The design was to make the main attack upon the enemy's left—at least to create a diversion in favor of the main attack, with the hope of something more, by assailing the enemy's right—and, as soon as one or both of the flank movements were fully successful, to attack their center with any reserve I might then have in hand.

McClellan's report covering his whole career in the war, dated August 4th, 1863 (and published February, 1864, after warm controversies had arisen and he had become a political character), modifies the above statement in some important particulars. It says:

> My plan for the impending general engagement was to attack the enemy's left with the

Union men patrol the area near the stone bridge over the Antietam Creek.

corps of Hooker and Mansfield, supported by Sumner's, and if necessary by Franklin's, and as soon as matters looked favorably there to move the corps of Burnside against the enemy's extreme right upon the ridge running to the south and rear of Sharpsburg, and having carried their position, to press along the crest toward our right, and whenever either of these flank movements should be successful, to advance our center with all the forces then disposable.

The opinion I got from Burnside as to the part the Ninth Corps was to take was fairly consistent with the design first quoted, viz., that when the attack by Sumner, Hooker, and Franklin should be progressing favorably, we were "to create a diversion in favor of the main attack, with the hope of something more." It would also appear probable that Hooker's movement was at first intended to be made by his corps alone, taken up by Sumner's two corps as soon as he was ready to attack, and shared in by Franklin if he reached the field in time, thus making a simul-

Hooker's corps crosses the upper fords of the Antietam.

taneous oblique attack from our right by the whole army except Porter's corps, which was in reserve, and the Ninth Corps, which was to create the "diversion" on our left and prevent the enemy from stripping his right to reënforce his left. It is hardly disputable that this would have been a better plan than the one actually carried out. Certainly the assumption that the Ninth Corps could cross the Antietam alone at the only place on the field where the Confederates had their line immediately upon the stream which must be crossed under fire by two narrow heads of column, and could then turn to the right along the high ground occupied by the hostile army before that army had been broken or seriously shaken elsewhere, is one which would hardly be made till time had dimmed the remembrance of the actual positions of Lee's divisions upon the field.

The evidence that the plan did not originally include the wide separation of two corps to the right, to make the extended turning movement, is found in Hooker's incomplete report, and in the wide interval in time between the marching of his corps and that of Mansfield. Hooker was ordered to cross the Antietam at about 2 o'clock in the afternoon of the 16th by the bridge in front of Keedysville and the ford below it. He says that after his troops were over and in march, he rode back to McClellan, who told

Brigadier General Joseph Hooker

him that he might call for reënforcements and that when they came they should be under his command. Somewhat later McClellan rode forward with his staff to observe the progress making, and Hooker again urged the necessity of reënforcements. Yet Sumner did not receive orders to send Mansfield to support Hooker till evening, and the Twelfth Corps marched only half an hour before midnight, reaching its bivouac, about a mile and a half in rear of that of Hooker, at 2 A.M. of the 17th. Sumner was also ordered to be in readiness to march with the Second Corps an hour before day, but his orders to move did not reach him till nearly half-past 7 in the morning. By this time, Hooker had fought his battle, had been repulsed, and later in the morning was carried wounded from the field. Mansfield had fallen before his corps was deployed, and General Alpheus S. Williams who succeeded him was fighting a losing battle at all points but one—where Greene's division held the East Wood.

After crossing the Antietam, Hooker had shaped his course to the westward, aiming to reach the ridge upon which the Hagerstown turnpike runs, and which is the dominant feature of the landscape. This ridge is some two miles distant from the Antietam, and for the first mile of the way no resistance was met. However, Hooker's progress had been observed by the enemy, and Hood's two brigades were taken from the center and passed to the left of D. H. Hill. Here they occupied an open wood (since known as the East Wood), north-east of the Dunker Church. Hooker was now trying to approach the Confederate positions, Meade's division of the Pennsylvania Reserves being in the advance. A sharp skirmishing combat ensued and artillery was also brought into action on both sides, the engagement continuing till after dark. On our side Seymour's brigade had been chiefly engaged, and had felt the enemy so vigorously that Hood supposed he had repulsed a serious effort to take the wood. Hooker was, however, aiming to pass quite beyond the flank, and kept his other divisions north of the hollow beyond the wood, and upon the ridge which reaches the turnpike near the largest reëntrant bend of the Potomac, which is here only half a mile distant. Here he bivouacked upon the northern slopes of the ridge, Doubleday's division resting with its right upon the turnpike, Ricketts's division upon the left of Doubleday, and Meade covering the front of both with the skirmishers of Seymour's brigade. Between Meade's skirmishers and the ridge were the farmhouse and barn of J. Poffenberger on the east of the road, where Hooker made his own quarters for the night. Half a mile farther in front was the farm of D. R. Miller, the dwelling on the east, and the barn surrounded by stacks on the west of the road. Mansfield's corps, marching as it did late in the night, kept farther to the right than Hooker's but moved on a nearly parallel course and bivouacked upon the farm of another J. Poffenberger near the road which, branching from the Hagerstown turnpike at the Dunker Church, intersects the one running from

Keedysville through Smoketown to the same turnpike about a mile north of Hooker's position.

On the Confederate side, Hood's division had been so severely handled that it was replaced by Jackson's (commanded by J. R. Jones), which, with Ewell's, had been led to the field from Harper's Ferry by Jackson, reaching Sharpsburg in the afternoon of the 16th. These divisions were formed on the left of D. H. Hill and almost at right angles to his line, crossing the turnpike and facing northward. Hood's division, on being relieved, was placed in reserve near the Dunker Church, and spent part of the night in cooking rations, of which its supply had been short for a day or two. The combatants on both sides slept upon their arms, well knowing that the dawn would bring bloody work.

When day broke on Wednesday morning, the 17th, Hooker, looking south from the Poffenberger farm along the turnpike, saw a gently rolling landscape, of which the commanding point was the Dunker Church, whose white brick walls appeared on the west side of the road backed by the foliage of the West Wood, which came toward him, filling a slight hollow which ran parallel to the turnpike, with a single row of fields between. Beyond the Miller house and barns, the ground dipped into a little depression. Beyond this was seen a large corn-field between the East Wood and the turnpike, rising again to the higher level. There was, however, another small dip beyond, which could not be seen from Hooker's position; and on the second ridge, near the church, and extending across the turnpike eastward into the East Wood, could be seen the Confederate line of gray, partly sheltered by piles of rails taken from the fences. They seemed to Hooker to be at the farther side of the cornfield and at the top of the first rise of ground beyond Miller's. It was plain that the high ground about the little white church was the key of the enemy's position, and if that could be carried Hooker's task would be well done.

The Confederates opened the engagement by a rapid fire from a battery near the East Wood as soon as it was light, and Hooker answered the challenge by an immediate order for his line to advance. Doubleday's division was in two lines, Gibbon's and Phelps's brigades in front, supported by Patrick and Hofmann. Gibbon had the right and guided upon the turnpike. Pattrick held a small wood in his rear, which is upon both sides of the road a little north of Miller's house. Some of Meade's men were supposed to be in the northernmost extension of the West Wood and thus to cover Gibbon's right flank as he advanced. Part of Battery B, 4th United States Artillery (Gibbon's own battery), was run forward to Miller's barn and stack-yard on the right of the road, and fired over the heads of the advancing regiments. Other batteries were similarly placed more to the left. The line moved swiftly forward through Miller's orchard and kitchen garden, breaking through a stout picket fence on the near side, down into the moist ground of the hollow, and up through the corn, which was higher than their heads, and shut out

Major General Joseph Mansfield

everything from view. At the southern side of the field they came to a low fence, beyond which was an open field, at the farther side of which was the enemy's line. But Gibbon's right, covered by the corn, had outmarched the left, which had been exposed to terrible fire, and the direction taken had been a little oblique, so that the right wing of the 6th Wisconsin, the flanking regiment, had crossed the turnpike and was suddenly assailed by a sharp fire from the West Wood on its flank. They swung back into the road, lying down along the high, stout post-and-rail fence, keeping up their fire by shooting between the rails. Leaving this little band to protect their right, the main line, which had come up on the left, leaped the fence at the south edge of the cornfield and charged across the open at the enemy in front. But the concentrated fire of artillery and musketry was more than they could bear. Men fell by scores and hundreds, and the thinned lines gave way and ran for the shelter of the corn. They were rallied in the hollow on the north side of the field. The enemy had rapidly extended his left under cover of the West Wood, and now made a dash at the right flank and at Gibbon's exposed guns. His men on the right faced by that flank and followed him bravely, though with little order, in a dash at the Confederates, who were swarming out of the wood. The gunners double-charged the cannon with canister, and under a terrible fire of both artillery and rifles the enemy broke and sought shelter.

Patrick's brigade had come up in support of Gibbon, and was sent across the turnpike into the West Wood to cover that flank. They pushed forward, the enemy retiring, until they were in advance of the principal line in the corn-field, upon which the Confederates were now advancing. Patrick faced his men to the left, parallel to the edge of the wood and to the turnpike, and poured his fire into the flank of the enemy, following it by a charge through the field and up to the fence along the road. Again the Confederates were driven back, but only to push in again by way of these woods, forcing Patrick to resume his original line of front and to retire to the cover of a ledge at right angles to the road near Gibbon's guns. Farther to the left Phelps's and Hofmann's brigades had had similar experience, pushing forward nearly to the Confederate lines, and being driven back with great loss when they charged over open ground against the enemy. Ricketts's division entered the edge of the East Wood; but here, at the salient angle, where D. H. Hill and Lawton joined, the enemy held the position stubbornly, and the repulse of Doubleday's division made Ricketts glad to hold even the edge of the East Wood, as the right of the line was driven back.

It was now about 7 o'clock, and Mansfield's corps (the Twelfth) was approaching, for that officer had called his men to arms at the first sound of Hooker's battle and had marched to his support. The corps consisted of two divisions, Williams's and Greene's. It contained a number of new and undrilled regiments, and in hastening to the field in columns of battalions in mass, proper intervals for deployment had not been preserved, and time was necessarily lost before the troops could be put in line. General Mansfield fell mortally wounded before the deployment was complete, and the command devolved on General Williams. Williams had only time to take the most general directions from Hooker, when the latter also was wounded. The Twelfth Corps attack seems to have been made obliquely to that of Hooker, and facing more to the westward, for General Williams speaks of the post-and-rail fences along the turnpike being a great obstruction in their front. Greene's division, on his left, moved along the ridge leading to the East Wood, taking as the guide for his extreme left the line of the burning house of

Mumma, which had been set on fire by D. H. Hill's men. Doubleday, in his report, notices this change of direction of Williams's division, which had relieved him, and says Williams's brigades were swept away by a fire from their left and front, from behind rocky ledges they could not see. Our officers were deceived in part as to the extent and direction of the enemy's line by the fact that the Confederate cavalry commander, Stuart, had occupied a commanding hill west of the pike and beyond our right flank, and from this position, which, in fact, was considerably detached from the Confederate line, he used his batteries with such effect as to produce the belief that a continuous line extended from this point to the Dunker Church. Our true lines of attack were convergent ones, the right sweeping southward along the pike and through the narrow strip of the West Wood, while the division which drove the enemy from the East Wood should move upon the commanding ground around the church. This error of direction was repeated with disastrous effect a little later, when Sumner came on the ground with Sedgwick's corps.

When Mansfield's corps came on the field, Meade, who succeeded Hooker, withdrew the First Corps to the ridge north of Poffenberger's, where it had bivouacked the night before. It had suffered severely, having lost 2470 in killed and wounded, but it was still further depleted by straggling, so that Meade reported less than 7000 men with the colors that evening. Its organization was preserved, however, and the story that it was utterly dispersed was a mistake.

Greene's division, on the left of the Twelfth Corps, profited by the hard fighting of those who had preceded it, and was able to drive the enemy quite out of the East Wood and across the open fields between it and the Dunker Church. Greene even succeeded, about the time of Sumner's advance, in getting a foothold about the Dunker Church itself, which he held for some time. But the fighting of Hooker's and Mansfield's men, though lacking unity of force and of purpose, had cost the enemy dear. J. R. Jones, who commanded Jackson's division, had been wounded; Starke, who succeeded Jones, was killed; Lawton, who followed Starke, was wounded. Ewell's division, commanded by Early, had suffered hardly less. Hood was sent back into the fight to relieve Lawton, and had been reënforced by the brigades of Ripley, Colquitt, and McRae (Garland's), from D. H. Hill's division. When Greene reached the Dunker Church, therefore, the Confederates on that wing had suffered more fearfully than our own men. Nearly half their numbers were killed and wounded, and Jackson's famous "Stonewall" division was so completely disorganized that only a handful of men under Colonels Grigsby and Stafford remained and attached themselves to Early's command. Of the division under Early, his own brigade was all that retained much strength, and this, posted among the rocks in the West Wood and vigorously supported by Stuart's horse artillery on the flank, was all that covered the left of Lee's army. Could Hooker and Mansfield have attacked together,—or, still better, could Sumner's Second Corps have marched before day and united with the first onset,—Lee's left must inevitably have been crushed long before the Confederate divisions of McLaws, Walker, and A. P. Hill could have reached the field. It is this failure to carry out any intelligible plan which the historian must regard as the unpardonable military fault on the National side. To account for the hours between 4 and 8 on that morning, is the most serious responsibility of the National commander.

Sumner's Second Corps was now approaching the scene of action, or rather two divisions of it—Sedgwick's and French's—Richardson's being still delayed till his place could be filled by Porter's troops, the strange tardiness in sending orders being noticeable in regard to every part of the army. Sumner met Hooker, who was being carried from the field, and the few words he could exchange with the wounded general were enough to make him feel the need of haste, but not sufficient to give him any clear idea of the position.

Both Sedgwick and French marched their divisions by the right flank, in three columns, a brigade in each column, Sedgwick leading. They crossed the Antietam by Hooker's route, but did not march as far to the north-west as Hooker had done. When the center of the corps was opposite the Dunker Church and nearly east of it, the change of direction was given; the troops faced to their proper front and advanced in line of battle in three lines, fully deployed, and 60 or 70 yards apart, Sumner himself being in rear of Sedgwick's first line, and near its left. When they approached the position held by Greene's division at Dunker Church, French kept on so as to form on Greene's left, while Sedgwick, under Sumner's immediate lead, diverged somewhat to the right, passing through the East Wood, crossing the turnpike on the right of Greene and of the Dunker Church, and plunged into the West Wood. At this point there were absolutely no Confederate troops in front of them. Early was farther to the right, opposing Williams's division of the Twelfth Corps, and now made haste under cover of the woods to pass around Sedgwick's right and to get in front of him to oppose his progress. This led to a lively skirmishing fight in which Early was making as great a demonstration as possible, but with no chance of solid success. At this very moment, however, McLaws's and Walker's divisions came upon the field, marching rapidly from Harper's Ferry. Walker charged headlong upon the left flank of Sedgwick's lines, which were soon thrown into confusion, and McLaws, passing by Walker's left, also threw his division diagonally upon the already broken and retreating lines of Sumner. Taken at such a disadvantage, these never had a chance; and in spite of the heroic bravery of Sumner and Sedgwick, with most of their officers (Sedgwick being severely wounded), the division was driven off to the north with terrible losses, carrying along in the rout part

Brigadier General Edwin Sumner

of Williams's men of the Twelfth Corps, who had been holding Early at bay. All these troops were rallied at the ridge on the Poffenberger farm, where Hooker's corps had already taken position. Here some thirty cannon of both corps were concentrated, and, supported by the organized parts of all three of the corps which had fought upon this part of the field, easily repulsed all efforts of Jackson and Stuart to resume the aggressive or to pass between them and the Potomac. Sumner himself did not accompany the routed troops to this position, but as soon as it was plain that the division could not be rallied, he galloped off to put himself in communication with French and with the headquarters of the army and try to retrieve the misfortune. From the flag-station east of the East Wood he signaled to McClellan: "Reënforcements are badly wanted. Our troops are giving way." It was between 9 and 10 o'clock when Sumner entered the West Wood, and in fifteen minutes, or a little more, the one-sided combat was over.

The enemy now concentrated upon Greene at the Dunker Church, and after a stubborn resistance he too was driven back across the turnpike and the open ground to the edge of the East Wood. Here, by the aid of several batteries gallantly handled, he defeated the subsequent effort to dislodge him. French had come up on his left, and both his batteries and the numerous ones on the Poffenberger hill swept the open ground and the corn-field over which

Franklin's column advances to support Sumner's corps in line of battle in the middle-ground.

Hooker had fought, and he was able to make good his position. The enemy was content to regain the high ground near the church, and French's attack upon D. H. Hill was now attracting their attention.

The battle on the extreme right was thus ended before 10 o'clock in the morning, and there was no more serious fighting north of the Dunker Church. French advanced on Greene's left, over the open farm lands, and after a fierce combat about the Roulette and Clipp farm buildings, drove D. H. Hill's division from them. Richardson's division came up on French's left soon after, and foot by foot, field by field, from hill to hill and from fence to fence, the enemy was pressed back, till after several hours of fighting the sunken road, since known as "Bloody Lane," was in our hands, piled full of the Confederate dead who had defended it with their lives. Richardson had been mortally wounded, and Hancock had been sent from Franklin's corps to command the division. Barlow had been conspicuous in the thickest of the fight, and after a series of brilliant actions was carried off desperately wounded. On the Confederate side equal courage had been shown and a magnificent tenacity exhibited. But it is not my purpose to describe the battle in detail. I limit myself to such an outline as may make clear my interpretation of the larger features of the engagement and its essential plan.

The head of Franklin's corps (the Sixth) had arrived about 10 o'clock and taken the position near the Sharpsburg Bridge which Sumner had occupied. Before noon Smith's and Slocum's divisions were ordered to Sumner's assistance, and early in the afternoon Irwin and Brooks, of Smith's, advanced to the charge and relieved Greene's division and part of French's, holding the line from Bloody Lane by the Clipp, Roulette, and Mumma houses to the East Wood and the ridge in front. Here Smith and Slocum remained till Lee retreated, Smith's division repelling a sharp attack. French and Richardson's battle may be considered as ended at 1 or 2 o'clock.

It seems to me very clear that about 10 o'clock in the morning was the great crisis in this battle. The sudden and complete rout of Sedgwick's division was not easily accounted for, and with McClellan's theory of the enormous superiority of Lee's numbers, it looked as if the Confederate general had massed overwhelming forces on our right. Sumner's notion that Hooker's corps was utterly dispersed was naturally accepted, and McClellan limited his hopes to holding on at the East Wood and the Poffenberger hill where Sedgwick's batteries were massed and supported by the troops that had been rallied there. Franklin's corps as it came on the field was detained to support the threatened right center, and McClellan determined to help it further by a demonstration upon the extreme left by the Ninth Corps. At this time, therefore (10 A.M.), he gave his order to Burnside to try to cross the Antietam and attack the enemy, thus creating a diversion in favor of our hardpressed right. Facts within my own recollection strongly sustain this view that the hour was 10 A.M.

I have mentioned the hill above the Burnside Bridge where Burnside took his position, and to which I went after the preliminary orders for the day had been issued. There I remained until the order of attack came, anxiously watching what we could see at the right, and noting the effect of the fire of the heavy guns of Benjamin's battery.

From that point we could see nothing that occurred beyond the Dunker Church, for the East and West Woods, with farm-houses and orchards between, made an impenetrable screen. But as the

morning wore on we saw lines of troops advancing from our right upon the other side of the Antietam, and engaging the enemy between us and the East Wood. The Confederate lines facing them now rose into view. From our position we looked, as it were, down between the opposing lines as if they had been the sides of a street, and as the fire opened we saw wounded men carried to the rear and stragglers making off. Our lines halted, and we were tortured with anxiety as we speculated whether our men would charge or retreat. The enemy occupied lines of fences and stone-walls, and their batteries made gaps in the National ranks. Our long-range guns were immediately turned in that direction, and we cheered every well-aimed shot. One of our shells blew up a caisson close to the Confederate line. This contest was going on, and it was yet uncertain which would succeed, when one of McClellan's staff rode up with an order to Burnside. The latter turned to me, saying we were ordered to make our attack. I left the hill-top at once to give personal supervision to the movement ordered, and did not return to it, and

First Maryland artillery batteries at Antietam

my knowledge by actual vision of what occurred on the right ceased. The manner in which we had waited, the free discussion of what was occurring under our eyes and of our relation to it, the public receipt of the order by Burnside in the usual and business-like form, all forbid the supposition that this was any reiteration of a former order. It was immediately transmitted to me without delay or discussion, further than to inform us that things were not going altogether well on the right, and that it was hoped our attack would be of assistance to that wing. If then we can determine whose troops we saw engaged, we shall know something of the time of day; for there has been a general agreement reached as to the hours of movement during the forenoon on the right. The official map settles this. No lines of our troops were engaged in the direction of Bloody Lane and the Roulette farm-house, and between the latter and our station on the hill, till French's division made its attack. We saw them distinctly on the hither side of the farm buildings, upon the open ground, considerably nearer to us than the Dunker Church or the East Wood. In number we took them to be a corps. The place, the circumstances, all fix it beyond controversy that they were French's men, or French's and Richardson's. No

McClellan rides the line of battle at Antietam.

others fought on that part of the field until Franklin went to their assistance at noon or later. The incident of their advance and the explosion of the caisson was illustrated by the pencil of the artist, Forbes, on the spot and placed by him at the time Franklin's head of column was approaching from Rohrersville, which was about 10 o'clock.

McClellan truly said, in his original report, that the task of carrying the bridge in front of Burnside was a difficult one. The depth of the valley and the shape of its curve made it impossible to reach the enemy's position at the bridge by artillery fire from the hill-tops on our side. Not so from the enemy's

position, for the curve of the valley was such that it was perfectly enfiladed near the bridge by the Confederate batteries at the position now occupied by the national cemetery. The Confederate defense of the passage was intrusted to D. R. Jones's division of four brigades, which was the one Longstreet himself had disciplined and led till he was assigned to a larger command. Toombs's brigade was placed in advance, occupying the defenses of the bridge itself and the wooded slopes above, while the other brigades supported him, covered by the ridges which looked down upon the valley. The division batteries were supplemented by others from the reserve, and the valley, the bridge, and the ford below were under the direct and powerful fire of shot and shell from the Confederate cannon. Toombs speaks in his report in a characteristic way of his brigade holding back Burnside's corps; but his force, thus strongly supported, was as large as could be disposed of at the head of the bridge, and abundantly large for resistance to any that could be brought against it. Our advance upon the bridge could only be made by a narrow column, showing a front of eight men at most. But the front which Toombs deployed behind his defenses was three or four hundred yards both above and below the bridge. He himself says in his report: "From the nature of the ground on the other side, the enemy were compelled to approach mainly by the road which led up the river for near three hundred paces parallel with my line of battle and distant therefrom from fifty to a hundred and fifty feet, thus exposing his flank to a destructive fire the most of that distance."

Under such circumstances, I do not hesitate to affirm that the Confederate position was virtually impregnable to a direct attack over the bridge, for the column approaching it was not only exposed at pistol-range to the perfectly covered infantry of the enemy and to two batteries which were assigned to the special duty of supporting Toombs, and which had the exact range of the little valley with their shrapnel, but if it should succeed in reaching the bridge its charge across it must be made under a fire plowing through its length, the head of the column melting away as it advanced, so that, as every soldier knows, it could show no front strong enough to make an impression upon the enemy's breastworks, even if it should reach the other side. As a desperate sort of diversion in favor of the right wing, it might be justifiable; but I believe that no officer or man who knew the actual situation at that bridge thinks a serious attack upon it was any part of McClellan's original plan. Yet, in his detailed official report, instead of speaking of it as the difficult task the original report had called it, he treats it as little different from a parade or march across, which might have been done in half an hour.

Burnside's view of the matter was that the front attack at the bridge was so difficult that the passage by the ford below must be an important factor in the task; for if Rodman's division should succeed in getting across there, at the bend in the Antietam, he would come up in rear of Toombs, and either the whole of D. R. Jones's division would have to advance to meet Rodman, or Toombs must abandon the bridge. In this I certainly concurred, and Rodman was ordered to push rapidly for the ford. It is important to remember, however, that Walker's Confederate division had been posted during the earlier morning to hold that part of the Antietam line, and it was probably from him that Rodman suffered the first casualties which occurred in his ranks. But, as we have seen, Walker had been called away by Lee only an hour before, and had made the hasty march by the rear of Sharpsburg, to fall upon Sedgwick. If, therefore, Rodman had been sent to cross at 8 o'clock, it is safe to say that his column fording the stream in the face of Walker's deployed division would never have reached the farther bank,—a contingency that McClellan did not consider when arguing long afterward the favorable results that might have followed an earlier attack. As Rodman died upon the field, no full report for his division was made, and we only know that he met with some resistance from both infantry and artillery; that the winding of the stream made his march longer than he anticipated, and that, in fact, he only approached the rear of Toombs's position from that direction about the time when our last and successful charge upon the bridge was made, between noon and 1 o'clock.

The attacks at Burnside's Bridge were made under my own eye. Sturgis's division occupied the center of our line, with Crook's brigade of the Kanawha Division on his right front, and Willcox's division in reserve, as I have already stated. Crook's position was somewhat above the bridge, but it was thought that by advancing part of Sturgis's men to the brow of the hill they could cover the advance of Crook, and that the latter could make a straight dash down the hill to our end of the bridge. The orders were accordingly given, and Crook advanced, covered by the 11th Connecticut (of Rodman), under Colonel Kingsbury, deployed as skirmishers. In passing over the spurs of the hills, Crook came out on the bank of the stream above the bridge and found himself under a heavy fire. He faced the enemy and returned the fire, getting such cover for his men as he could and trying to drive off or silence his opponents. The engagement was one in which the Antietam prevented the combatants from coming to close quarters, but it was none the less vigorously continued with musketry fire. Crook reported that his hands were full, and that he could not approach closer to the bridge. But later in the contest, and about the time that the successful charge at the bridge was made, he got five companies of the 28th Ohio over by a ford above. Sturgis ordered forward an attacking column from Nagle's brigade, supported and covered by Ferrero's brigade, which took position in a field of corn on one of the lower slopes of the hill opposite the head of the bridge. The whole front was carefully covered with skirmishers, and our batteries on the heights overhead were ordered to keep down the fire of the enemy's artillery. Nagle's effort was gallantly made, but it failed, and his men were forced to seek cover behind the spur of the hill from which they had advanced. We were constantly hoping to hear something from Rodman's advance by the ford, and would gladly have waited for some more certain knowledge of his progress, but at this time McClellan's sense of the necessity of relieving the right was such that he was sending reiterated orders to push the assault. Not only were these forwarded to me, but to give added weight to my instructions, Burnside sent direct to Sturgis urgent messages to carry the bridge at all hazards. I directed Sturgis to take two regiments from Ferrero's brigade, which had not been engaged, and make a column by moving them by the flank, the one left in front and the other right in front, side by side, so that when they passed the bridge they could turn to left and right, forming line as they advanced on the run. He chose the 51st New York, Colonel Robert B. Potter, and the 51st Pennsylvania, Colonel John F. Hartranft (both names afterward greatly distinguished), and both officers and men were made to feel the necessity of success. At the same time Crook succeeded in bringing a light howitzer of Simmonds's mixed battery down from the hill-tops, and placed it where it had a point-blank fire on the farther end of the bridge. The howitzer was one we had captured in West Virginia, and had been added to the battery, which was partly made up of heavy rifled Parrott guns. When everything was ready, a heavy skirmishing fire was opened all along the bank, the howitzer threw in double charges of canister, the two regiments charged up the road in column with fixed bayonets, and in scarcely more time than it takes to tell it, the bridge was passed and Toombs's brigade fled through the woods and over the top of the hill. The charging regiments were advanced in line to the crest above the bridge as soon as they were deployed, and the rest of Sturgis's division, with Crook's brigade, were immediately brought over to strengthen the line. These were soon joined by Rodman's division with Scammon's brigade, which had crossed at the ford, and whose presence on that side of the stream had no doubt made the final struggle of Toombs's men less obstinate than it would otherwise have been, the fear of being taken in rear having always a strong moral effect upon even the best of troops. It was now about 1 o'clock, and nearly three hours had been spent in a bitter and bloody contest across the narrow stream. The successive efforts to carry the bridge had been made as closely following each other as possible. Each had been a fierce combat, in which the men, with wonderful courage, had not easily accepted defeat, and even when not able to cross the bridge had made use of the walls at the end, the fences, and every tree and stone as cover, while they strove to reach with their fire their well-protected and nearly concealed opponents. The lulls in the fighting had been short, and only to prepare new efforts. The severity of the work was attested by our losses, which, before the crossing was won, exceeded five hundred men and included some of our best officers, such as Colonel Kingsbury, of the 11th Connecticut; Lieutenant-Colonel Bell, of the 51st Pennsylvania, and Lieutenant-Colonel Coleman, of the 11th Ohio, two of them commanding regiments. The proportion of casualties to the number engaged was much greater than common, for the nature of the task required that comparatively few troops should be exposed at once, the others remaining under cover.

Our first task was to prepare to hold the height we had gained against the return assault of the enemy which we expected, and to reply to the destructive fire from the enemy's abundant artillery. The light batteries were brought over and distributed in the line. The men were made to lie down behind the crest to save them from the concentrated artillery fire which the enemy opened upon us as soon as Toombs's regiments succeeded in reaching their main line. But McClellan's anticipation of an overwhelming attack upon his right was so strong that he determined still to press our advance, and sent orders accordingly. The ammunition of Sturgis's and Crook's men had been nearly exhausted, and it was imperative that they should be freshly supplied before entering into another engagement. Sturgis also reported his men so exhausted by their efforts as to be unfit for an immediate advance. On this I sent to Burnside the request that Willcox's division be sent over, with an ammunition train, and that Sturgis's division be replaced by fresh troops, remaining, however, on the west side of the stream as a support to the others. This was done as rapidly as was practicable, where everything had to pass down the steep hill road and through so narrow a defile as the bridge. Still, it was 3 o'clock before these changes and preparations could be made. Burnside had personally striven to hasten them, and had come over to the west bank to consult and to hurry matters, and took his share of personal peril, for he came at a time when the ammunition wagons were delivering cartridges, and the road where they were, at the end of the bridge, was in the range of the enemy's constant and accurate fire. It is proper to mention this because it has been said that he did not cross the stream. The criticisms made by McClellan as to the time occupied in these changes and movements will not seem forcible, if one will compare them with any similar movements on the field; such as Mansfield's to support Hooker, or Sumner's or Franklin's to reach the scene of the action. About this, however, there is fair room for difference of opinion; what I personally know is that it would have been folly to advance again before Willcox had relieved Sturgis, and that as soon as the fresh troops reported and could be put in line, the order to advance was given. McClellan is in accord with all other witnesses in declaring that when the movement began, the conduct of the troops was gallant beyond criticism.

Willcox's division formed the right, Christ's brigade being north and Welsh's brigade south of the road leading from the bridge to Sharpsburg. Crook's brigade of the Kanawha Division supported Willcox. Rodman's division formed on the left, Harland's brigade having the position on the flank, and Fairchild's uniting with Willcox at the center. Scammon's brigade of the Kanawha Division was the reserve for Rodman on the extreme left. Sturgis's division remained and held the crest of the hill above the bridge. About half the batteries of the divisions accompanied the movement, the rest being in position on the hill-tops east of the Antietam. The advance necessarily followed the high ground toward Sharpsburg, and as the enemy made strongest resistance toward our right, the movement curved in that direction, the six brigades of D. R. Jones's Confederate division being deployed diagonally across our front, holding the stone fences and crests of the cross ridges and aided by abundant artillery, in which arm the enemy was particularly strong. The battle was a fierce one from the moment Willcox's men showed themselves on the open ground. Christ's brigade, taking advantage of all the cover the trees and inequalities of surface gave them, pushed on along the depression in which the road ran, a section of artillery keeping pace with them in the road. The direction of movement brought all the brigades of the first line in échelon, but Welsh soon fought his way up beside Christ, and they, together, drove the enemy successively from the fields and farm-yards till they reached the edge of the village. Upon the elevation on the right of the road was an orchard in which the shattered and diminished force of Jones made a final stand, but Willcox concentrated his artillery fire upon it, and his infantry was able to push forward and occupy it. They now partly occupied the town of Sharpsburg, and held the high ground commanding it to the south-east, where the national cemetery now is. The struggle had been long and bloody. It was half-past 4 in the afternoon, and ammunition had again run low, for the wagons had not been able to accompany the movement. Willcox paused for his men to take breath again, and to fetch up some cartridges; but meanwhile affairs were taking a serious turn on the left.

As Rodman's division went forward, he found the enemy before him seemingly detached from Willcox's opponents, and occupying ridges upon his left front, so that he was not able to keep his own connection with Willcox in the swinging movement to the right. Still, he made good progress in the face of stubborn resistance, though finding the enemy constantly developing more to his left, and the interval between him and Willcox widening. In fact his movement became practically by column of brigades. The view of the field to the south was now obstructed by fields of tall Indian corn, and under this cover Confederate troops approached the flank in line of battle. Scammon's officers in the reserve saw them as soon as Rodman's brigades écheloned, as these were toward the front and right. This hostile force proved to be A. P. Hill's division of six brigades, the last of Jackson's force to leave Harper's Ferry, and which had reached Sharpsburg since noon. Those first seen by Scammon's men were dressed in the National blue uniforms which they had captured at Harper's Ferry, and it was assumed that they were part of our own forces till they began to fire. Scammon quickly changed front to the left, drove back the enemy before him, and occupied a line of stone fences, which he held until he was withdrawn from it. Harland's brigade was partly moving in the cornfields. One of his regiments was new, having been organized only three weeks, and the brigade had somewhat lost its order and connection when the sudden attack came. Rodman directed Colonel Harland to lead the right of the brigade, while he himself attempted to bring the left into position. In performing this duty he fell mortally wounded, and the brigade broke in confusion after a brief effort of its right wing to hold on. Fairchild, also, now received the fire on his left, and was forced to fall back and change front.

Being at the center when this break occurred on the left, I saw that it would be impossible to continue the movement to the right, and sent instant orders to Willcox and Crook to retire the left of their line, and to Sturgis to come forward into the gap made in Rodman's. The troops on the right swung back in perfect order; Scammon's brigade hung on at its stone-wall with unflinching tenacity till Sturgis

had formed on the curving hill in rear of them, and Rodman's had found refuge behind. Willcox's left, then united with Sturgis and Scammon, was withdrawn to a new position on the left flank of the whole line. That these manœuvres on the field were really performed in good order is demonstrated by the fact that, although the break in Rodman's line was a bad one, the enemy was not able to capture many prisoners, the whole number of missing, out of the 2340 casualties which the Ninth Corps suffered in the battle, being 115, which includes wounded men unable to leave the field. The enemy were not lacking in bold efforts to take advantage of the check we had received, but were repulsed with severe punishment, and as the day declined were content to entrench themselves along the line of the road leading from Sharpsburg to the Potomac at the mouth of the Antietam, half a mile in our front. The men of the Ninth Corps lay that night upon their arms, the line being one which rested with both flanks near the Antietam, and curved outward upon the rolling hill-tops which covered the bridge and commanded the plateau between us and the enemy. With my staff I lay upon the ground behind the troops, holding our horses by the bridles as we rested, for our orderlies were so exhausted that we could not deny them the same chance for a little broken slumber.

G. MOXLEY SORREL
The Battle of Sharpsburg

During the Antietam Campaign Maj. G. Moxley Sorrel (see "The Peninsula and the Battle of Williamsburg") was acting adjutant general of Confederate Lt. Gen. James Longstreet's corps.

His account of the battle, during which he was wounded, is abridged from his Recollections of a Confederate Staff Officer.

On the night before the battle we were getting some sleep under thick trees when a stampede of horses nearly trampled us. It was a very surprising thing that happened to the Jeff Davis Legion. The regiment was well lined and picketed in front, part of the officers and men asleep, guards and pickets on good watch, and everything deadly quiet and still, the night well on.

Suddenly something seemed to pass through the animals like a quiver of motion, a faint sound as of a sign, and then the wildest scene ensued. The horses for no reason that could be found had become stampeded, in the greatest panic and excitement. They broke away from their picket ropes, and droves of

different sizes, some few, some many, were thundering along over the country and about the army in wild confusion. Fortunately, they drew to our rear, and the troopers were all night and part of the next day recovering them. Duncan has well described to me this extraordinary stampede, the like of which did not occur during the four years' war.

The morning of September 17 opened with battle before us, presaged by the booming of cannon already beginning their noisy work.

Longstreet held the right center, the other wing being trusted to Jackson, Hood, Richard H. Anderson, McLaws, and other divisions. The fall of Harper's Ferry had released the attacking forces and

President Lincoln and McClellan meet after the battle.

enabled Jackson and part of his command to join Lee, but only after great exhaustion and fatal straggling. The enemy called this battle Antietam, from the little stream that traverses the field. We gave it the name of Sharpsburg, the village that nestled in the hills by the turnpike some little distance back of Antietam. It was a dreadful day of fighting. Beginning early, we were at it until nightfall. Outnumbered three to one, it seemed that at almost any time a strong effort by McClellan would drive us back, but that effort was not made. A third of his fine army did not fire a rifle.

In the early afternoon, Lee, Longstreet, and D. H. Hill ascended a little acclivity near the turnpike to make some observations. All others—staff and orderlies—were kept back under the brow of the hill to avoid drawing fire on the three generals. In truth, they did look conspicuous on the crest, silhouetted

against the bright skies, and the shot of course came, a little wide, but the second was from a good gunner. This shot struck the front legs of Hill's horse, cutting them sharp off at the knees. The poor beast did not fall immediately, and made no sound, but put his nose into the grass, nibbling at it seemingly.

The small general in a high-cantled saddle could not get his leg over in the position of the horse until Longstreet helped him down. There is occasional talk of groans and shrieks of horses when wounded. I have seen many badly hurt, but cannot recall an instance in which the animal made any noise. This "gunning" has recently been associated with another incident on the field with which it has really no connection. It was rather later in the day that we came on two of Miller's Washington Artillery guns that had been doing splendid work, but were now silent.

Lieutenant General James Longstreet

The gunners had fallen by their places, which were temporarily without cannoneers. Longstreet was with us. Fairfax, Goree-Manning, Walton, myself, and perhaps some others took our horses' bridles as we leaped from them to the guns. The position was most important and it would never do for those "barkers" to be dumb, even for a minute; so at it we went, the improvised gunners, and were afterwards cheered by being told we did it well and could always get a gunner's berth when we might want it. I had the rammer, No. 1, I think it is in the drill. Our fire was really strong and effective, until some reliefs from the Washington Artillery came up "ventre à terre," and with hearty shouts took their guns in hand. The enemy opened a severe fire on us, but fortunately none of our party was hurt. We mounted again with cheerful grins at our sudden adventure, and Longstreet, much pleased, turned his attention to other imperiled points. . . .

Longstreet, whose eyes were everywhere, had noticed a regiment well advanced that had been fighting steadily for hours. It had gathered a few rails and stones for a chance protection to its brave fellows, all the time keeping up a good steady fire on the force in front of them, whose ranks looked so thick as to make one wonder they did not walk over our poor little regiment. Longstreet never failed to encourage good work; he praised freely and liberally where he thought it due, constantly recommending meritorious young officers for promotion. There was no illiberality about him, and the officers knew it and tried for his notice. "Major Sorrel," he said, "go down to that regiment with my compliments to the colonel. Say he has fought splendidly and must keep it up. We are hard pressed and if he loses his position there is nothing left behind him; his men have made noble sacrifices, but are to do still more."

It was Col. John R. Cooke, commanding a North Carolina regiment, that received this message. There were many dead along his lines and some severely wounded who could not be got away. My horse was wounded on the way to him, and the enemy's rifle firing was incessant, while from the saddle Longstreet's praises and encouragement were given this brave officer.

Profanity is justly considered objectionable. I do not approve of it, but there are times when it may be overlooked, and never did such words sound so sweet as when I looked into Cooke's eyes and heard him: "Major, thank General Longstreet for his good words, but say, by ——— almighty, he needn't doubt me! We will stay here, by J. C., if we must all go to hell together! That ——— thick line of the enemy has been fighting all day, but my regiment is still ready to lick this whole ——— outfit. Start away, Major, quick, or you'll be getting hurt too, exposed as you are on that horse!" This is only a faint reproduction of the Colonel's gift of language, but it left with me no doubt that the position would stand until that gallant heart gave the word to leave it. He stuck there until ordered off at night. It was some time before I was able to send a report to Longstreet, the hour being about 5 p.m., but he had Cooke promoted immediately. I had scarcely drawn my hand from Cooke's when a shell burst over us and a fragment struck me senseless from my horse. . . .

Toombs's brigade of Georgians had fought well at the bridge on the right. It was contested all day and was the scene of some bloody encounters. Some fresher men under A. P. Hill at last came up late, almost dark, and a general advance on the enemy's lines persuaded the timorous McClellan that we were not done fighting, and he ceased his operations. Lee was left, after the long day's work, with thin ranks holding the ground he stood on in the morning, and nothing lost by us in guns, colors, or prisoners. The casualties, however, were very heavy, our list of wounded and killed being awful. Here fell my dear personal friends of school days, McIntosh and Parkman. I had lost several in the battles preceding and my heart was heavy.

Longstreet's conduct on this great day of battle was magnificent. He seemed everywhere along his extended lines, and his tenacity and deep-set resolution, his inmost courage, which appeared to swell with the growing peril to the army, undoubtedly stimulated the troops to greater action, and held them in place despite all weakness. My staff comrades described to me later his appearance and reception by Lee when they met at night after firing ceased. Longstreet, big, heavy, and red, grimly stern after this long day's work, that called for all we could stomach, rolled in on his clumsy carpet slippers. Lee immediately welcomed him with unconcealed joy. "Here comes my war horse just from the field he has done so much to save!" his arm affectionately around "Peter's" shoulder. The latter should surely have been proud and well satisfied. Lee held his ground that night and all the next day (the 18th), caring for his wounded and burying his dead. On the night of the 18th he quietly moved out and successfully passed the Potomac to Virginia ground without loss. That McClellan with his great army, a third of which had taken no part in the two battles, permitted this escape is unaccountable. In olden times generals lost their heads for such stupidities. "Little Mac" lost his place instead, being soon superseded by Burnside. . . .

When struck down by that bursting shell, Colonel Cooke had me immediately carried off on a stretcher to a less exposed place, and on regaining consciousness good old Fairfax was pouring whiskey down my throat. We had been severed by one of those unnecessary camp differences and were not on good terms. Needless to say all that was now forgotten and we were comrades once more. He managed to get an ambulance and sent me off to the army field-infirmary. There was another officer stretched by me in the ambulance, very bloody and very terribly wounded. I did not think I was hurt badly, but seemed to have no motion or feeling about the legs. We were soon at the surgeon's camp, Dr. Guild medical director in charge. I knew him well, a cheerful soul. "What, you too!" he cried. "Now, turn over." And he began pinching my legs unmercifully. I kicked and cried out loudly, and he laughed and said: "O, you are quite right, I feared for your back. Now away to the rear across the river; you will be on duty again in a fortnight." The hurt was a violent contusion below the right shoulder and made the whole side of the body black and blue with extravasated blood. Off we started and came up with my staff comrade, Walton, slowly trotting to the rear with a bullet in his shoulder. He took charge of things energetically, managed by threats and bullying to get a boat, and had us ferried across the river at Shepherdstown. There Walton got some men to carry me, hunting a resting place; he tried everywhere, his wound paining him all the time. The little town was full of wounded and it looked as if we should have to lie out in the street, but some gentle hearts were melted. At the house of the Hamtrammocks, already crowded with wounded, the ladies gave up their last room and put us in it, fed and cheered us, providing that sweet sympathy and goodness that was ever present among the noble women of battle-torn Virginia.

The Hamtrammock family was unknown to me, but stood very well in the village and all through the Valley. It was said that their father, long dead, had commanded a Virginia regiment in the Mexican War. The only members of the family we saw were the two pleasant girls, Elsie and Florence, and an aunt, Miss Sheperd. That evening the doctor relieved Walton of acute suffering by cutting out the bullet, which had buried itself in the muscles of the shoulder, and dressed my battered back. So we awoke next morning refreshed and easier, charmed with our luck in such good quarters. We were soon quite ready to be entertained by the young ladies, and they were nothing loth after the nurses had made us presentable. There was a Georgian in the house, Captain D'Antignac, badly wounded in the head, and in charge of Miss Sheperd. She would sometimes rush into our room, laughing immoderately; the poor fellow was out of his head and talking all sorts of nonsense. Our hostesses were very gracious, gay, happy, well educated girls; they played and sang prettily, and were such Confederates! We had much curiosity to know how they had fared during the night, since they had been robbed of their rooms; it finally came out that they had shared the bathroom between them. But this elysium could not last long, for next day the enemy planted some guns on the river bank and began shelling everything. The wounded were in great peril and the surgeons hurried them to the rear. An ambulance was sent at once for us, and with grateful farewells to our friends, we were taken away to a little old farmhouse fifteen miles distant, behind Lee's army.

JOHN B. GORDON
Antietam

Col. John B. Gordon (see "The First Winter of the War") commanded his regiment, the 6th Alabama, during the Antietam Campaign. A part of Daniel H. Hill's division, Gordon and his men fought at South Mountain. At Antie-tam they formed part of the center of Lee's lines. Gordon's vivid account of the battle, from which he emerged seriously wounded, is drawn from his Reminiscences of the Civil War.

Like two mighty giants preparing for a test of strength, the Union and Confederate armies now arrayed themselves for still bloodier encounters. In this encounter the one went down, and in that the other; but each rose from its fall, if not with renewed strength, at least with increased resolve. In the Southwest, as well as in Virginia, the blows between the mighty contestants came fast and hard. Both were in the field for two and a half years more of the most herculean struggle the world has ever witnessed.

At Antietam, or Sharpsburg, as the Confederates call it, on the soil of Maryland, occurred one of the most desperate though indecisive battles of modern times. The Union forces numbered about 60,000, the Confederates about 35,000. This battle left its lasting impress upon my body as well as upon my memory.

General George B. McClellan, after his displacement, had been again assigned to the command of the Union forces. The restoration of this brilliant soldier seemed to have imparted new life to that army. Vigorously following up the success achieved at South Mountain, McClellan, on the 16th day of September, 1862, marshalled his veteran legions on the eastern hills bordering the Antietam. On the opposite slopes, near the picturesque village of Sharpsburg, stood the embattled lines of Lee. As these vast American armies, the one clad in blue and the other in gray, stood contemplating each other from the adjacent hills, flaunting their defiant banners, they presented an array of martial splendor that was not equalled, perhaps, on any other field. It was in marked contrast with other battle-grounds. On the open plain, where stood these hostile hosts in long lines, listening in silence for the signal summoning them to battle, there were no breastworks, no abatis, no intervening woodlands, nor abrupt hills, nor hiding-places, nor impassable streams. The space over which the assaulting columns were to march, and on which was soon to occur the tremendous struggle, consisted of smooth and gentle undulations and a narrow valley covered with green grass and growing corn. From the position assigned me near the centre of Lee's lines, both armies and the entire field were in view. The scene was not only magnificent to look upon, but the realization of what it meant was deeply impressive. Even in times of peace our sensibilities are stirred by the sight of a great army passing in review. How infinitely more thrilling in the dread moments before the battle to look upon two mighty armies upon the same plain, "beneath spread ensigns and bristling bayonets," waiting for the impending crash and sickening carnage!

Behind McClellan's army the country was open and traversed by broad macadamized roads leading to Washington and Baltimore. The defeat, therefore, or even the total rout of Union forces, meant not necessarily the destruction of that army, but, more probably, its temporary disorganization and rapid retreat through a country abounding in supplies, and toward cities rich in men and means. Behind Lee's Confederates, on the other hand, was the Potomac River, too deep to be forded by his infantry, except at certain points. Defeat and total rout of his army meant, therefore, not only its temporary disorganization, but its possible destruction. And yet that bold leader did not hesitate to give battle. Such was his confidence in the steadfast courage and oft-tested prowess of his troops that he threw his lines across McClellan's front with their backs against the river. Doubtless General Lee would have preferred, as all prudent commanders would, to have the river in his front instead of his rear; but he wisely, as the sequel proved, elected to order Jackson from Harper's Ferry, and, with his entire army, to meet McClellan on the eastern shore rather than risk the chances of having the Union commander assail him while engaged in crossing the Potomac.

On the elevated points beyond the narrow valley the Union batteries were rolled into position, and the Confederate heavy guns unlimbered to answer them. For one or more seconds, and before the first sounds reached us, we saw the great volumes of white smoke rolling from the mouths of McClellan's artillery. The next second brought the roar of the heavy discharges and the loud explosions of hostile shells in the midst of our lines, inaugurating the great battle. The Confederate batteries promptly responded; and while the artillery of both armies thundered, McClellan's compact columns of infantry fell upon the left of Lee's lines with the crushing weight of a land-slide. The Confederate battle line was too weak to withstand the momentum of such a charge. Pressed back, but neither hopelessly broken nor dismayed, the Southern troops, enthused by Lee's presence, reformed their lines, and, with a shout as piercing as the blast of a thousand bugles, rushed in counter-charge upon the exulting Federals, hurled them back in confusion, and recovered all the ground that had been lost. Again and again, hour after hour, by charges and counter-charges, this portion of the field was lost and recovered, until the green corn that grew upon it looked as if it had been struck by a storm of bloody hail.

Up to this hour not a shot had been fired in my front. There was an ominous lull on the left. From sheer exhaustion, both sides, like battered and bleeding athletes, seemed willing to rest. General Lee took advantage of the respite and rode along his lines on the right and centre. He was accompanied by Division Commander General D. H. Hill. With that wonderful power which he possessed of divining the plans and purposes of his antagonist, General

Lee had decided that the Union commander's next heavy blow would fall upon our centre, and those of us who held that important position were notified of this conclusion. We were cautioned to be prepared for a determined assault and urged to hold that centre at any sacrifice, as a break at that point would endanger his entire army. My troops held the most advanced position on this part of the field, and there was no supporting line behind us. It was evident, therefore, that my small force was to receive the first impact of the expected charge and to be subjected to the deadliest fire. To comfort General Lee and General Hill, and especially to make, if possible, my men still more resolute of purpose, I called aloud to these officers as they rode away: "These men are going to stay here, General, till the sun goes down or victory is won." Alas! many of the brave fellows are there now.

General Lee had scarcely reached his left before the predicted assault came. The day was clear and beautiful, with scarcely a cloud in the sky. The men in blue filed down the opposite slope, crossed the little stream (Antietam), and formed in my front, an

Confederate dead lie on Sunken Road.

assaulting column four lines deep. The front line came to a "charge bayonets," the other lines to a "right shoulder shift." The brave Union commander, superbly mounted, placed himself in front, while his band in rear cheered them with martial music. It was a thrilling spectacle. The entire force, I concluded, was composed of fresh troops from Washington or some camp of instruction. So far as I could see, every soldier wore white gaiters around his ankles. The banners above them had apparently never been discolored by the smoke and dust of battle. Their gleaming bayonets flashed like burnished silver in the sunlight. With the precision of step and perfect alignment of a holiday parade, this magnificent array moved to the charge, every step keeping time to the tap of the deep-sounding drum. As we stood looking upon that brilliant pageant, I thought, if I did not say, "What a pity to spoil with bullets such a scene of martial beauty!" But there was nothing else to do. Mars is not an aesthetic god; and he was directing every part of this game in which giants were the contestants. On every preceding field where I had been engaged it had been my fortune to lead or direct charges, and not to receive them; or else to move as the tides of battle swayed in the one direction or the other. Now my duty was to move neither to the front nor to the rear, but to stand fast, holding that centre under whatever pressure and against any odds.

Every act and movement of the Union commander in my front clearly indicated his purpose to discard bullets and depend upon bayonets. He essayed to break through Lee's centre by the crushing weight and momentum of his solid column. It was my business to prevent this; and how to do it with my single line was the tremendous problem which had to be solved, and solved quickly; for the column was coming. As I saw this solid mass of men moving upon me with determined step and front of steel, every conceivable plan of meeting and repelling it was rapidly considered. To oppose man against man and strength against strength was impossible; for there were four lines of blue to my one of gray. My first impulse was to open fire upon the compact mass as soon as it came within reach of my rifles, and to pour into its front an incessant hail-storm of bullets during its entire advance across the broad, open plain; but after a moment's reflection that plan was also discarded. It was rejected because, during the few minutes required for the column to reach my line, I could not hope to kill and disable a sufficient number of the enemy to reduce his strength to an equality with mine. The only remaining plan was one which I had never tried but in the efficacy of which I had the utmost faith. It was to hold my fire until the advancing Federals were almost upon my lines, and then turn loose a sheet of flame and lead into their faces. I did not believe that any troops on earth, with empty guns in their hands, could withstand so sudden a shock and withering a fire. The programme was fixed in my own mind, all the horses were sent to the rear, and my men were at

once directed to lie down upon the grass and clover. They were quickly made to understand, through my aides and line officers, that the Federals were coming upon them with unloaded guns; that not a shot would be fired at them, and that not one of our rifles was to be discharged until my voice should be heard from the centre commanding "Fire!" They were carefully instructed in the details. They were notified that I would stand at the centre, watching the advance, while they were lying upon their breasts with rifles pressed to their shoulders, and that they were not to expect my order to fire until the Federals were so close upon us that every Confederate bullet would take effect.

There was no artillery at this point upon either side, and not a rifle was discharged. The stillness was literally oppressive, as in close order, with the commander still riding in front, this column of Union infantry moved majestically in the charge. In a few minutes they were within easy range of our rifles, and some of my impatient men asked permission to fire. "Not yet," I replied. "Wait for the order." Soon they were so close that we might have seen the eagles on their buttons; but my brave and eager boys still waited for the order. Now the front rank was within a few rods of where I stood. It would not do to wait another second, and with all my lung power I shouted "Fire!"

My rifles flamed and roared in the Federals' faces like a blinding blaze of lightning accompanied by the quick and deadly thunderbolt. The effect was appalling. The entire front line, with few exceptions, went down in the consuming blast. The gallant commander and his horse fell in a heap near when I stood—the horse dead, the rider unhurt. Before his rear lines could recover from the terrific shock, my exultant men were on their feet, devouring them with successive volleys. Even then these stubborn blue lines retreated in fairly good order. My front had been cleared; Lee's centre had been saved; and yet not a drop of blood had been lost by my men. The result, however, of this first effort to penetrate the Confederate centre did not satisfy the intrepid Union commander. Beyond the range of my rifles he reformed his men into three lines, and on foot led them to the second charge, still with unloaded guns. This advance was also repulsed; but again and again did he advance in four successive charges in the fruitless effort to break through my lines with the bayonets. Finally his troops were ordered to load. He drew up in close rank and easy range, and opened a galling fire upon my line.

I must turn aside from my story at this point to express my regret that I have never been able to ascertain the name of this lion-hearted Union officer. His indomitable will and great courage have been equalled on other fields and in both armies; but I do not believe they have ever been surpassed. Just before I fell and was borne unconscious from the field, I saw this undaunted commander attempting to lead his men in another charge.

The fire from these hostile American lines at

close quarters now became furious and deadly. The list of the slain was lengthened with each passing moment. I was not at the front when, near nightfall, the awful carnage ceased; but one of my officers long afterward assured me that he could have walked on the dead bodies of my men from one end of the line to the other. This, perhaps, was not literally true; but the statement did not greatly exaggerate the shocking slaughter. Before I was wholly disabled and carried to the rear, I walked along my line and found an old man and his son lying side by side. The son was dead, the father mortally wounded. The gray-haired hero called me and said: "Here we are. My boy is dead, and I shall go soon; but it is all right." Of such were the early volunteers.

My extraordinary escapes from wounds in all the previous battles had made a deep impression upon my comrades as well as upon my own mind. So many had fallen at my side, so often had balls and shells pierced and torn my clothing, grazing my body without drawing a drop of blood, that a sort of blind faith possessed my men that I was not to be killed in battle. This belief was evidenced by their constantly repeated expressions: "They can't hurt him." "He's as safe one place as another." "He's got a charmed life."

If I had allowed these expressions of my men to have any effect upon my mind the impression was quickly dissipated when the Sharpsburg storm came and the whizzing Miniés, one after another, began to pierce my body.

The first volley from the Union lines in my front sent a ball through the brain of the chivalric Colonel Tew, of North Carolina, to whom I was talking, and another ball through the calf of my right leg. On the right and the left my men were falling under the death-dealing crossfire like trees in a hurricane. The persistent Federals, who had lost so heavily from repeated repulses, seemed now determined to kill enough Confederates to make the debits and credits of the battle's balance-sheet more nearly even. Both sides stood in the open at short range and without the semblance of breastworks, and the firing was doing a deadly work. Higher up in the same leg I was again shot; but still no bone was broken. I was able to walk along the line and give encouragement to my resolute riflemen, who were firing with the coolness and steadiness of peace soldiers in target practice. When later in the day a third ball pierced my left arm, tearing asunder the tendons and mangling the flesh, they caught sight of the blood running down my fingers, and these devoted and big-hearted men, while still loading their guns, pleaded with me to leave them and go to the rear, pledging me that they would stay there and fight to the last. I could not consent to leave them in such a crisis. The surgeons were all busy at the field-hospitals in the rear, and there was no way, therefore, of stanching the blood, but I had a vigorous constitution, and this was doing me good service.

A fourth ball ripped through my shoulder, leaving its base and a wad of clothing in its track. I could

Shell startles citizens taking shelter in a cellar.

still stand and walk, although the shocks and loss of blood had left but little of my normal strength. I remembered the pledge to the commander that we would stay there till the battle ended or night came. I looked at the sun. It moved very slowly; in fact, it seemed to stand still. I thought I saw some wavering in my line, near the extreme right, and Private Vickers, of Alabama, volunteered to carry any orders I might wish to send. I directed him to go quickly and remind the men of the pledge to General Lee, and to say to them that I was still on the field and intended to stay there. He bounded away like an Olympic racer; but he had gone less than fifty yards when he fell, instantly killed by a ball through his head. I then attempted to go myself, although I was bloody and faint, and my legs did not bear me steadily. I had gone but a short distance when I was shot down by a fifth ball, which struck me squarely in the face and passed out, barely missing the jugular vein. I fell forward and lay unconscious with my face in my cap and it would seem that I might have been smothered by the blood running into my cap from this last wound but for the act of some Yankee, who, as if to save my life, had at a previous hour during the battle, shot a hole through the cap, which let the blood out.

I was borne on a litter to the rear, and recall nothing more till revived by stimulants at a late hour of the night. I found myself lying on a pile of straw at an old barn, where our badly wounded were gathered. My faithful surgeon, Dr. Weatherly, who was my devoted friend, was at my side, with his fingers on my pulse. As I revived, his face was so expressive of distress that I asked him: "What do you think of my case, Weatherly?" He made a manly effort to say that he was hopeful. I knew better, and said: "You are not honest with me. You think I am going to die; but I am going to get well." Long afterward, when the danger was past, he admitted that this assurance was his first and only basis of hope.

General George B. Anderson, of North Carolina, whose troops were on my right, was wounded in the foot, but it was thought, not severely. That superb man and soldier was dead in a few weeks, though his wound was supposed to be slight, while I was mercifully sustained through a long battle with wounds the combined effect of which was supposed to be fatal. Such are the mysterious concomitants of cruel war.

Mrs. Gordon was soon with me. When it was known that the battle was on, she had at once started toward the front. The doctors were doubtful about the propriety of admitting her to my room; but I told them to let her come. I was more apprehensive of the effect of the meeting upon her nerves than upon mine. My face was black and shapeless—so swollen that one eye was entirely hidden and the other nearly so. My right leg and left arm and shoulder were bandaged and propped with pillows. I knew she would be greatly shocked. As she reached the door and looked, I saw at once that I must reassure her. Summoning all my strength, I said: "Here's your handsome (?) husband; been to an Irish wedding." Her answer was a suppressed scream, whether of anguish or relief at finding me able to speak, I do not know. Thenceforward, for the period in which my life hung in the balance, she sat at my bedside, trying to supply concentrated nourishment to sustain me against the constant drainage. With my jaw immovably set, this was exceedingly difficult and discouraging. My own confidence in ultimate recovery, however, was never shaken until erysipelas, that deadly foe of the wounded, attacked my left arm. The doctors told Mrs. Gordon to paint my arm above the wound three or four times a day with iodine. She obeyed the doctors by painting it, I think, three or four hundred times a day. Under God's providence, I owe my life to her incessant watchfulness night and day, and to her tender nursing through weary weeks and anxious months.

VI

FREDERICKSBURG

STRATEGICALLY ANTIETAM WAS A DEFEAT FOR THE UNION. ONCE AGAIN MCCLELLAN had failed to take advantage of a decidedly favorable situation, letting Lee's army slip away to fight again. Nevertheless the battle had significant consequences. It raised Northern morale, it strengthened the image of the Union abroad, and it prompted Lincoln to issue The Emancipation Proclamation, promising the abolition of slavery in any territory still in rebellion at the onset of the new year. In addition, Antietam marked the end of McClellan's active career, for Lincoln was determined to remove him. But getting rid of McClellan proved easier than finding a replacement for him. In the end, the choice came down to Maj. Gen. Ambrose E. Burnside, who had done well in an independent command on the North Carolina coast, though less well commanding a corps at Antietam. Burnside was reluctant to accept the job, but allowed himself to be talked into it by Lincoln and several of the other commanders. Assuming command in November, Burnside's tenure at the head of The Army of the Potomac was neither long, nor glorious. The principal operation was an attempt to get across the Rappahannock at Fredericksburg in December. Burnside's plan was sound, but complex. He intended to elude Lee, leaving him in north central Virginia, and march rapidly to Fredericksburg, there to conduct a surprise crossing of the Rappahannock, getting in a position to sever Lee's communications with Richmond. But things went awry and time was lost, causing Lee to become aware of the dangerous maneuver. Rather than cancel the operation, Burnside attempted to carry it out anyway.

G. MOXLEY SORREL
The Fredericksburg Campaign

By the time Burnside was ready to undertake his first offensive with The Army of the Potomac, Confederate Maj. Gilbert Moxley Sorrel (see "The Peninsula and the Battle of Williamsburg" and "The Battle of Sharpsburg") had recovered from the wound he had received at Antietam and returned to active duty as acting

adjutant general to Lt. Gen. James Longstreet, whose command was now formally designated I Corps of the Army of Northern Virginia. Sorrel's perceptive account of the campaign is from his excellent Recollections of a Confederate Staff Officer.

The new commander of the Army of the Potomac was one of the most highly respected officers of the United States Army, but he was not equal to the command, and so stated to the officers who brought him Mr. Lincoln's commission and orders.

McClellan was of decided ability in many respects; timorous, but safe; and there was no better organizer. He seemed to hate battle, and it is surprising that with such a record he should have secured

and retained the devotion and confidence of his men to the very end. There was no lack of physical courage; it was a mental doubt with him.

Burnside had no prominent reputation, but made a success of an unimportant expedition into North Carolina. He conspicuously failed at Sharpsburg, where all day the bridge on the right was the scene of combat, without his movement to seize it. His great corps, held idly in hand, was equal to it ten times

Fredericksburg was an old aristocratic Virginia town.

over. But he may have been waiting on McClellan, with whom he was in the closest intimacy of friendship.

At all events, Burnside could and would fight, even if he did not know how, and after "Little Mac" this was what Mr. Lincoln was trying for. He was a handsome man, from Rhode Island, of fine, courteous bearing. . . .

A pause in the operations ensued while we lay about Bunker Hill and Winchester [in the Shenandoah Valley]. But Lee had, in the first half of November, decided where he should make Burnside fight. It was Fredericksburg. Longstreet had previously sent McLaws's division east of the mountains to the vicinity of Culpeper, and about November 16 started him for the old town on the Rappahannock, following a day or two later from his Valley camps with the remainder of the corps.

The gaps of the Blue Ridge were well occupied and defended by Jackson and Stuart's cavalry during Lee's transfer of his army in this delicate strategical operation.

I parted from Longstreet for a day or two, and arrived near Fredericksburg with some of the leading troops, before him.

My ride was in the worst weather, roads deep in mud, with rain in torrents. Fredericksburg is one of the oldest and most aristocratic of the Virginia towns. A dwindling trade had thinned the population and quieted its ambitions. At this time the place was the home of families of historical importance and present interest, with a thorough knowledge of good living, and still respectable cellars of old Madeira that had been imported by them many years before.

The enemy had a small garrison there and a provost marshal, an elderly United States officer, kind and gentle in his authority, and much liked by the citizens.

From this officer I received a request to meet him under flag of truce, and we made acquaintance in a little block-house just outside of town. The good old General Patrick was quite in ignorance apparently of the great operation that was then culminating. Expecting to hold the city with his little garrison he wished to avert any shelling of the town by our guns.

His friends had not yet made their appearance on the Falmouth Hills, commanding the town on the left bank of the river. We had outstripped their march.

General Patrick was informed that he must at once withdraw from Fredericksburg, that we should occupy it in force. He smiled, thinking it a bluff, and wanted to know where the soldiers were. On this

point he got no information, of course, and we parted. However, he was soon to see our men pouring forward, and McLaws's division seizing the city and posting his gallant Mississippians on the river front, under the intrepid Barksdale.

Patrick's little gang had, of course, immediately slipped away when they saw what was coming.

This I think was about November 21. The entire army soon after arrived and took position behind the Rappahannock, a wide, undulating plain for the most part stretching between our lines and the river itself. Longstreet took the left and Jackson the right; the former's most important point being the stone wall and sunken road at the foot of Marye's Hill.

Looking back at the situation, it seems surprising that we did so little in the way of defensive fieldworks. The enemy in great masses were crowding the Falmouth Hills, and we knew intended to cross and strike us. But yet we contented ourselves with the little stone wall (which proved helpful), and two

Union soldier surveys Confederate prisoners from horseback.

or three tiers of light trenchwork extended on the slope of the hill behind and on our left.

The like observation applies to Jackson, whose lines were about the same as ours in strength, except the stone wall.

Later in the war such a fault could not have been found. Experience had taught us that to win, we must fight; and that fighting under cover was the thing to keep up the army and beat the enemy. He knew it, too, and practised it, so later on veterans no

sooner got to facing each other than they began to dig, if ever so little; a little trench, a tiny hillock is often a very helpful defense and protection.

The march to Fredericksburg in bad weather and over almost bottomless roads had caused great suffering to the men and some losses among the animals. It was then that Longstreet told his men of an expedient that as an old soldier he had often resorted to. "Rake," he sent word to the men, "the coals and ashes from your cooking fires and sleep on that

Union charges Fredericksburg.

ground; it will be dry and warm." And so it proved. Also, there being many barefooted men, "Take the rawhides of the beef cattle, killed for food; cut roughly for a moccasin-like covering for the feet, and there you are with something to walk in." But this did not go. This foot-wear had nothing like soles of stiffening, and in the mud and icy slush of the Virginia roads the moist, fresh skins slipped about as if on ice. The wearers, constantly up or down, finally kicked them aside and took the road as best they could, barefooted or wrapped with rags or straw. . . .

It was awfully nasty work getting down to that stone wall for giving orders or receiving information, the way swept by the enemy's volume of fire over every foot. Once at the wall it was fairly snug, but the coming back was still worse, and one drew a long breath on emerging safely from that deadly fusilade.

We could only manage it on foot by making short rushes from point to point, affording perhaps some little cover. It was on such a duty that my friend Lord King was killed. He was A. D. C. to McLaws, of the family of Kings of southern Georgia. . . .

But now it is time to sketch something of the remarkable battle that the quiet waters of the Rappahannock were to see fiercely fought in torrents of blood across the plain that bordered the stream. I attempt no description, limiting myself to some stray observations.

The enemy had finally massed his great force (122,500 men) on Stafford Heights, and was to force the passage of the river. Franklin had wisely advised Burnside to do the work with half the army against our right, and Burnside, at first assenting, then resumed his original intention to attack our center with Sumner's grand division. Well for us that he did so!

On December 11 his movement began by attempting to set his pontoon bridge opposite the city for the crossing.

It was opposed by General Barksdale's Mississippi Brigade of McLaw's division, and stands as one of the finest acts of heroism and stubborn resistance in our military annals.

Burnside first poured an artillery fire in the devoted town and defending brigade—that was literally an "enfer."

There had been nothing like it before in this war. Every shot, all kinds of missiles, were thrown at the Mississippians to dislodge them. The brave fellows were there, however, to stay. They hid themselves in cellars, wells, holes of any kind where they could get a little cover, while their rifles picked off the pontooners pluckily trying to throw their boats across the stream. The latter fell in great numbers and this went on nearly all day. The Confederates would not budge, although so stubborn a defense had been no part of our expectation. We knew the town would be seized.

Quite late the bridge effort was abandoned by the Federal engineers. Calling for volunteers to fill the boats and cross in mass, it was gallantly answered. A number of them were quickly crowded, and not-withstanding our fire their landing was soon made and the town occupied, but not before Barksdale had safely withdrawn his hard-fighting fellows.

They had the cheers of the army for their day's brave work.

Then began that night and all next day and night the movement of Burnside's great army across the river. More brigades were added and there were several in Franklin's possession. He had no trouble in laying what he wanted in his front.

Thus stood Burnside, his army facing us with nothing between, on December 13, and bitter cold, Franklin operating on his left against Jackson. Sumner in the center and center-right against Longstreet, who also guarded the lines extended considerably to our left. Hooker's grand division was held on Stafford Heights during the night of the 12th.

But Marye's Hill was our strong point. Burnside wanted it and there he threw his men in blind and impotent fury. It was held by T. R. R. Cobb's brigade of Georgians behind a stone wall at first and another brigade in support. The front here was quite narrow. Ranson's and Cook's North Carolina brigades were in light trenches higher up the hill, but in position to deliver deadly fire, and did so. The defense at the stone wall was also kept carefully reinforced as needed. There was some artillery in pits near the crest of the hill that did effective service.

General Lee's position with his staff during the day was on a small hill with a good plateau, from which he had a fair view of Sumner's attack on Longstreet, as well as Franklin's on Jackson. Longstreet was much of the time with him. Before the hot work began, "Stonewall" rode up to have a word with Lee. As he dismounted we broke into astonished smiles. He was in a spick and span new overcoat, new uniform with rank marks, fine black felt hat, and a handsome sword. We had never seen the like before, and gave him our congratulations on his really fine appearance. He said he "believed it was some of his friend Stuart's doings."

Franklin was in great masses before Jackson, and before mounting, Longstreet called out, "Jackson, what are you going to do with all those people over there?" "Sir," said Stonewall, with great fire and spirit, "we will give them the bayonet."

There is really now but little more to be said in detail of the battle. In front of us it was hammer and tongs all day from 11 a.m. until finally Burnside had to desist in sheer weariness of slaughter. His troops advanced to their assaults with the finest intrepidity, but it was impossible for them to stand before our fire. I afterwards saw that perhaps not more than half a dozen of their men had got within sixty yards of our wall and dropped there. Not once was there any sign of faltering or weakness among our troops; the solid bodies of troops attacking might easily have made it otherwise with unseasoned soldiers.

On our right Franklin had been more successful. He managed to pierce a salient that should have been corrected and worsted a considerable number of Jackson's men. The line was retaken and restored, but with some loss, among whom was Captain Edward Lawton, a young brother of General Lawton, of Georgia. We also lost at Marye's Hill General Cobb (T. R. R.), of Georgia, deeply mourned as one of the most promising officers and whole-souled patriots of the South.

When darkness fell on this great tragedy, hostile movements ceased and the two armies were caring for the "butcher's bill." Ours was small comparatively, but the enemy had lost very heavily.

A thick fog or mist also arose and enveloped the enemy's movements in strangeness and uncertainty. They were actually started on hastily recrossing the river, but we don't appear to have known it. Most of the day of the 14th it was thick and misty, but all the time he was preparing for his retreat.

He was not attacked while in this exposed position. Why not? It is generally thought it would have been fatal to the Federals and it is indisputable that they were in hourly dread of it. Some say Jackson proposed a night attack, but I doubt it, and am glad it was not made.

It is impossible to describe the confusion of such an attempt or to anticipate what might happen. . . .

But why did we not attack on the 14th in daylight? Not my part to attempt this explanation, but it looks much as if we were "building a bridge of gold for the flying enemy."

On the night of the 17th Burnside withdrew his army to his old camp in the Falmouth Hills.

We lost in killed and wounded—Longstreet, 1,519; Jackson, 2,682; total, 4,201. Jackson was also reported as having lost in missing 526. These figures are also adopted by Ropes, and he gives Burnside's army as 122,500, ours as 78,500. I do not think that more than half of our forces were engaged on the 13th. The Federal losses, attacks on Marye's Hill, 8,000; loss of whole army, Federal, 12,650 killed and wounded. (Ropes's figures.)

The hill referred to as affording General Lee at Fredericksburg a point of view, had a light trench in which was mounted a 30-pounder Parrott gun, made in Richmond. The 10-pounder guns of that make had done well, but those of heavy caliber were treacherous. The one on "Lee's Hill," as it came to be called, burst after a few discharges. Happily it did not send fragments flying about, and no one was hurt. The immense breech just appeared to have split into a dozen pieces of various sizes and then fallen heavily to the ground. We were rather glad to have done with such a piece of metal.

The old wines of the good people of Fredericksburg have been referred to. They suffered in the fortunes of war. A few nights before the opening of the battle, which was then imminent, considerable quantities of fine old Madeira and other varieties were taken out of cellars and bins, and sent by the citizens to our fellows in camp, equally ready for drink or for battle. It was known that the town would be shelled and occupied by the Federals, probably looted and plundered; therefore it was thought safest to see priceless old vintages passed around

Major General Ambrose Burnside.

campfires and quaffed in gulps from tincups. Of course the men would have better liked whiskey, but they did not refuse the wine.

An incident on the river may bear telling. It was after the battle, when the pickets had resumed their posts and had become friendly; more given to trading than shooting each other at less than one hundred yards. The authorities had to set their faces sternly against this trading. It led to desertion. A fine Federal band came down to the river bank one afternoon and began playing pretty airs, among them the Northern patriotic chants and war songs. "Now give us some of ours!" shouted our pickets, and at once the music swelled into Dixie, My Maryland, and the Bonnie Blue Flag. Then, after a mighty cheer, a slight pause, the band again began, all listening; this time it was the tender melting bars of Home, Sweet Home, and on both sides of the river there were joyous shouts, and many wet eyes could be found among those hardy warriors under the flags. "One touch of nature makes the whole world kin."

A pontoon bridge is constructed at Fredericksburg.

Union charges Fredericksburg.

Union guns bombard Fredericksburg on December 11.

R.F. Zogbaum

EVANS

D. AUGUSTUS DICKERT
Incidents of the Fredericksburg Campaign

D. Augustus Dickert (1844–1917), a native of South Carolina, joined the 3rd South Carolina as a private on the outbreak of the Civil War. He proved a brave and able soldier, being wounded four times and rising to the rank of captain and acting regimental commander by the end of the war. Afterwards becoming a farmer, the self-educated Dickert also managed to establish himself as a writer of some skill and was active in the Ku Klux Klan. His most important work is the rare History of Kershaw's Brigade *(Newberry, S.C., 1899), one of the best unit histories to come out of the war, from which his account of Fredericksburg has been excerpted.*

Many incidents of courage and pathos could be written of this, as well as many other battles, but one that I think the crowning act of courage and sympathy for an enemy in distress is due was that of a Georgian behind the wall. In one of the first charges made during the day a Federal had fallen, and to protect himself as much as possible from the bullets of his enemies, he had by sheer force of will pulled his body along until he had neared the wall. Then he failed through pure exhaustion. From loss of blood and the exposure of the sun's rays, he called loudly for water. "Oh, somebody bring me a drink of water!—water! water!!" was the piteous appeals heard by those behind the stone wall. To go to his rescue was to court certain death, as the housetops to the left were lined with sharpshooters, ready to fire upon anyone showing his head above the wall. But one brave soldier from Georgia dared all, and during the lull in the firing leaped the walls, rushed to the wounded soldier, and raising his head in his arms, gave him a drink of water, then made his way back and over the wall amid a hail of bullets knocking the dirt up all around him.

The soldier, like the sailor, is proverbial for his superstition. But at times certain incidents or coincidents take place in the life of the soldier that are inexplicable, to say the least. Now it is certain that every soldier going into battle has some dread of death. It is the nature of man to dread that long lost sleep at any time and in any place. He knows that death is a master of all, and all must yield to its inexorable summons, and that summons is more likely to come in battle than on ordinary occasions. That at certain times soldiers do have a premonition of their coming death, has been proven on many occasions. Not that I say all soldiers foretell their end by some kind of secret monster, but that some do, or seem to do so. Captain Summer, of my company, was an unusually good-humored and lively man, and while he was not what could be called profane, yet he had little predilection toward piety or the Church. In other battles he advanced to the front as light-hearted and free from care as if going on drill or inspection. When we were drawn up in line of battle at Fredericksburg the first morning an order came for the Captain. He was not present, and on enquiry, I was told that he had gone to a cluster of bushes in the rear. Thinking the order might be of importance, I hastened to the place, and there I found Captain Summer on his knees in prayer. I rallied him about his "sudden piety," and in a jesting manner accused him of "weakening." After rising from his kneeling posture, I saw he was calm, pale, and serious—so different from his former moods in going into battle. I began teasing him in a bantering way about being a "coward." "No," said he, "I am no coward, and will show I have as much nerve, if not more, than most men in the army, for all have doubts of death, but I have none. I will be killed in this battle. I feel it as plainly as I feel I am living, but I am no coward, and shall go in this battle and fight with the same spirit that I have always shown." This was true. He acted bravely, and for the few moments that he commanded the regiment he exhibited all the daring a brave man could, but he fell shot through the brains with a minnie ball. He had given me messages to his young wife, to whom he had been married only about two months, before entering the services, as to the disposition of his effects, as well as his body after death.

Another instance was that of Lieutenant Hill, of Company G, Third South Carolina Regiment. The day before the battle he asked permission to return to camp that night, a distance perhaps of three miles. With a companion he returned to the camp, procured water, bathed himself, and changed his underclothing. On being asked by his companion why he wished to walk three miles at night to simply bathe and change his clothing, with perfect unconcern he replied: "In the coming battle I feel that I

Troops cross river at Fredericksburg in blowing rain.

Considerable human suffering is in evidence at Fredericksburg Union field hospital.

will be killed, and such being the case, I could not bear the idea of dying and being buried in soiled clothes." He fell dead at the first volley. Was there ever such courage as this—to feel that death was so certain and that it could be prevented by absenting themselves from battle, but allowed their pride, patriotism, and moral courage to carry them on to sure death?

In the case of a private in Company C, Third Regiment, it was different. He did not have the moral courage to resist the "secret monitor," that silent whisperer of death. He had always asserted that he would be killed in the first battle, and so strong was this conviction upon him, that he failed to keep in line of battle on another occasion, and had been censured by his officers for cowardice. In this battle he was ordered in charge of a Sergeant, with instructions that he be carried in battle at the point of the bayonet. However, it required no force to make him keep his place in line, still he continued true to his convictions, that his death was certain. He went willingly, if not cheerfully, in line. As the column was moving to take position on Mayree's Hill, he gave instructions to his companions as he advanced what messages should be sent to his wife, and while giving those instructions and before the command reached its position he fell pierced through the heart. . . .

In looking back at the incidents of the War Between the States, it is with great pleasure that an incident highly honorable to the African slave race is recalled.

It was on the 13th of December, 1862, when the Third South Carolina Regiment of Infantry was ordered from the position at the foot of Lee's Hill, at Fredericksburg, Va., to Mayree's House, near but to the right of the sunken road protected by the rock fence, that in going down the Telegraph Road the regiment was for a time exposed to the fire of the Federal batteries on the Stafford Heights. A shell from those batteries was so accurately directed that it burst near by Company C, of that regiment, and one of the results was that Lieutenant James Spencer Piester, of that company, was instantly killed. His body lay in that road and his faithful body servant, Simpson Piester, went to the body of his master and tenderly taking it into his arms, bore it to the rear, so that it might be sent to his relatives in Newberry, South Carolina. Anyone who had occasion to go upon the Telegraph Road in that day must appreciate the courage and fidelity involved in the act performed by Simpson Piester. . . .

★★★

JOSHUA L. CHAMBERLAIN
Night on the Field of Fredericksburg

Joshua L. Chamberlain (1828–1914) was one of the best amateur soldiers of the war. A native of Maine, he chose an academic career and was a professor at Bowdoin College on the outbreak of the Civil War. Passing up a chance to study in Europe, he entered the Union Army as lieutenant colonel of the 20th Maine in mid-1862. He fought with his regiment through all the battles in the eastern theater until Gettysburg, where his defense of Little Round Top earned him a Medal of Honor. He served thereafter as a brigade and division commander and ended the war as a brigadier general with a brevet major generalcy. He afterwards became president of Bowdoin, was active in the development of Florida, wrote extensively on a variety of subjects, and was four times elected governor of Maine. Some years after the war Chamberlain contributed a piece to **Camp-Fire Sketches and Battlefield Echoes** (Springfield, MA, 1887), one of many works on the war which appeared at about that time. This dealt with the aftermath of Fredericksburg.*

The desperate charge was over. We had not reached the enemy's fortifications, but only that fatal crest where we had seen five lines of battle mount but to be cut to earth as by a sword-swoop of fire. We had that costly honor which sometimes falls to the "reserve"—to go in when all is havoc and confusion, through storm and slaughter, to cover the broken and depleted ranks of comrades and take the battle from their hands. Thus we had replaced the gallant few still struggling on the crest, and received that withering fire, which nothing could withstand, by throwing ourselves flat in a slight hollow of the ground, within pistol shot of the enemy's works; and, mingled with the dead and dying that strewed the field, we returned the fire till it reddened into night, and at last fell away through darkness into silence.

But out of that silence from the battle's crash and roar rose new sounds more appalling still; rose or fell, you knew not which, or whether from the earth or air; a strange ventriloquism, of which you could not locate the source, a smothered moan that seemed to come from distances beyond reach of the natural sense, a wail so far and deep and wide, as if a thousand discords were flowing together into a key-note weird, unearthly, terrible to hear and bear, yet startling with its nearness; the writhing concord broken by cries for help, pierced by shrieks of paroxysm; some begging for a drop of water; some calling on God for pity; and some on friendly hands to finish what the enemy had so horribly begun; some with delirious, dreamy voices murmuring loved names, as if the dearest were bending over them; some gathering their last strength to fire a musket to

Over the appalling cries of men in agony the crash and roar of battle sounds.

call attention to them where they lay helpless and deserted; and underneath, all the time, that deep bass note from closed lips too hopeless or too heroic to articulate their agony.

Who could sleep, or who would? Our position was isolated and exposed. Officers must be on the alert with their command. But the human took the mastery of the official; sympathy of soldiership. Command could be devolved; but pity, not. So with a staff officer I sallied forth to see what we could do where the helpers seemed so few. Taking some obser-

vations in order not to lose the bearing of our own position, we guided our steps by the most piteous of the cries. Our part was but little; to relieve a painful posture; to give a cooling draught to fevered lips; to compress a severed artery, as we had learned to do, though in bungling fashion; to apply a rude bandage, which yet might prolong the life to saving; to take a token or farewell message for some stricken home; it was but little, yet it was an endless task. We had moved towards the right and rear of our own position—the part of the field immediately above the city. The farther we went the more the need deepened, and the calls multiplied. Numbers half wakening from the lethargy of death, or of despair, by sounds of succor, begged us to take them quickly to a surgeon; and when we could not do that, imploring us to do the next most merciful service and give them quick dispatch out of their misery. Right glad were we when, after midnight, the shadowy ambulances came gliding along, and the kindly hospital stewards, with stretchers and soothing appliances, let us feel that we might return to our proper duty.

And now we were aware of other figures wandering, ghostlike, over the field. Some on errands like our own, drawn by compelling appeals; some seeking a lost comrade, with uncertain steps amidst the unknown, and ever and anon bending down to scan the pale visage closer, or, it may be, by the light of a brief match, whose blue flickering flame scarcely can give the features a more recognizable or more human look; some man, desperately wounded, yet seeking, with faltering step, before his fast ebbing blood shall have left him too weak to move, some quiet or sheltered spot out of sound of the terrible appeals he could neither answer nor endure, or out of reach of the raging battle coming with the morning; one creeping, yet scarcely moving, from one lifeless form to another, if, perchance, he might find a swallow of water in the canteen still swung from the dead soldier's side; or another, was with just returning or just remaining consciousness, vainly striving to rise from a mangled heap, that he may not be buried with them while yet alive; or some man, yet sound of body, but pacing feverishly his ground because in such a bivouac his spirit could not sleep. And so we picked our way back, amidst the stark, upturned faces, to our little living line.

The night chill had now woven a misty veil over the field. Fortunately, a picket fence we had encountered in our charge from the town had compelled us to abandon our horses, and so had saved our lives on the crest; but our overcoats had been strapped to the saddles, and we missed them now. Most of the men, however, had their overcoats or blankets—we were glad of that. Except the few sentries along the front, the men had fallen asleep—the living with the dead. At last, outwearied and depressed with the desolate scene, my own strength sunk, and I moved two dead men a little and lay down between them, making a pillow of the breast of a third. The skirt of his overcoat drawn over my face helped also to shield me from the bleak winds. There was some comfort even

BATTLE OF
FREDERICKSBURG,
DEC. 13, 1862.

Federal reserves wait to go into action at Fredericksburg.

Confederates at Hamilton's Crossing prepare to meet Meade's advancing Pennsylvanians.

in this companionship. But it was broken sleep. The deepening chill drove many forth to take the garments of those who could no longer need them, that they might keep themselves alive. More than once I was startled from my unrest by some one turning back the coat-skirt from my face, peering, half vampire-like, to my fancy, through the darkness, to discover if it too were of the silent and unresisting; turning away more disconcerted at my living word than if a voice had spoken from the dead.

Having held our places all the night, we had to keep to them all the more closely the next day, for it would be certain death to attempt to move away. As it was, it was only by making breastworks and barricades of the dead men that covered the field that we saved any alive. We did what we could to take a record of these men. A testament that had fallen from the breast pocket of the soldier who had been my pillow, I sent soon after to his home—he was not of my command—and it proved to be the only clue his parents ever had to his fate.

The next midnight, after thirty-six hours of this harrowing work, we were bidden to withdraw into the town for refreshment and rest. But neither rest nor motion was to be thought of till we had paid fitting honor to our dead. We laid them on the spot which they had won, on the sheltered edge of the crest, and committed their noble forms to the earth, and their story to their country's keeping.

We buried them darkly, at dead of night,
The sod with our bayonets turning.

Splinters of boards torn by shot and shell from the fences we had crossed served as headstones, each name hurriedly carved under brief match lights anxiously hidden from the foe. It was a strange scene around that silent and shadowy sepulture. "We will give them a starlight burial," it was said; but heaven ordained a more sublime illumination. As we bore them in dark and sad procession, their own loved North took up the escort and lifting all her glorious lights led the triumphal march over the bridge that spans the worlds—an aurora borealis of marvelous majesty! fiery lances and banners of blood and flame, columns of pearly light, garlands and wreaths of gold, all pointing upward and beckoning on. Who would not pass on as they did, dead for their country's life, and lighted to burial by the meteor splendors of their native sky?

Field hospital

VII

WINTER, 1862–1863

ALTHOUGH BURNSIDE ESSAYED TWO OPERATIONS AFTER FREDERICKSBURG, THE ONSET of winter impeded any serious resumption of campaigning. It had been a hard year, opening with bright hopes for swift victory on both sides. After much maneuver and much bloodshed, the situation did not seem very much altered from what it had been at the outset. Yet much had occurred. And as the armies settled into winter quarters one of the most momentous events of the war took place.

D. AUGUSTUS DICKERT
Snow Ball Fight

Winter quarters was a cold, boring experience for everyone, officer and enlisted man alike, Yankee or Rebel. Efforts to relieve the boredom were common, as recounted by D. Augustus Dickert, in a selection from his History of Kershaw's Brigade.

Guard duty around camp was abolished for the winter; so was drilling, only on nice, warm days; the latter, however, was rarely seen during that season. The troops abandoned themselves to base ball, snow fights, writing letters, and receiving as guests in their camps friends and relatives, who never failed to bring with them great boxes of the good things from home, as well as clothing and shoes for the needy soldiers. Furloughs were granted in limited numbers. Recruits and now the thoroughly healed of the wounded from the many engagements flocked to our ranks, making all put on a cheerful face.

That winter in Virginia was one of the most severe known in many years, but the soldiers had become accustomed to the cold of the North, and rather liked it than otherwise, especially when snow fell to the depth of twelve to sixteen inches and remained for two or three weeks. So the reader can see that the soldier's life has its sunny side, as well as its dark. The troops delight in "snow balling," and revelled in the sport for days at a time. Many hard battles were fought, won, and lost; sometimes company against company, then regiment against regiment, and sometimes brigades would be pitted against rival brigades. When the South Carolinians were against the Georgians, or the two Georgia brigades against Kershaw's and the Mississippi brigades, then the blows would fall fast and furious. The fiercest fight and the hardest run of my life was when Kershaw's Brigade, under Colonel Rutherford, of the Third, challenged and fought Cobb's Georgians. Colonel Rutherford was a great lover of the sport, and wherever a contest was going on he would be sure to take a hand. On the day alluded to Colonel Rutherford martialed his men by the beating of drums and the bugle's blast; officers headed their companies, regiments formed, with flags flying, then when all was ready the troops were marched to the brow of a hill, or rather half way down the hill, and formed line of battle, there to await the coming of the Georgians. They were at that moment advancing across the plain that separated the two camps. The men built great pyramids of snow balls in their rear, and awaited the assault of the fast approaching enemy. Officers cheered the men and urged them to stand fast and uphold the "honor of their State," while the officers on the other side besought their men to sweep all before them off the field.

The men stood trembling with cold and emotion, and the officers with fear, for the officer who was luckless enough to fall into the hands of a set of "snow revelers," found to his sorrow that his bed was not one of roses. When the Georgians were within one hundred feet the order was given to "fire." Then shower after shower of the fleecy balls filled the air. Cheer after cheer went up from the assaulters and the assaultant—now pressed back by the flying balls, then to the assault again. Officers shouted to the men, and they answered with a "yell." When some, more bold than the rest, ventured too near, he was caught and dragged through the lines, while his comrades made frantic efforts to rescue him. The poor prisoner, now safely behind the lines, his fate problematical, as down in the snow he was pulled, now on his face, next on his back, then swung round and round by his heels—all the while snow being pushed down his back or in his bosom, his eyes, ears, and hair thoroughly filled with the "beautiful snow." After a fifteen minutes' struggle, our lines gave way. The fierce looks of a tall, muscular, wild-eyed Georgian, who stood directly in my front, seemed to have singled me out for sacrifice. The stampede began. I tried to lead the command in the rout by placing myself in the front of the boldest and stoutest squad in the ranks, all the while shouting to the men to "turn boys turn." But they continued to charge to the rear, and in the nearest cut to our camp, then a mile off, I saw the only chance to save myself from the clutches of that wild-eyed Georgian was in continual and rapid flight. The idea of a boy seventeen years old, and never yet tipped the beam at one hundred, in the grasp of that monster, as he now began to look to me, gave me the horrors. One by one the men began to pass me, and while the distance between us and the camp grew less at each step, yet the distance between me and my pursuer grew less as we proceeded in our mad race. The broad expanse that lay between the men and camp was one flying, surging mass, while the earth, or rather the snow, all around was filled with men who had fallen or been overtaken, and now in the last throes of a desperate snow battle. I dared not look behind, but kept bravely on. My breath grew fast and thick, and the camp seemed a perfect menage, now near at hand then far in the distance. The men who had not yet fallen in the

A severe Virginia winter made fires a necessity no matter where the men spent the night.

hands of the reckless Georgians had distanced me, and the only energy that kept me to the race was the hope that some mishap might befall the wild-eyed man in my rear, otherwise I was gone. No one would have the temerity to tackle the giant in his rage. But all things must come to an end, and my race ended by falling in my tent, more dead than alive, just as I felt the warm breath of my pursuer blowing on my neck. I heard, as I lay panting, the wild-eyed man say, "I would rather have caught that d—n little Captain than to have killed the biggest man in the Yankee army."

★★★

JOHN N. OPIE
The Art of Confiscation

In 1861 the 17-year-old John N. Opie found the prospects of joining the Confederate cavalry more enticing than analytic geometry. He had an eventful career as a trooper, mostly in the Shenandoah Valley until 1864, when he was captured. He barely survived his imprisonment at Elmira. After the war he took up law and served in the Virginia state senate. His memoirs, A Rebel Cavalryman with Lee, Stuart, and Jackson *(Chicago, 1899), is eminently readable and full of the commonplace things of a soldier's life, as revealed in his account of foraging during the winter of 1862–1863.*

While we are in winter quarters and passing the dull times in perfect quiet, I will relate a few instances showing the manner in which we confiscated the necessaries of life which could not otherwise be obtained. This art was learned and practiced by our men as soon as they began to suffer from want. The principal subjects of confiscation were fence-rails, corn, apples, onions, chickens, hogs, turkeys and horses.

We were compelled to imitate Napoleon when in Italy—to wit, live on the country we occupied. When camped near Winchester, on a certain occasion, three of us went out on a voyage of discovery, and, when about two miles from camp, the man on the lookout saw a flock of turkeys roosting in a tree in a farmer's back yard. We needed a turkey at that time, so we drew lots, and the other two arranged it so that it fell upon me to confiscate one. I crept stealthily up to the fence, when the dogs barked, the ducks quacked and the farmer shot; but I secured the prize. The next morning we cut the turkey up and fried it, as we had no other means of cooking it, and divided it out among our mess. There was a young man, Edward Waddell, a member of our mess, who would not eat of the confiscated food. We threw him down upon the floor of the tent, forced his mouth open with a bayonet and thrust into it a leg of the turkey; but still the delicious morsel tempted not the stomach of the pious young soldier. We prodded him with bayonets and played tattoo upon him, yet he would not eat. Subsequently, he got bravely over his squeamishness.

On another occasion, a cavalryman from Berkeley County informed another soldier and myself that, near the Potomac river, there lived a Union man who owned some fine horses. We agreed that it was our patriotic duty to confiscate them; and he undertook to pilot us through the lines, and did so successfully. When we reached the man's barn it was empty, but, in riding through the fields to make a closer inspection, a magnificent young stallion ran up to us, rearing and charging. We made frequent but unavailing efforts to catch him, when, finally, I proposed to ride up in a corner of a field, when the others should drive him up to my side, and throwing the horses across the corner in our rear, I would get upon him from my horse while thus hemmed in. This all worked to perfection, until the horse, finding me upon his back, whirling abruptly around, rushed through the barricade and began to penetrate the surrounding darkness with lightning rapidity, plunging from the earth, ever and anon, like a ricocheting cannon ball. I endeavored to reach his throat, and thus choke him to submission; but his throat was a thing unattainable, and I soon realized that, as there was no bridle or halter on him, I was not master of the situation. Finally, the horse rushed up to a fence, and, thinking it was his purpose to leap, I prepared to go with him, when he stopped so suddenly and unexpectedly that I went over his head and over the fence, feeling as if I had fallen into another hemisphere. The horse, having gotten rid of his unwelcome burden, galloped off in the darkness, and, when my comrades came up, I was lifted upon my horse, supposing that my leg was broken, and we sorrowfully returned into our own country, having utterly failed in our patriotic efforts.

While in winter quarters in the Luray Valley, a member of our company informed me that he had discovered a hogshead of oats hidden under a straw stack. I imparted this valuable information to four or five of my mess, and after dark we followed our guide out of camp. Having been taught a severe lesson by Swindler, I carried my revolver. When some distance from camp we reached a rail fence, where our guide halted and whispered to me, "We are too late: other soldiers are ahead of us." I jumped up on the fence, and fired in the air, calling out in a loud voice, "What are you doing, stealing my oats?" There were five or six soldiers standing around an inverted hogshead, in which a soldier had crawled, and was engaged in scraping out the remainder of the oats, the bulk of which had been bagged. When I fired, the fellow in the hogshead, being taken by surprise, struck his head on the side of the hogshead, giving out a sound like that of a cannon ball when thrown against a barn, and they all fled across the field, in terror, from the supposed owner of the oats. I fired several shots, in order to hasten their departure.

Two of our party being in the rear, and hearing the firing and the shouting, believed that it came from the owner of the oats, and that the shooting was at us, fled ingloriously to the camp and reported that we had been attacked by the citizens. The rest of us shouldered the bags of oats and started back to camp. When about half way on our return, we halted and sat upon our bags to rest, when a soldier with his hat in his hand and tongue hanging out, came rapidly running by, and, on seeing us, he halted and asked what we had there, to which he received no reply. He then exclaimed, "Them is oats!" Seeing no way out of the dilemma, I remarked, "Yes; thet are oats. What of it?" "You d—d fellows scared us away from the straw rick and took our oats." I inquired of him what title he had to them, which question puzzled him into silence; and I then gave him a bag of the oats, and told him to hold his peace, which entirely pacified him. I met this man, Sergeant Veach by name, at Elmira prison the last winter of the war. The next day an officer informed me that the farmer had procured an order from General Jones, and was searching the regiment. We occupied a Sibley tent, with a stove in the center, which our beds encircled. When we received this timely information, we took up our blankets and poured the oats upon the ground and replaced the blankets. The old countryman soon appeared, and, looking around him, exclaimed, "No oats in here!" and moved on.

=★★★=

ABRAHAM LINCOLN
The Emancipation Proclamation

In the aftermath of Antietam, Lincoln issued a proclamation that freed the slaves in all areas still in rebellion on New Year's Day. There were several reasons for this proclamation. In one sense it was a final attempt to compromise on slavery, a summons to the seceded states to resume their loyalty to the Union and thus avoid the penalty of abolition. More importantly, it served a significant political purpose.

Lincoln—and the leaders of the South—well knew that the institution could not be partially abolished and partially preserved. No Southern state could possibly take up his offer. Sentiment for abolition had been growing stronger as the war progressed. On January 1, 1863, the Emancipation Proclamation was put in force, establishing the abolition of slavery as a major Union war aim.

Whereas, on the twenty second day of September, in the year of our Lord one thousand eight hundred and sixty two, a proclamation was issued by the President of the United States, containing, among other things, the following, towit:

That on the first day of January, in the year of our Lord one thousand eight hundred and sixty-three, all persons held as slaves within any State or designated part of a State, the people whereof shall then be in rebellion against the United States, shall be then, thenceforward, and forever free; and the Executive Government of the United States, including the military and naval authority thereof, will recognize and maintain the freedom of such persons, and will do no act or acts to repress such persons, or any of them, in any efforts they may make for their actual freedom.

That the Executive will, on the first day of January aforesaid, by proclamation, designate the States and parts of States, if any, in which the people thereof, respectively, shall then be in rebellion against the United States; and the fact that any State, or the people thereof, shall on that day be, in good faith, represented in the Congress of the United States by members chosen thereto at elections wherein a majority of the qualified voters of such State shall have participated, shall, in the absence of strong countervailing testimony, be deemed conclusive evidence that such State, and the people thereof, are not then in rebellion against the United States.

Now, therefore, I, Abraham Lincoln, President of the United States, by virtue of the power in me vested as Commander-in-Chief, of the Army and Navy of the United States in time of actual armed rebellion against authority and government of the United States, and as a fit and necessary war measure for suppressing said rebellion, do, on this first day of January, in the year of our Lord one thousand eight hundred and sixty three, and in accordance with my purpose so to do publicly proclaimed for the full period of one hundred days, from the day first above mentioned, order and designate as the States and parts of States wherein the people thereof respectively, are this day in rebellion against the United States, the following, towit:

Arkansas, Texas, Louisiana, (except the Parishes of St. Bernard, Plaquemines, Jefferson, St. Johns, St. Charles, St. James, Ascension, Assumption, Terrebonne, Lafourche, St. Mary, St. Martin, and Orleans, including the City of New-Orleans) Mississippi, Alabama, Florida, Georgia, South-Carolina, North-Carolina, and Virginia, (except the for-

tyeight counties designated as West Virginia, and also the counties of Berkley, Accomac, Northampton, Elizabeth-City, York, Princess Ann, and Norfolk, including the cities of Norfolk & Portsmouth) and which excepted parts are, for the present, left precisely as if this proclamation were not issued.

And by virtue of the power, and for the purpose aforesaid, I do order and declare that all persons held as slaves within said designated States, and parts of States, are, and henceforward shall be free; and that the Executive government of the United States, including the military and naval authorities thereof, will recognize and maintain the freedom of said persons.

And I hereby enjoin upon the people so declared to be free to abstain from all violence, unless in necessary self-defence; and I recommend to them that, in all cases when allowed, they labor faithfully for reasonable wages.

And I further declare and make known, that such persons of suitable condition, will be received into the armed service of the United States to garrison forts, positions, stations, and other places, and to man vessels of all sorts in said service.

And upon this act, sincerely believed to be an act of justice, warranted by the Constitution, upon military necessity, I invoke the considerate judgment of mankind, and the gracious favor of Almighty God.

In witness whereof, I have hereunto set my hand and caused the seal of the United States to be affixed.

Done at the City of Washington, this first day of January, in the year of our Lord one thousand eight hundred and sixty three, and of the Independence of the United States of America the eighty-seventh.
By the President: Abraham Lincoln
   William H. Seward, Secretary of State

Abraham Lincoln, the Great Emancipator

SOURCES

Alexander, E. P. "From the Peninsula to Cedar Mountain." In *Military Memoirs of a Confederate: A Critical Narrative*. pp. 175–184. New York, 1907.

Chamberlain, Joshua L. "Night on the Field of Fredericksburg." *Camp-Fire Sketches and Battlefield Echoes*, edited by W. C. King and W. P. Derby, pp. 127–130. Springfield, Mass., 1887.

Cox, Jacob D. "The Battle of Antietam." In *Battles and Leaders of the Civil War*, edited by Robert U. Johnson and Clarence C. Buell, vol. 2, pp. 630–656. New York, 1887.

Dickert, D. Augustus. "Incidents of the Fredericksburg Campaign." In *History of Kershaw's Brigade*, pp. 196–203. Newberry, S.C., 1889.

—————. "Snow Ball Fight." *Ibid.*, pp. 205–207.

Gibbon, John. "Second Bull Run." In *Personal Recollections of the Civil War*, pp. 43–70. New York, 1928.

Gordon, John B. "Antietam." *Reminiscences of the Civil War*, pp. 81–91. New York, 1904.

—————. "The First Winter of the War." *Ibid.*, pp. 48–52.

Goss, Warren Lee. "Yorktown and Williamsburg." In *Battles and Leaders of the Civil War*, edited by Robert U. Johnson and Clarence C. Buell, vol. 2, pp. 189–194. New York, 1887.

Hill, Daniel H. "The Battle of South Mountain, or Boonesboro'." In *Battles and Leaders of the Civil War*, edited by Robert U. Johnson and Clarence C. Buell, vol. 2, pp. 560–577. New York, 1887.

Howe, Julia Ward. "The Writing of 'The Battle Hymn of the Republic.'" *Reminiscences, 1819–1899*, pp. 273–276. Boston, 1899.

Imboden, John D. "Stonewall Jackson in the Shenandoah." In *Battles and Leaders of the Civil War*, edited by Robert U. Johnson and Clarence C. Buell, vol. 2, pp. 282–298. New York, 1887.

Law, Evander McI. "Lee Takes Command." In *The Southern Bivouac*, April 1867, pp. 649–651.

Lincoln, Abraham. *The Emancipation Proclamation*. The National Archives.

Longstreet, James. "'The Seven Days,' Including Frayer's Farm." In *Battles and Leaders of the Civil War*, edited by Robert U. Johnson and Clarence C. Buell, vol. 2, pp. 396–405. New York, 1887.

McClellan, George B. "The Antietam Campaign." In *Battles and Leaders of the Civil War*, edited by Robert U. Johnson and Clarence C. Buell, vol. 2, pp. 551–555. New York, 1887.

—————. "McClellan Takes Command." *Ibid.*, vol. 2, pp. 160–167.

—————. "The Movement to the Peninsula." *Ibid.*, vol. 2, pp. 168–170.

Opie, John N. "The Art of Confiscation." In *A Rebel Cavalryman with Lee, Stuart, and Jackson*, pp. 103–107. Chicago, 1899.

Porter, Fitz-John. "The Battle of Malvern Hill." In *Battles and Leaders of the Civil War*, edited by Robert U. Johnson and Clarence C. Buell, vol. 2, pp. 408–427. New York, 1887.

Sorrel, G. Moxley. "The Battle of Sharpsburg." In *Recollections of a Confederate Staff Officer*, pp. 110–119. New York, 1905.

—————. "The Fredericksburg Campaign." *Ibid.*, pp. 130–144.

—————. "The Peninsula and the Battle of Williamsburg." *Ibid.*, pp. 62–67.

Taylor, Richard. "With Jackson in the Valley." In *Destruction and Reconstruction: Personal Experiences of the Late War*, pp. 44–59. New York, 1879.